At Home With Computers

MATERIALIZING CULTURE
. . . .

Series Editors: Paul Gilroy, Michael Herzfeld and Danny Miller

Barbara Bender, *Stonehenge: Making Space*

Gen Doy, *Materializing Art History*

Laura Rival (ed.), *The Social Life of Trees: Anthropological Perspectives on Tree Symbolism*

Victor Buchli, *An Archaeology of Socialism*

Marius Kwint, Christopher Breward and Jeremy Aynsley (eds), *Material Memories: Design and Evocation*

Penny van Esterik, *Materializing Thailand*

Michael Bull, *Sounding Out the City: Personal Stereos and the Management of Everyday Life*

Anne Massey, *Hollywood beyond the Screen: Design and Material Culture*

Wendy Joy Darby, *Landscape and Identity: Geographies of Nation and Class in England*

Joy Hendry, *The Orient Strikes Back: A Global View of Cultural Display*

Judy Attfield, *Wild Things: The Material Culture of Everyday Life*

Daniel Miller (ed.), *Car Cultures*

Elizabeth Edwards, *Raw Histories: Photographs, Anthropology and Museums*

David E. Sutton, *Remembrance of Repasts: An Anthropology of Food and Memory*

Eleana Yalouri, *The Acropolis: Global Fame, Local Claim*

Elizabeth Hallam and Jeremy Hockey, *Death, Memory and Material Culture*

Sharon Macdonald, *Behind the Scenes at the Science Museum*

At Home With Computers

ELAINE LALLY

Oxford • New York

First published in 2002 by
Berg
Editorial offices:
150 Cowley Road, Oxford, OX4 1JJ, UK
838 Broadway, Third Floor, New York, NY 10003-4812, USA

Berg is the imprint of Oxford International Publishers Ltd.

Library of Congress Cataloging-in-Publication Data

Lally, Elaine.
 At home with computers / Elaine Lally.
    p. cm. – (Materializing culture, ISSN 1460-3349)
   ISBN 1-85973-561-4 (pbk.) – ISBN 1-85973-556-8
  1. Computers – Social aspects. 2. Information superhighway – Social
aspects. I. Title. II. Series.
   QA76.9.C66 L355 2002
   004–dc21

                                                        2002000063

British Library Cataloguing-in-Publication Data

A catalogue record for this book is available from the British Library.

ISBN 1 85973 556 8 (Cloth)
      1 85973 561 4 (Paper)

Typeset by JS Typesetting Ltd, Wellingborough, Northants.

Contents

List of Figures

Acknowledgements

This book had its origins in a doctoral thesis written at the University of Western Sydney (initially in the Department of Media and Cultural Studies, and subsequently in the School of Cultural Histories and Futures, following a university restructure). I would like to thank my PhD supervisors, Greg Noble and Zoë Sofoulis for challenging me to deepen my understanding of the phenomena I was investigating, to broaden my knowledge of the existing research and clarify the expression of my ideas. I am also grateful to the examiners of the thesis for their generous insights and feedback, which have enriched the present work. I would also like to thank a number of colleagues and friends who have acted as intellectual sounding boards, critical readers and motivators: Daniel Miller, Mandy Thomas, Fiona Allon, Helen Grace, Amanda Wise, Amanda Little, Jane Hobson, Lisa Law, Tanja Dreher, Sharon Chalmers and Joy Stevens. I am particularly grateful to Ien Ang for creating the stimulating intellectual environment of the Institute for Cultural Research at the University of Western Sydney, from which my research has benefited greatly.

This research would not have been possible without the input of the people who were interviewed for the study: although they must remain anonymous, I would like to thank them all for their generous contribution.

Finally, many of the observations about the everyday negotiations of domestic life which have found their way into this book emerged embryonically through my own home life. I am profoundly grateful to my children Holly and Hugh Evans and especially to my partner Paul Evans for supporting and enabling this process.

Introduction

> Indeed, things are perhaps the most faithful witnesses of all, and in their fidelity to us they function as extensions of ourselves, reflections and echoes of who we are, were, and will become. Those things in your room, for example, those simple, ordinary things mirror who and what you are, and situated in that room they give a shape to its space, they form it into a place, they outline a world . . . Staying in their place, they give us our place, and without such things in our lives we would have no place at all. (Romanyshyn 1989: 193–4)

Computers are, on the one hand, technologies that are profoundly reshaping the world around us and powerful cultural symbols of futurity, and, on the other hand, they are concrete elements of everyday life and personal items which can be bought and owned by house-holders. As a highly technological object, the home computer takes on an association with processes of globalization and sociotechnical development, and is symbolically linked with imaginaries of the future. As commodity, the home computer is embedded in contemporary production and consumption processes, and its acquisition is generally a contribution to a household's 'home-building', its ongoing project of maintenance and reproduction. As an everyday domestic object, the home computer is distinguished by its technological character, but must also find its place among a variety of other kinds of household objects, many of which are not normally thought of as technologies.

This book explores the social life of the computer in contemporary domestic life, based on interviews with the members of computer-own-ing households in western Sydney. It explores how such objects move from anonymous and alien commodities to become powerfully inte-grated into the lives of their users. It is centrally about technology and home-building, but the conceptual thread which links these is that of *ownership*, considered as an activity and a relationship, which is by its very nature complicated, multilayered, even at times contradictory.

1

Ownership is seen as an activity, rather than as an attribute. This notion is derived from Simmel (1990: 303–6): our relationship with our personal possessions is not static, but is constituted in and through the ongoing activities of our everyday lives. Such relationships of ownership between people and their personal domestic possessions are constructed and maintained through the incorporation of these objects into the times and spaces and patterns of activity of the household, a complex process which may take place over an extended period of time. In other words, ownership is explored as 'living with things' (Dant 1999), which occurs within the domestic arena, often in negotiation between household members, rather than in terms of a legal concept of rights.

It is therefore not just about appropriating objects to the self, but is about how we make ourselves at home in our everyday environments, how we make them habitable and comfortable, and use objects to manage the social world. In the contemporary world, technological objects play an important part in making our everyday living spaces habitable, and increasingly in mediating social relationships and cultural forms.

Information Technology in the Home

High tech commodities such as the home computer are important contemporary cultural forms. Both symbolic and material, techno-logical objects are complex and multifaceted in use, and can give us insights which are applicable across a broad range of contemporary domestic objects. They are brought into the domestic space as mass-produced objects, but they also provide a point of articulation into the outside world, through the channel that they establish into the home for mass media and other messages.

This dual role of information and communication technologies has been referred to as their 'double articulation' (Morley and Silverstone 1990). However, many household objects which are not normally thought of as information and communication technologies (such as books and newspapers) are also 'doubly articulated'; also, a variety of household objects act as information storage, organization and retrieval technologies (filing cabinets, the front of the fridge, notice-boards and so on). Although it is an information and communication technology in the conventional sense, the home computer is also a domestic object which interacts with the information management and communication functions of other domestic objects such as the dining room table (a common homework workstation). With some household objects the home computer has a collaborative relationship. With others the relationship is competitive, and indeed some objects are being displaced (in the sense of a relocation, rather than a supplanting) by the use of a computer in the home (just as the domestic role of radio changed with the introduction of television). Although new technologies displace earlier ones, that displacement is neither complete nor simple.

Indeed, it is argued in later chapters that the ensemble of domestic objects within the material context of the home itself may be seen as a kind of domestic appliance, or 'machine for living'. The physical infrastructure of home is fabricated from 'found objects' of the cultural environment, assembled within the space of the dwelling itself, as a process of continuous bricolage, rather than as something that is built and then lived in. This construction supports and structures the activities and interactions of those who live in it, and the home as a 'machine for living' is therefore also a form of social organization.

Technological objects and media, such as the home computer, are becoming more and more important in adding information and communications functionality to the home. While home computing in the mid-1980s was primarily a hobbyist activity, an image of the home computer as a kind of software 'player' for the home emerged in the late 1980s (Haddon 1988). During the 1990s, a further transformation took place in the representations, discourses and public understandings of home computing. The home computer, as a novel kind of 'information appliance' for the home, and the Internet as an 'information utility' have become important contemporary media for the development of work-related skills, new entertainment forms and ways of being creative at home. Computers are now well integrated into domestic commodity marketing. Home computers are portrayed in advertising and other public representations as indispensable to the modern home, and as time- and labour-saving (Centre for International Economics 2001). As we will see, however, these discourses often acknowledge and attempt to defuse cultural anxieties about the pace and inevitability of technological progress and about our growing dependence on these technologies to support the infrastructure of everyday life in the contemporary world.

The experiences recounted by the people I interviewed for this study seem both to adopt and contradict these widely circulating views of home computing. People give many reasons for acquiring a home computer. For some it is a way of extending their professional life into the domestic space, for others an investment in their children's education. In addition to these reasons, and often in conjunction with them, it is common for people to say that they feel the need to keep up with these new technologies because otherwise they may be 'left behind'. Often an individual will express a contradictory set of feelings about the computer – frustration and fear mixed with fascination and excitement. People also say that they do not feel that they are making the most of the computer, that they know that it can do lots of things that they either are not aware of or do not know how to make it do. Parents say that their children know more about the computer than they do, but also that the children only know enough to cause problems, not to fix them. Pre-purchase expectations about what owning a home computer will be like challenge the subsequent reality in complex ways. While the novelty of exploring what the computer can do keeps people up into the early hours of the morning, this contrasts with the frustration of trying to solve problems using only the manuals or the technician at the other end of the helpline.

When this study started in 1995–6, all the householders participating had a general awareness of the Internet, and some had access either at work or at home. However, the dominant understanding of the Internet was via the notion of the 'information superhighway', which was widely represented and discussed in the media at the time. The metaphor of the highway engaged the popular imagination, but in the abstract terms of its growing importance, rather than in giving people something concrete to envisage as part of their lives. At that time, a number of people told me that they couldn't see there being anything of interest to them in the Internet. Yet within two or three years, that had changed, and the same people who had been unable to conceive of anything of interest to them had enthusiastically taken up Internet use, and some had even published their own web pages.

In 1996 and 1997, a transformation took place in the way the Internet was represented and understood by consumers, with the widespread appearance of URLs (Universal Resource Locators) in billboard, newspaper and television advertising. The first two such public representations I saw were in 1996. They were a billboard advertisement for a newspaper classifieds section, and an advertisement for the film *Independence Day*. The latter simply gave the cryptic link http://www.id4.com/ and left it to the resourceful viewer to make the connection to the film, or to follow the link to find out what it referred to. These developments were important in naturalizing the Internet into the cultural landscape, and in providing a more 'domesticated' image of the Internet than that of the highway.

The effect of this cultural transformation is also reflected in the statistics on the uptake of home computer ownership and home Internet access. In February 1994, a home computer was used in 23 per cent of Australian households. By November 2000 this proportion had reached 56 per cent. Home Internet access is now increasing at a much faster rate than home computer acquisition, almost doubling between November 1998 and November 2000, to 37 per cent. The Australian Bureau of Statistics projects that half of Australian households will have Internet access by the end of 2001 (ABS 2001a: 4). In 2000, for the first time, the home overtook other sites as the most likely place for an individual to access the Internet in Australia (ABS 2001a: 3). Home Internet access appears to be even more common in the USA and Sweden (ABS 2001a: 3).

This book attempts to reach behind these statistics, to look at how householders understand and respond to these rapid cultural changes, and to examine the nature of domestic information and communications technologies as material culture.

Technology, in particular, is an important contemporary medium for imagining the future. While computers have long had an association with science fiction, the Internet seems to have come to 'represent a utopian future conjunction of personal freedoms, market freedoms, global mobility and cultural identity' (Miller and Slater 2000: 16). An engagement with technology is also potentially an intense emotional engagement, either positively or negatively, and often involving a mixture of these extremes. Staudenmaier (1995) refers to this mix of emotions as 'technological ambiguity' – 'a seemingly contradictory but remarkably stable mix of emotion: exuberant delight and purposeful energy entangled with discomfort and solipsistic retreat'. He sees this

> bonding of exultation with anxiety, personal power with personal impotence, as a kind of affective escape mechanism. It operates with a back and forth rocking movement from exultation to intimidation, that inculcates in ordinary people a feeling of power and betterment even as it warns them not to get in the way of Progress. (149–50)

As we will see, there is both excitement and hope for the future in these technologies, and anxiety and fear of failure, both at the level of individuals' engagements with the technology, and within public discourses and representations about sociotechnical change. Information technology is therefore an important contemporary medium by which individuals and communities project themselves into the future, both figuratively and practically.

Miller and Slater (2000) describe this potential in terms of two dynamics: the dynamic of expansive realization and the dynamic of expansive potential. In expansive realization, 'the Internet is viewed as a means through which one can enact – often in highly idealized form – a version of oneself or culture that is regarded as old or even originary but can finally be realized: through these new means, one can become what one thinks one really is (even if one never was)' (Miller and Slater 2000: 10). This mode of engagement with the technology is exemplified in the current study by Doug Fowler, who calls himself a 'futurist' and says that he has had a passion for computers every since he knew they were around. (It should be noted that pseudonyms have been used for the study participants wherever they are named.) Doug's home computer ownership simply confirms him as the person he always thought he was 'really'. In the dynamic of expansive potential, 'the encounter with the expansive connections and possibilities of the Internet may allow one to envisage a quite novel vision of what one could be' (Miller and Slater 2000: 11). One of the study participants, a retired high school principal, referred to her home computer as like having 'a handle on the future'.

The central issue to be explored in this book is that of how home computers are able to have these effects on the everyday lives of people throughout the contemporary world, through coming into close and intimate relationships with us. Pragmatic questions are raised about how contemporary artefacts, particularly those such as the home computer which are initially encountered as mass-produced commodities, come to be built into everyday life, to the point at which it is possible to say that the object is one which is 'owned'.

Ownership

What do we mean by ownership? At one extreme, a pure, legally enforceable definition in terms of the system of property rights exists in various jurisdictions. Indeed, Macpherson insists that property *is* rights, not things (1978: 2), and it is the common usage asserting the converse that is flawed. Property is distinguished from mere possession in that it refers to a socially enforceable claim arising by 'custom or convention or law' (3). On the other hand, in ordinary language we use the term very broadly. We talk about having a sense of ownership of public places or of a sense of belonging to communities and organizations. Ownership in this broad sense may take many forms, and be expressed through many different modalities. While a purely 'economic' form of ownership, for example, may be attained simply by a legal transfer of title to goods in exchange for a financial consideration, this form of ownership is often only the beginning of the establishment of a deeper and more complex, multimodal relationship of ownership, which is manifested in everyday activities and interactions, and which often involves an affective dimension.

It is clear that property relations in contemporary western societies are culturally and historically specific forms. Historically, private property rights arose from the possession of land and from work, both of which have been seen as the conduits by which property rights could be established. All other kinds of property stem from these 'canonical' forms of legitimization of property rights (Ryan 1984). The transformation of property rights from a predominantly political to a largely economic category is primarily a consequence of the growth of a capitalist economy (Ryan 1984: 47). The legal arrangements in place to enforce particular property rights in contemporary industrial societies are therefore a legacy of earlier times, when property was generally tangible and concrete, and the securing of property rights was essential to ensuring political stability. These arrangements have now been distorted beyond recognition as 'wealth' is increasingly based on intangible assets. All sorts of rights are now transferred via modern property law 'whose social implications are quite removed from eighteenth or nineteenth-century ideas about what it means to be a man of property' (Ryan 1984: 13).

However, as Ryan points out, the English legal system discouraged a question which Roman law encouraged, namely, '"What is it to be the *owner* of something?" or "How does a thing become Mine?"' (1984: 7). The concept of property *as* rights rather than things is far from our sense of ownership of our personal domestic possessions. To see ownership simply in terms of a system of property rights tends to conflate ownership with the economic consequences of possession. Legally binding property rights are just one aspect of the relationship we have to our possessions. Property rights are not, therefore, the place to *start* to think about what ownership means as a cultural phenomenon. Rather we need to look at what kinds of relationships with objects (or other cultural forms) can be translated into ones which entail socially recognized privileges, and through what kinds of processes these rights are won.

Romanyshyn's warning (quoted at the beginning of this chapter) that without personal possessions we would have no personalized place in the world, and would have no way of knowing who we are or were or might become, evocatively summons up a relational image of the self, as self-in-relation to these objects. The notion that personal possessions can be regarded in some way as an integral part of the self, or as a kind of extension of the self, is not a new one:

> It is clear that between what a man calls *me* and what he simply calls *mine* the line is difficult to draw. We feel and act about certain things that are ours very much the same as we feel and act about ourselves . . . *In its widest possible sense, however, a man's Self is the sum total of what he CAN call his*, not only his body and his psychic powers, but his clothes and his house, . . . his reputation and his works, his lands and horses, and yacht and bank account. (James 1981: 279–80)

It is not just that our intimate possessions belong to us, but that we in a sense (at least sometimes) belong to them too. This conceptualization of ownership is continuous with our sense of belonging to communities, our sense that the forms of knowledge we have expertise in belong to us, and our communal sense of ownership over public spaces.

Romanyshyn's evocative description of our possessions, staying in their place to give us our place, however, seems stiflingly static and lacking in the depth and complexity of the contemporary social and cultural contexts of everyday life. We construct our place in the world through our interactions with a dynamic social, cultural and material environment, filled with technologies, mass media, mass-produced commodities, abstract objects such as knowledges, and other people.

The approach to ownership developed in this book elaborates on the image of possessions a kind of scaffolding for the self by introducing a dynamic sense of everyday life as process, and by recognizing that we create our personal place in the world from social and cultural materials which are not of our own making. Individual relationships to material objects resonate with larger cultural structures of meaning and are conducted within social contexts and institutions.

Home-building

As we will see, a home computer is brought into a domestic context which is already organized around structures and hierarchies of age, gender and other specific roles, with pre-existing patterns of interaction and activity, and which already contains a large number of objects and other technologies. These structures provide the household's existing patterns of activity with a considerable momentum. The household is thus a complex structure which sustains, often nurtures, but frequently constrains the behaviour of its members. Further, the household is articulated into wider social processes and institutions and therefore cannot be thought of in isolation from the economic, political and cultural structures within which it is embedded, including its involvement in processes of consumption for a large part of its infrastructural maintenance. Information and communications technologies take on an important role in constructing and maintaining these structures in the contemporary world (Silverstone and Hirsch 1992).

Douglas (1991) suggests that, fundamentally, the construction of home is about bringing space and time under control, to provide an infrastructure for the development of the household as a proto-community. However, as we will see throughout this book, this control does not arise spontaneously, but is achieved through what Hage (1997) calls 'home-building' as social practice. Home-building practices are directed towards 'the building of a feeling of being "at home"', and a deep subconscious familiarity with our everyday living spaces arises as a result:

> The feeling of familiarity is generated by a space where the deployment of our bodily dispositions can be maximised . . . This involves the creation of a space where one possesses a maximal practical know-how: knowing what everything is for and when it ought to be used. It also involves the creation of a space where one possesses a maximal spatial knowledge: knowing almost unthinkingly where one is, and where one needs to go for specific purposes and how to get there. (102–3)

Hage illustrates the point: 'If I get up at night, my feet can take me to the toilet or to the fridge without me really having to wake up and think where to go' (147). Indeed, while this phenomenon is perhaps at its most developed in our homes, it operates in our sense of feeling 'at home' throughout our familiar environments of everyday living, including, in the contemporary world, shopping malls, mediascapes and institutions such as schools, universities and other workplaces.

If home-building practices are directed towards feeling 'at home', it is clear that they are not directed only towards the management of the affective relationships of home. They are also material practices by which the physical domestic environment is assembled as a *bricolage* of objects and materials brought together, usually over an extended period of time (perhaps even over the lifespan of the individuals who constitute the household), from a diverse range of sources. As Bachelard

(1994: 4) expresses it, the objects of our personal domestic environment do not simply provide us with a static backdrop to our everyday lives: the home is an *inhabited* place. Indeed, Bachelard goes further than this, seeing home as the archetype of inhabited space: 'all really inhabited space bears the essence of the notion of home' (5). The relationship we have with our personal domestic environment is based on continuing processes of interaction: for Bachelard, we need to investigate 'how we inhabit our vital space, in accord with all the dialectics of life, how we take root, day after day, in a "corner of the world"' (4).

Within this book I am considering primarily the home-building practices of people who have a stable location within which they can construct a home. There are, of course, people without such a place: the homeless, refugees, long-term travellers, but it seems inevitable that over a period of time strategies and spatial practices which involve the appropriation of objects and space may be developed by these individuals. Dant observes, for example, that people who were formally homeless but living in hostels emphasized control over what they were allowed to do, such as being able to make a cup of coffee, in relating what 'home' meant to them (1999: 70). Home-building is not solely conducted at home: when we personalize our workplaces by bringing personal items or by customizing our work computer we are also undertaking home-building activities.

Within the physical space of the dwelling, the material home is constructed through the assembly and configuration of objects, such as furniture, decorative items and technologies. These organizations of objects are not static, but interact dynamically with those who inhabit them, as the material substrate to their patterns of everyday life. Although the materials from which it is built are brought into it from outside, the home is 'modeled by fine touches', and is, in the final analysis, 'a house built by and for the body . . . in an intimacy that works physically'. The process of home-building is like that of the bird's nest described by Michelet:

> The form of the nest is commanded by the inside. 'On the inside,' he
> continues, 'the instrument that prescribes a circular form for the nest is
> nothing else but the body of the bird. It is by constantly turning round
> and round and pressing back the walls on every side, that it succeeds in
> forming this circle.' The female, like a living tower, hollows out the house,
> while the male brings back from the outside all kinds of materials, sturdy
> twigs and other bits. . . . Michelet points out how the home is modeled
> by fine touches, which make a surface originally bristling and composite

into one that is smooth and soft. (Bachelard, 1994: 100–2; including quoted material from Michelet 1858: 208)

In the contemporary western world, our possessions generally start life as mass-produced commodities. Importantly, they are not just material objects, but also have symbolic associations (such as the link between technological imaginaries and the future), and they are generally also involved in broader projects of domestic development, maintenance and reproduction. This is clear in the case of the home computer, which is often expressly acquired because of its association with work-related skills and activities, and with educational applications for both children and adults. Consumers may have the sense of acting freely when they choose to acquire a home computer. However, the broad social context within which personal computers are produced and marketed, and incorporated into social institutions such as schools and workplaces, leaves many consumers feeling that the choice *not* to acquire a home computer is an untenable option.

A Case Study: the Manfredotti Family

Domestic Material Culture

Many of the themes which will recur throughout the book, linking technology, home-building and ownership, can be illustrated through the experiences of the Manfredotti family. Laura and Max Manfredotti have four children: Angelica (fifteen), Paul (fourteen), Steven (eleven) and Josh (six). The two older children are at high school, while the two younger are in primary school. Max left school at the age of fifteen, and drives a truck in the sand and gravel industry. Laura works part-time (eight hours per week) in health care. Their computer, an Apple Macintosh LCIII, was bought just over two years before my interview with them, exclusively, Laura explains, to contribute to the children's education. She sees education as crucial to her children's future life choices, and feels that her husband's limited formal education has severely constrained his career options. She is anxious that her children should not be limited in the same way:

> My husband didn't get an education, he has no formal education. He left school at fifteen to help his parents on the family farm. He drove the tractor, loved it, every minute of it. And it's only been in the last ten years that his lack of education has really created problems, and I don't want

Figure 1 The Manfredotti household's computer is located in a corner of their dining room. The chair to the right of the computer is Laura Manfredotti's 'spot', from which she can monitor her sons' use of the computer.

that to happen to my boys, I don't want that to happen to my kids. So for me, that's a big thing. I don't want them to be limited like their dad, very very limited, he could not do any other job than what he's doing, unless he was a farm-hand or something like that. I think that's a real shame, and I don't want that to happen.

Not having a computer, Laura feels, puts children at an educational disadvantage, particularly once they reach high school. The computer was bought at the beginning of Angelica's second year in high school, after she had had some limited computer tuition at school the previous year, and had been encouraged to progress further. One of the teachers commented that it was 'such a shame' that Angelica had no chance to practise her computer skills outside the limited access at school, and advised that she would 'go ahead in leaps and bounds if only she could practise'.

The first time she had computers in Year 7 it was a compulsory thing every now and again, and she sat there in front of it, couldn't use the keyboard. Everyone else had started, and she had to ask the teacher 'where do I turn it on?' She didn't have a clue. Yet by the end of the year she was so far ahead that she was invited then to do computer studies as a course, it was by invitation only. They were saying to us, you know, 'it's such a shame Angelica doesn't have a keyboard to use, because just looking at her once or twice a week for the hour, her head's in it, she knows what to do but she can't practise'. So that was a big incentive, and they said 'she'll go ahead leaps and bounds if only she could practise'. So, we thought at one stage of just buying a typewriter, but that was already, for a good one, with a keyboard like that, was already several hundred dollars, and so we thought 'no, no. We'll stick it out and get the computer.'

I asked Laura whether there was a feeling at all of not wanting to be left behind in their home computer purchase:

Oh, definitely. Not for myself, but for the kids . . . For me, education was very important, and . . . I didn't want Angelica in five or six years time, saying, I could have done better if I'd had the facilities at hand. So I want to make sure that those important things, that she's got them.

They plan for it to see their children through their high school education, and then, Laura feels, they won't need it any more: 'That's it, we never expected to use it ourselves. If they weren't here we never would have bought it, we have no need of it.'

What comes through clearly within this narrative is the powerful motivational cocktail of parental hopes and fears for their children and the sense of responsibility for providing them with the infrastructural basis they will need to take advantage of life opportunities. To these forces must be added the subtle encouragement given by the school, and the broad sense that these are changes which must be kept up with or risk being left behind.

The process of research and investigation leading up to the actual purchase of the computer shows an attention to detailed research and investigation. In this household, as in many others, there was a need to prioritize the purchase among other possible uses for the money, and a significant delay between the initial decision that a home computer would be a good idea and the acquisition itself. Laura and her daughter Angelica spent about six months collecting information about computers before making the final decision jointly. Friends and acquaintances were asked what sort of computer they had, what they used it for and what their experience had been. A number of different computer shops were visited, and brochures and advertising leaflets collected.

Laura found the difficulty of making a decision about such a sizeable investment very stressful: 'I found it terrible, I was a wreck. I was so worried, I just wanted to choose the best that I could afford for my family . . . I wouldn't like to go through it again.' Although, at $3,000, the computer purchase was a large financial commitment for this family, who saved for a year to buy it, Laura feels that she is also equally careful about smaller purchases: 'I have just as much trouble getting the best value for money school bag . . . I'm stressed like that all the time, when it comes to things like that.'

The range of models to choose from and the issue of whether to go for an IBM-compatible or Apple Macintosh were very confusing. Laura's strategy, like that of many other computer purchasers, was to keep asking questions in different places until something like a consistent picture emerged. At one particular large retailer:

> they had too many choices, and we didn't know enough about each. They told us not to go for Apple Mac because we wouldn't be able to swap games or anything like that. They told us that's the expensive way around and that Apple Mac would be phased out eventually and be totally taken over by IBM and that eventually there'd be no games or anything made for Apple Mac because that was a dying thing.

In the end, one of the advantages from Laura's point of view was the relative lack of circulation in pirate Macintosh software: neighbours had had a problem with a computer virus which was attributed to the children swapping games and programs with friends. The Apple retailer who eventually sold them their computer offered a different perspective, pointing out that most of the local schools had Apple Macintoshes.

Laura feels that this process of researching the purchase left her feeling cynical and distrustful of the sales staff in most of the outlets they visited: 'They were there to make a sale . . . He wasn't really interested in what we were looking at but my problem was that I wasn't going to go buying a big four or five thousand dollar computer.' The major deciding factor in where they eventually bought from was Laura's confidence in one particular staff member at the local Apple reseller, who, for Laura, fell outside the distrusted category of sales person:

> He wasn't a salesman, he used to go around to all the schools. A very big, old man, lovely person . . . I was nervous and feeling like an idiot because I didn't know anything. Anyway, when Norman came over he was far more interested, he wanted to know a bit about us first, what we

were looking for and then he said 'well you don't need this and you don't need that and this isn't going to do the job and you've got a choice of these'.

Norman's interest in and attention to their personal needs, and his apparent lack of concern at the level of the eventual sale won Laura's trust. They had initially wanted to buy a computer with CD-ROM installed, but were talked out of it by Norman. His argument was: 'Don't present the children with all the challenges at the same time' and that with this model they could buy an external CD-ROM drive later.

Two years down the track, at the time of my interview with them, the Manfredottis were going through a similar process of researching the purchase of a CD-ROM drive for their computer. Norman was no longer employed by the Apple reseller, and the staff there advised the Manfredottis that they should have bought the CD-ROM at the same time as the computer, since, they said, their computer was too limited in speed and memory capacity to take one of the currently available CD-ROM drives. The Apple dealer suggested that, rather than upgrading their existing computer, they should trade it in on a new one with a CD-ROM installed.

I asked Laura whether, with hindsight, she felt that Norman's advice not to buy the CD-ROM with the initial purchase had been sound. After a long pause, she said 'I don't know', and paused again. Then 'Yeah, probably, because the children weren't interested in a CD-ROM'. Along with other processes of researching the purchase, a sense of trust and confidence in the people who provide advice is clearly very important as a strategy for minimizing the risk associated with a major purchase like a computer, and maintaining a sense of control over the incorporation of such technological innovations into the life of the household (Silverstone and Haddon 1996: 60). Inexperienced computer consumers must navigate a minefield of conflicting messages in negotiating this new cultural terrain, which is highly stressful but is seen as a necessary parental responsibility.

As this example illustrates, everyday consumption practices are inherently contradictory, although these contradictions may remain unacknowledged and unexamined. Laura still speaks positively about the salesman she thinks of as 'not a salesman' even though they may not (with hindsight) have been given good advice. Consumers must develop their own strategies for coping with these situations, and although the practices and institutions of consumption are organized in such a way as to provide defences against such anxiety (Robins 1994), they are clearly still sources of stress for many consumers.

The purchase of a computer is also not a single isolated act. It is instead a process which may take place over an extended period of time, commencing with the initial recognition that a computer purchase is something the household might benefit from, through saving for and researching the process, to the final decision on which computer to buy and where to buy it from. The acquisition of a computer, then, is a process commencing well before the act of acquisition itself, and continues as the computer is incorporated into the everyday life of the household.

Integrating the Computer into the Household's 'Pattern of Life'

Laura reports that the computer is used mainly for school work, as intended when it was purchased. As in other households with school-aged children, school work takes priority over other uses of the computer. Angelica is the principal user of the computer, although fourteen-year-old Paul's use is increasing since he started high school too. Laura uses the computer sometimes to do wordprocessing in connection with her voluntary work as treasurer of a local community association, while her husband Max doesn't use the computer at all. Game playing is a secondary use of the computer, although Laura reports that the children tend to see the computer as for 'serious' use and use their Nintendo games console instead for playing games, only playing games on the computer if the Nintendo is already in use.

In order to build up an ongoing and relatively stable relationship of interaction between the members of the household and the novel acquisition, a computer must find its place within the existing patterns of activity and routine within the household. The establishment of the place of the computer within the household does not happen immediately on bringing it home, but is built up over a period of time, and through changing temporalities of the household (Silverstone 1993). When a new computer is brought home, there is often a pronounced sense of its novelty, which is reflected in a period of exploration and investigation of what the computer can do. After a period of time, the novelty 'wears off'. Within the Manfredotti household, for example, the computer was used much more for playing games, when it was new than it was by the time, two years later, that they were interviewed:

> Originally, because it was a novelty, but like I say we've only got three or four games, and then a couple of others which have lost their challenge, it's like playing Monopoly over and over again, they get bored. And they

might not play it for ages, and then all of a sudden, they'll have a competition going, and they'll keep a running record over three or four days of who's got the best score and all of that . . . But that, after a while, will get boring too. (Laura Manfredotti)

The patterning of home computer use is structured, then, by the temporal routines of the household, but as is shown here, even a relatively stable pattern of activity within the household will maintain some flexibility. A period of intense engagement in some area of everyday activity may reach a kind of saturation point, when boredom sets in and the activity is set aside. Then, perhaps because of school holidays, or a period of wet weather, the activity that had previously become unattractive may suddenly seem interesting again.

Term-time patterns of use (which tend to centre around school homework) are different from those which emerge during school holidays. The weekday pattern in this household is different from that at weekends and differs between the household members:

> The boys [use it] very little during the week, because Angelica needs to do her school work. Anyone who has to do school work has priority but at the weekends it comes in fits and starts, mostly the games. If they get on it, they'll be on it for an hour and then they'll be bored with it. They'll have a go at everything and then they'll be bored with it. Then it might only be off for five minutes and someone else will want a turn. So I'd say in half-hour or hour lots it would be on quite a bit.

Over an extended period of time, then, temporal patterns emerge out of the ebb and flow of everyday household activity. These are also, however, actively managed to a significant degree as part of the parental role, and in particular illustrate strategies through which domestic structures are kept under control. The household's pattern of life is manifested in its routines of activity, but also in the balance of interpersonal relationships between household members, in their patterns of interaction, and through the construction and maintenance of domestic hierarchies of power.

While the computer must find its place within the household's routines of activity, and within the structures of interpersonal relationship between household members, it must also establish a relationship to both the physical layout of the house and other household objects. Computers generally are fairly large objects which are usually located in a fixed location within the house, and are associated with furniture and other objects such as a desk and chair, disks, books, papers and so on. The Manfredottis' computer is located in a corner of their dining room (see figure 1). Dining rooms are often seen as suitable locations for computers, despite the apparent paradox of the universal injunction against food and drink around them, an issue which will be explored in chapter 10.

The home computer, as a new kind of domestic appliance – an 'information appliance' – may be like the vacuum cleaner (which is generally switched on only during the time it is in use), or more like the fridge, which is left on all the time. Television sets provide a useful comparison here: while in many households the television may be left on even when no-one is watching it, in others it must be switched off when whoever was watching it is finished. Behaviour around the computer, it seems, is similar to this, in that in some households it is switched on and left on, while in others, the Manfredotti household included, this is never the case: 'They must turn it off.' The rules around one technology do not necessarily translate simply across to others, however. In this household, the computer is categorized with the Nintendo games machine rather than the television, since, in general, once the television is switched on it tends to be left on.

While some kinds of household objects such as furniture and other items are allied collaboratively with the computer, for other objects there is a more competitive relationship. Some commentators have suggested, for example, that the introduction of a computer into the household may result in a reduction in the amount of television watched by householders (Wheelock 1992). Just as the introduction of television redefined the role of radio within the household (Taachi 1998), the computer may be seen to be transforming the role of a range of other kinds of household objects, such as the typewriter and perhaps unexpected objects, such as board games. The complementarity of computer game-playing and the use of dedicated equipment such as the Nintendo and Sony platforms is instructive here. In the Manfredotti household, for example, the computer has been redefined as for 'serious' use over time, rather than for playing games. The children tend to use the Nintendo for playing games instead:

> The children now don't see it as a toy. They go on the Nintendo for the toy and they go to the computer for work. They still play the games that we have there but I think they get a lot more use out of it . . . They still play some games on the computer, particularly if it's the weekend, and my son will have a friend over and the younger boy will come in with a

friend expecting to play and they'll have to wait their turn, so we'll have one group over here and two sitting over there playing with that and then we play swaps, and the kitchen timer comes in there.

Laura Manfredotti had initially been 'panicky' around the computer, and monitored closely her children's use of it. In figure 1, the place Laura would take up to monitor her children's use of the computer can be seen on the right-hand side of the computer workstation:

> I sat next to whoever was on it, monitoring my $3000 worth. I was terrified of it, didn't know what they could do, what they couldn't do. Angelica was way ahead of me, and there was a lot of arguments because she had the confidence and I didn't have the confidence in her ability, and I had that manual and we couldn't make head nor tail of it at the beginning because we didn't know anything about computers. And Angelica was able to explain a few things and I was getting frustrated because we'd had a couple of problems that the children had done which made me so upset, so nervous. Because they were naturally curious, because they were doing things that . . . I was out of control.

At this early stage Laura did not know very much about the computer herself, and therefore felt that control over the technology itself was out of her reach. It is clear, however, that she was able to develop strategies for retaining the level of domestic control she feels comfortable with, even if this meant physically taking up a position next to whoever was using it.

We can also see again the same anxiety as we saw above in relation to the Manfredottis' acquisition of the computer, and Laura's development of strategies which give her more control over the computer and its place in the household. This control necessarily means, for Laura in her role as parent, that she feels the need to maintain parental authority and retain the prerogative to regulate access to the computer. This tension between Laura's need to stay in control and Angelica's greater knowledge of the computer, and its threat to the general balance of their relationship, resulted in this case in overt conflicts – 'a lot of arguments' – around the computer.

Laura's anxiety was, in fact, exacerbated in the early days with the computer, because there had been problems caused by the children's curiosity. After one particularly nasty problem, which required the complete reinstallation of the software and a home visit from a staff member of the retailer who had sold them the machine, they installed a program to limit access to the system by the boys (but not Laura or Angelica). Laura also enrolled in a computer course:

> I used to get so upset – crying and wishing that we'd never bought this thing. Anyway that seemed to end after I went to the course, I had more confidence and by that time Angelica was getting these glowing reports all the time. And by then I knew the boys couldn't get in and do any damage. They can play the games, they can't get into Clarisworks or anything like that . . . So I'm back in control now.

While Laura initially felt the need to monitor closely all use of the computer, further down the track she was no longer concerned that one of the children would do something to damage the computer. She still feels sometimes, however, that she needs to keep a close eye on the children's application to their homework, particularly as far as her sons are concerned. This is because, she explains, she feels that Angelica understands the importance of achieving a good education, but 'my boys would do no school work at all if I wasn't onto them from the time they get home'.

In this, as in many of the households in the study, there is explicit regulation by the parents of their children's use of the home computer. Indeed, Wood and Beck (1994) argue that the presence of children in the household makes explicit rules necessary. Hawkins also argues that such rules are an important part of the 'intimate economy of value' (1998: 123) of the home, contributing to the pedagogic transmission of value. What may start as explicit injunctions, however, eventually become techniques of self-management: 'rules survive by becoming naturalized, by ceasing to be imposed and becoming instead meaning, order, rationality, the "way we do things here"' (131).

A prohibition against food and drink around the home computer – which generally applies to children but not to adults – appears to be almost universal. In the Manfredotti household, this rule is allied with more general controls about which parts of the house food and drink are allowed to be taken into:

> No food, and no drink [around the computer]. But that rule applies to a lot of areas. We've no food or drink upstairs, they either eat outside, at the table, or in the kitchen, not on the lounges, only Max and I are allowed to do that. That's me, I'm afraid, we don't have much and I want to keep what we have as nice as possible, you know, we keep everything simple. So I've gotta have rules.

Parents often also serve a gate-keeping function and resolve disputes around the computer, including conflicts over whose turn it is to use it. Laura Manfredotti reports that disputes over the computer had largely died out by the time of our interview, but that, when the computer was new and was more of a novelty, she would allocate time on the computer amongst the children by using the kitchen timer:

> I used to use the kitchen timer. I did it wrong, we used to have 'you play one game and then it's someone else's turn', but Angelica could make a game last half an hour where Josh would be out in five minutes. So we started using the kitchen timer to time half-hour lots. I don't have to do that any more, the children now don't see it as a toy.

In many households one person emerges as a kind of 'local expert' or local manager of the computer. In the Manfredotti household it is Angelica who looks after the organization of things on the computer, including managing the administration of the software which limits access to the younger children to a few specified programs. Laura is happy for her to do this, since she has confidence in her ability:

> She's put this Clarisworks alias over here [on the desktop] for some reason, I don't know why. I don't question her, because I've got the confidence now that she knows what she's doing . . . Everything that's on there stays on there, she hasn't done anything where she's had to come and say 'Mum?' like all three boys have done.

Ownership of the Manfredottis' Computer

As part of the process of integration of the computer into this household, a differentiated sense of ownership of the computer has emerged. The computer was explicitly bought for the family as a whole, and particularly for the use of the children to assist with their school work, and it therefore, in the pure sense of property rights, belongs to them all. Laura feels, however, that she has to tread carefully in order not to reinforce a sense that Angelica has more proprietary rights over it than the rest of the children:

> She's the one that uses it the most [and] anything that she uses the most, eventually she considers it her own, so if we say that it's hers then the boys will feel that they have to ask her permission to use it . . . and that's probably my instigation because I made the rule . . . that anyone who

has homework gets priority before games, even if one of them has got a friend over. I try to be accommodating but if Angelica says 'I've got to get this done and I have to go to work tomorrow night and I need it for Wednesday morning' – 'Off, on the Nintendo or outside, Angelica has priority.' And that would not only be Angelica, it's happened with the others too, with Paul, and then Steven.

While Angelica may have a privileged sense of proprietorship over the computer compared with the other children (which may exist even though Laura resists it), it is clear that, over the time that the computer has been in the household, Laura's own relationship with the computer has also evolved. While in the beginning the computer was clearly an object which was outside her domestic control, and indeed was an object to be feared, by the time of the interview she again felt that she was 'back in control'. For Laura, then, ownership of the computer is tied up with her sense of ownership over the domestic space as a whole, as a space of comfort and control which may be disrupted by such 'alien' presences (in the sense of an object which is *not* owned) as the computer initially was.

As these aspects of computer use in the Manfredotti household show, the computer may be the focus of different kinds of interpersonal negotiation, all of which are implicated in how each member of the household is able to construct for themselves a personal relationship with the technology. In many households, these social or interpersonal negotiations also involve people who live outside the household. Once people have reached the limit of their own expertise with the computer, and if there is no-one else within the household who takes on the 'local expert' role, there is often a further line of defence outside the household. This often takes the form of a network of friends, relatives or acquaintances who can be called on for assistance or advice (as, indeed, we saw above in the case of the advice sought before purchasing the computer). For children, the computer may also be the focus of social activity with their friends – getting together at each other's houses and engaging in computer-based activities such as playing games. Angelica Manfredotti's friends, for example, sometimes come over to do joint school work together using the computer.

Over a period of time, then, the computer within the Manfredotti household has established its place within the domestic pattern of life. Rather than happening all at once on its arrival, the computer's location within this structure is emergent, through both explicit negotiation and more subtle and implicit adaptation to changing circumstances.

Although there is a role for parental intervention in these processes (which in this household is largely taken on, particularly in relation to the computer, by Laura), this is by no means the only (or even the most important) factor in how the computer's location within the household is arrived at.

The same object may be differentially taken up by the members of the household. Angelica Manfredotti, for example, had managed to develop a personal sense of proprietary rights over the computer through becoming its main user and through her role as the 'administrator' of the computer's security provisions. For the three sons in the household, the computer had become an integral part of their 'serious' school-related work at home, to be contrasted with the Nintendo machine on which they play games. For Laura Manfredotti, although she herself uses the computer at times, the most important aspect of her relationship with the computer was that it had become integral to the domestic domain, within which the children's developmental needs are provided for. Max Manfredotti does not use the computer at all, and we might therefore conclude that, although in an economic sense the computer belongs to him (as to all the family members), he has not developed a subjective sense of ownership of it at all.

Since the construction of a personal relationship of ownership involves an ongoing negotiation between the object and its owner(s), through which they come into an established relationship with each other, it is possible for this process to stall. Sometimes consumers are not successful in staking their claim to ownership, which may indeed be the case for people like Max Manfredotti who do not use the computer in their home:

> There are certain goods that the consumer never successfully lays claim to because the consumer never successfully lays claim to their symbolic properties. The good becomes a paradox: the consumer owns it without possessing it. (McCracken 1988: 85)

McCracken distinguishes here between ownership in the legal form of property rights, and possession as the subjective relationship of ownership. It is this second sense which this book aims to elaborate, of possession as a complex and multidimensional relationship, formed through interaction and activity and involving affective attachments.

Conclusion

Macpherson is partially correct in insisting that property is not things (1978: 2). It does not, however, purely consist of rights, either. Possession is not simply an attribute either on the part of the owner or the object owned, but is constructed through the activities and interactions through which we each come into a personal and subjective relationship with the material culture we bring into the domestic space. Material culture shapes subjectivities and social identities through the profoundly relational engagements we form with our everyday personal environments of action and interaction. It is not that the objects of material culture act as a 'human mirror', passively reflecting or marking identity, but that they are actively involved in the construction of human subjects in the social and cultural world. Possession is more, however, than the simple appropriation of domestic objects. The ownership of objects which start life as mass-produced commodities, as illustrated by the Manfredotti case study and as will become clear throughout this book, is implicated in the household's interactions with a broad range of external social institutions and cultural forms. They are one of the principal means, in contemporary western society, by which the household maintains and reproduces itself, through processes of home-building.

The Relationship of Ownership

As suggested in chapter 1, personal possessions must be seen in essentially relational terms, and ownership viewed as an activity, rather than an attribute. One of the central paradoxes of the contemporary world, however, is that most of the objects which become our personal possessions originate as generic and impersonal mass-produced commodities. This chapter develops a theoretical model for the ownership of personal possessions by extending Miller's (1987) conception (derived from Hegel) of *objectification* as a dynamic and dialectical process through which both socialized human subjects and the objects of the cultural environment are mutually constituted. Material culture – the cultural environment in its broadest terms, including such 'virtual' cultural forms as media flows and ideologies – have the collective function of making meanings and values stable and visible, or in other terms, of making social experience meaningful.

However, because they operate largely through extra-linguistic modes of experience, the logics of material culture may not be readily available to conscious articulation and interrogation. Transcendent values and meanings which are otherwise intangible can be made concrete, culturally intelligible and given permanence and social effectiveness. Contradictions and paradoxes can be made liveable, both at the level of broad public discourse and representation and in everyday life and practice. It is suggested that evocative cultural objects like the home computer may be able to act as 'bridges' between the concrete, local and particular present and imagined alternative states or abstract and otherwise intangible entities. But material culture may also act in an 'anchoring' mode, as 'scaffolding' for the self, as placeholders which have a role for individuals in maintaining ontological security and a sense of self in everyday life.

The Objectness of Objects

We are surrounded by material objects. Most of them, particularly in industrialized countries, are mass-produced artefacts. Our homes, in particular, are full of objects. Contemporary mass consumption has seen an explosion of domestic objects: at the beginning of the nineteenth century, the home of a reasonably well-off family would have contained no more than 150 to 200 objects, including crockery and clothing. The home of a comparable family today might contain up to 3000 items, not counting individually such items as books and tapes (Branzi 1988: 14).

Despite their ubiquity these everyday objects are, for the most part, completely taken for granted, forming an invisible backdrop to our day-to-day lives. It has been suggested that this paradox, and the general neglect of material culture in academic discourse until very recently, may be a consequence of the very physicality of the material world. Artefacts may be difficult to investigate within intellectual traditions based profoundly on language and the language-like features of culture (Miller 1987: 100; McCracken 1988: 68). Taussig traces this neglect of what he calls the 'objectness of objects' to the Enlightenment's privileging of sight as the organ of knowledge acquisition. This led to an analytical separation and distancing between the observer and the object of study which has only recently been widely problematized in academic debate (Taussig 1993: 18). By reducing objects to identification with linguistic elements we ignore their role in reproducing kinaesthetic and emotional influences, and their significance as tools or environments experienced.

The fundamental characteristic of material objects is that, because they exist in a physically concrete form, they have presence with permanence from moment to moment which intra-psychic subjective experience may not have – 'staying in their place' as Romanyshyn puts it, to give us our place in the world. Miller (1987: 99) proposes that the materiality of artefacts may allow them to act as a bridge between the physical and mental worlds, and indeed between consciousness and the unconscious. McCracken (1988: 132) also suggests that the materiality of artefacts allows them to act as culturally conservative forms, effectively making ideology manifest, but in such a way that it is not available for conscious reflection and interrogation. Material culture 'allows culture to insinuate its beliefs and assumptions into the very fabric of daily life' (68).

Consumption is an active symbolic process within which social categories are continuously defined and redefined (Douglas and Isherwood 1996). Goods are needed for making the categories of culture visible and stable and making social experience and relationships meaningful, but each individual object or act of consumption only has meaning within the context of a structured system of objects and consumption practices taken as a whole (Baudrillard 1996). It is clear, however, that the selection of goods cannot be equated in any simple way with the construction of the self. It is not just that we use goods to project a particular identity and to communicate with others about who we are or would like to be, either consciously or unconsciously. The characteristics we incorporate as a result of the goods we consume are deeply internalized: as Douglas and Isherwood point out, culture fits us like a skin, not like a glove (1996: 62).

As Silverstone (1994: 1) has pointed out, running through recent theorizing on the nature of social life has been a stress on the social as a defence against anxiety. In particular, in contemporary life this includes institutions and practices of consumption (Robins 1994). If such defences against the inevitably anxiety-provoking aspects of everyday life are successful, then what Giddens has termed 'ontological security' is achieved: 'the confidence that most human beings have in the continuity of their self-identity and in the constancy of the surrounding social and material environments of action' (1990: 92). What is created is a space for everyday life that is safe and comfortable, because of its familiarity and proven trustworthiness – a psychological comfort zone.

In the work of psychoanalyst D.W. Winnicott, such a comfort zone arises out of the normal processes of individual development. At the earliest stages of life, an infant is not aware of the separation between itself and the external environment. Initially, the infant is under the illusion (maintained with the active co-operation of the mother or other care giver) of magical control over the environment – the breast appears almost as soon as the infant becomes aware of wanting it. As the infant develops cognitively and physically, and becomes more capable of independence, the mother undertakes a process of disillusionment, gradually withdrawing her adaptation to the baby's needs and introducing the outside world to the child. 'Independence is never absolute. The healthy individual does not become isolated, but becomes related to the environment in such a way that the individual and the environment can be said to be interdependent.' (Winnicott 1963).

This is a very slow maturational process, which continues throughout childhood and into adulthood, at first mediated primarily by the mother or other carers and continuing through the growing child's emerging involvement in school and other social institutions. At first, the child's world consists almost entirely of the home, but gradually broadens as more and more experiences and skills are acquired (Matthews 1992). In particular, familiarity with and skills in consumption activities (which start with the school canteen if not before) are an important part of what is essentially the process of socialization. This personal evolution continues, until eventually the individual becomes independently capable of seeking out and appropriating novel experiences, activities and objects to the self. However, the process is never actually completed, as there are always new and unfamiliar social and cultural contexts for the individual to come into contact with. In particular, in the complex globalizing contemporary world, the pace of change is such that we are continually challenged by new situations and experiences. The development of strategies and skills for responding to new experiences, cultural contexts and material objects is thus a crucial part of the maturational process.

The role of physical objects is crucial in the transition from total dependence to relative independence, in mediating the intermediate area between subjective experience and that which is objectively perceived. Of particular importance are what Winnicott calls 'transitional objects' – 'the first not-me possessions', often teddy bears and special blankets (1971: 96). These objects are not part of the infant's body yet are not fully recognized as belonging to external reality. Winnicott uses the term 'potential space' to describe the gradually evolving and expanding experiential sphere of perception and action which constitutes the individual's everyday world. This space, essentially the interface between the inner life of the individual and that individual's everyday interaction with external reality, is described by Winnicott as 'a place for living that is not properly described by either of the terms "inner" and "outer"' (1971: 106).

It is essential to the successful unfolding of potential space that the individual is able to have confidence in the continuity of his or her experience – that ontological security is maintained. In earliest infancy, this is achieved by the repetitive and reliable nature of parental management. As the child moves towards autonomy, continuity of experience is achieved by presenting the complexities of the social and cultural world to the infant a bit at a time: 'only on the basis of monotony can a mother profitably add richness' (Winnicott 1945). As the child grows, he or she is increasingly able, and is generally enthusiastic, to explore the world around in a series of forays from the safe and familiar base that is known and comfortable. Parental management of this developmental process includes the kinds of strategies of support for their children's development, but also a need to maintain control over the process, that we saw in the case of the Manfredotti household.

The developmental processes described by Winnicott therefore provide for a continuity of experience between infancy and adulthood, between having no sense of a separation between the self and the external environment and being aware of and able to act in and manipulate the environment autonomously. The familiar objects and routine activities of everyday life – everything that can be said to belong to an individual, both concrete and abstract – constitute the psychological comfort zone of the individual's ontological security. Potential space in Winnicott's terms could be said to be that essentially personal space of everyday life, familiar and largely taken for granted, trusted because of its proven reliability, the space of all that is truly 'mine'. Almost by definition, anything in the world outside this space is unfamiliar and in all likelihood will be anxiety-provoking. The objects and activities which are most likely to be taken up and appropriated to the self will tend, therefore, to be those on the (fuzzy) outskirts of personal space, those not already familiar and comfortable, but also not totally unfamiliar and threatening. As we will see in chapter 3, the processes of consumption, particularly discourses and representations around commodities and strategies on the part of commercial organizations, have precisely this function of making unfamiliar objects familiar, and hence more acceptable, to consumers. Indeed, it must also be recognized that the emotional response to objects and activities which are 'not quite' familiar is not a wholly negative one. There is also something of a *frisson* of anticipation and excitement which characterizes the response to the new, which is one of the engines which drives us forward to new experiences and explorations.

Our personal possessions and the routine activities of our everyday lives become, in a sense, the anchors for our personal place in the world. New social and cultural contexts, and interactions with unfamiliar technologies or other objects may play a role in reshaping and renegotiating the activities of everyday life, and thus provide opportunities for self-transformation by giving access to new areas of experience. The physical presence of material objects may therefore allow them to act as place-holders or mnemonics, as a kind of personal and cultural psychic scaffolding. It is important to emphasize that what is being proposed here is not simply a cognitive phenomenon, a mental mapping of the physical environment. What is being proposed is, in fact, a rejection of the Cartesian mind–body dualism: the embodied human subject is embedded within and interacts both mentally and materially with its proximate environment of perception.

The familiar quotidian environments which we inhabit, including our homes, are physical environments within which, because of our longstanding experience of them, we are no longer continuously conscious of the objects around us. These objects have retreated into the background of our consciousness of our environment, and we become aware of them only when, for some reason, they call attention to themselves by, for one reason or another, *not* appearing in their familiar places. Indeed, the largely habitual interaction we are able to sustain within the familiar physical environment might be called a kind of *cultural proprioception*. Just as the physical sense of proprioception gives us a continuous awareness of the arrangement of our limbs and location in space (so that I can close my eyes and still be able to put my finger to the end of my nose), the material continuity and perceptibility of cultural forms supports and structures our place in the social world, and mediates the way that we act in it.

If the materiality of the object world is able to provide us with this sort of psychic scaffolding, then perhaps it does so by providing permanence and tangibility to the structure of Winnicott's potential space. Everyday life is largely improvised on the basis of past experience and present expectations as incorporated in the embodied human subject. Structured crystallizations of practice (*habitus*, as Bourdieu (1977) calls them) tend to reproduce themselves, and hence innovations in social networks will result in practices which 'tend to be unreflectingly remodelled to conform with the "usual", "right" practices' (Glennie and Thrift 1996: 40–1). The sense of the self is

> inextricably linked with practices and practical knowledges because it involves being able to marshal a set of narratives, . . . appropriate segments of the object world (almost inevitably including nowadays all manner of consumer goods), a repertoire of bodily stances, and so on. Together, these resources generate a 'sense of belonging', a feeling that the agent does not have to qualify as a member of a network, being already competent in its spaces and times. (41)

This sense of belonging is essentially a feeling of *being at home* in the everyday social and cultural environments we inhabit. The taken-for-granted knowledge and deep subconscious familiarity which results from our 'home-building' activities (Hage 1997), as noted in chapter 1, has its parallel in the comfortable familiarity of the many and diverse cultural environments in whose spaces and times we are competent:

Every time we enter a hotel, a theme park, a freeway, a subway, a McDonald's restaurant, or an office building, we draw on a repertoire of gestures and interactive competencies in order to negotiate material space as well as communicate with others. (Gottdiener 1995: 73)

This comfort and familiarity has its converse in the stressful sense of disorientation we feel when faced with new cultural environments.

This view of the human subject as a culturally produced self-in-relation to its environment, whose 'belongings' include its competence in its familiar cultural environment, is in accord with the model of objectification developed by Miller (1987). As an irreducibly relational process which mutually constructs both human subjects and their sociocultural environment, the concept of objectification addresses the paradox of how it is that each of us is able to build a personalized place in the world, largely out of mass-produced objects.

Objectification

The objects we interact with as socialized subjects, including technologies and mass-produced commodities, appear from the point of view of the individual as socially and symbolically 'given'. Yet it is only through interacting with this social and cultural environment that we make our own personal place in the world. The concept of objectification recognizes that cultural phenomena which seem fixed and rigid are in reality dynamic social processes, providing a view of all cultural form as created by human activity, in a dynamic, dialectical and diachronic process. Social institutions and forms appear to individuals as existing outside of them and constraining their actions, but this seemingly autonomous and objective social reality in fact arises from individual, albeit collaborative, human initiative and activity.

Miller (1987) follows Hegel's *Phenomenology of Spirit* (1977) in seeing that individual and collective human activity creates the objects of the social world, from commodities to political and economic institutions and, of course, sociotechnical systems. Miller's aim is to provide a view of mass-produced commodities which recognizes their potential for personally and socially progressive effects. In particular, goods which are the product of commercial concerns and industrial processes may in certain circumstances be able to be appropriated and symbolically recontextualized by segments of the population who use them to create themselves in their own image. This potential is, however, bound up in already existing hierarchies and structures of social constraint and agency, and, in many cases:

people are forced to live in and through objects which are created through the images held of them by a different and dominant section of the population. The possibilities of recontextualization may vary for any given object according to its historical context, or for one particular individual according to his or her changing social environment. (1987: 175)

The process of objectification can be outlined briefly as follows. The development of the human subject (individual and collective) takes place through a progressive series of processes of externalization (or self-alienation) and sublation (reabsorption or reincorporation). Human subjects and the (material and immaterial) objects of their sociocultural environment form a subject–object relation which is mutually evolving, and through which they form a recursively defined, irreducible entity. This model emphatically rejects a dualism in the subject–object relation, by incorporating 'a refusal to allow for the existence of either subject or object except in a mutually constitutive relationship which itself exists only as part of the process of its own realization' (27).

This is not the same as asserting that there are no analytically distinguishable subjects or objects. Quite the contrary: the subject, object and process exist and can usefully be analytically distinguished but are ultimately inseparable from the point of view of any one aspect of the system determining the outcomes for the others. In other words, neither human action nor the material characteristics of the environment can fully determine the nature of the relationship between the two. This is because neither subjects nor objects can be abstracted from their historically specific context: this insistence on the historical embeddedness of the process is intrinsic to the notion of objectification.

The mutually constitutive relationship between human beings as subjects and the humanly-shaped environment is, indeed, what we call 'culture' in its broadest sense. The concept of objectification thus offers a dialectical model of culture as process by providing a mechanism for the articulation between society (as individuals and collective groups) and cultural form. The key to this articulation is the historical nature of the process of objectification. Indeed, Miller defines culture as 'the externalization of society in history through which it is enabled to embody and thus reproduce itself' (33). Objectification therefore describes the processes through which the socialized human subject is developed:

Culture is derived as a historical force prior to the existence of any individual subject, but is only realisable through agency. It is therefore the means by which the individual is socialized as a member of a given society, and is, in turn the form of all individual and social creativity. (81)

It is important to stress that the term objectification is used here in this analytically precise sense, rather than in the everyday sense of a concrete expression of something which is otherwise intangible, or pejorative senses in which the term is used. Indeed, the relationships between people and their environment which emerge through the processes of objectification are vastly more varied than is commonly associated with the term. Cultural forms encompassed include 'language, material culture, individual dreams, large institutions such as the nation state and religion' (180). Indeed the broadest possible range of subject–object relationships is implicated: the relations of producer–product, consumer–commodity, owner–possession, as well as those between people and their tools are all constructed through the interplay of these processes of objectification. It is also important to note that through these processes both concrete *and* abstract cultural objects are created.

Objectification in the sense in which it is used here (despite the term's commonplace usage) is not just about the production of concrete cultural form. It also results in highly abstract forms such as mathematical theories and 'virtual' forms. Indeed, the Internet is perhaps the contemporary medium *par excellence* for the production and circulation of 'immaterial' forms of material culture, through such electronic objects as email messages, image files, web pages, shareware downloads, MP3s and so on, which must be taken seriously as new electronic forms of material culture. It is therefore necessary to examine the ways they are both similar to and different from earlier forms.

This conception of objectification is, fundamentally, that of a metaphysics of culture as a process through which human activity results in the objective and perceptible structures of the social world, which then form the media for all individual and collective self-expression and construction of subjectivity. It is worth noting that this interpretation follows closely that of Hegel himself, according to Lukács: 'The entire development of society together with all the ideological formations which it creates in the course of history are the product of human activity itself, a manifestation of the self-production and reproduction of society' (1975: 75).

Further, the 'whole of human history together with all the social formations that are born and pass away, are the product of human activity', but 'all these formations get out of the control of man [*sic*] and become autonomous powers with an objectivity of their own' (82). Finally, 'Hegel's logic shows on the one hand that the objects which seem to be so fixed and rigid are in reality processes, and, on the other hand, it regards the objective nature of the objects as products of "externalization" on the part of the subject' (532).

Through processes of objectification, transcendent values and things that are otherwise intangible may be made concrete, culturally intelligible and given permanence and social effectiveness. In particular, it is possible for these structures to encompass and make liveable profound cultural contradictions, both at the level of broad public discourses and representations, and in the mundane domain of everyday domestic life. At the level of communities, for example, Miller and Slater suggest that, in relation to the Internet as both symbolic totality and practical multiplicity 'it would be misleading to assume that experience of the net in itself leads either to nationalism as it was previously constituted or to cosmopolitanism. Rather, the primary advantage of the net was that it became yet another means of reconciling and preventing contradictions between these two ideals.' (Miller and Slater 2000: 100) At the level of the individual and the household, Hawkins (1998) argues that cultural phenomena like television and the home computer are the focus of complex and contradictory systems of value and meaning. Television, for example, may be 'both dangerous and contaminating nuisance and special treat' (135). Such contradictions, she suggests, are an unavoidable feature of disjunctures between different spatialities and temporalities of the self, and the result of embodying and living these contradictions is a profound ambivalence towards these cultural forms. A similar ambivalence in relation to technology has been referred to as technological ambiguity (Staudenmaier 1995).

The artefactual world is therefore capable of manifesting – and making liveable and practical – transcendent or contradictory values and meanings. Miller's analysis of everyday provisioning illustrates how it is possible to analytically discern circuits or structures of objectification which link together, on the one hand, patterns of everyday activity and interaction with objects, and on the other, structures of meaning and value identifiable within representations, discourses and ideologies. Material culture may be able to communicate meanings that language cannot, since it acts to integrate the representative individual within the normative order of the larger social group, where it serves as a medium of intersubjective order inculcated as a generative practice through some version of 'habitus'. This order is continually objectified in the pattern or style of the artefactual world. (Miller 1987: 129–30)

Cultural definitions of the symbolic value of particular types of commodities, because they operate in an extra-linguistic mode, tend to be culturally conservative. Material culture 'allows for the representation of cultural categories, principles and processes without at the same time encouraging their innovative manipulation' (McCracken 1988: 68). The material world effectively makes ideology manifest, but in such a way that it is not generally available for conscious reflection and interrogation.

When Miller (1998b) writes of the household as the objectification of processes of social and biological reproduction, it is in this sense of a relationship which both constitutes its subjects (its participants) and its object (the 'household'), through complex collaborations of practice and discourse. For the elderly, for example, everyday acts of thrift constitute the relationship between themselves and absent descendants: 'the presence of the following generations is reconstituted on an almost daily basis by the act of thrift', even when contact with the descendants themselves is rare. To think of thrift as a means to an end is to misunderstand how the other may be objectified as a presence through such regimes of everyday practice: 'in some ways the absence of [actual] objects of love makes things easier, since the actual partner or child is often so far from the idealized object that they have to be "unthought" in order to be reconstituted as the proper recipients of love' (Miller 1998b: 102–3).

What this description captures is a sense of the household an entity which is amorphous and multifaceted, simultaneously both concrete and abstract, and which resists reduction to a single 'name':

[T]he house works as a metaphor for kindred, and this is found in many societies where the very concept of lineage is encapsulated within the house. The house may be a metaphor, but as with many metaphors it thereby helps constitute something which cannot easily be objectified, in this case a sense of transcendent identity to which individuals belong and devote their lives, or . . . flout at their peril. (133)

The household thus defined parallels in many important ways the Silverstone et al. model of the household as a 'moral economy' (Silverstone, Hirsch and Morley 1992). These perspectives both describe the household as a manifestation in objects and activities (including communicative acts) of meanings and values held in common by its members (although not homogeneously, since there can be negotiation and contestation of these), embedded within a broader social and cultural context.

It may be that everyday cultural forms are able to objectify transcendental values precisely *because* these abstractions resist reduction to language (Miller 1987: 100; see also McCracken 1988: 57–70). This resistance is exemplified by the awkwardness of Miller's use of the term 'love' within his analysis of shopping to encapsulate a category of interpersonal and social relationship which is complex and contradictory and which must remain largely unexamined in order for it to work properly, but which is able to be stably constructed and maintained through the complex interplay of ideologies and public discourses, everyday practices and its embodiment in material objects. Provisioning the household through the everyday activity of shopping, can therefore be

> primarily an act of love, that in its daily conscientiousness becomes one of the primary means by which relationships of love and care are constituted by practice. That is to say, *shopping does not merely reflect love, but is a major form in which love is manifested and reproduced* . . . One could use other terms than love. Care, concern, obligation, responsibility and habit play their roles in these relationships. So also may resentment, frustration and even hatred. Can these latter be the ingredients we may properly term love? As long as it is clear that we understand by this term 'love' a normative ideology manifested largely as a practice within long-term relationships and not just some romantic vision of an idealized moment of courtship, then the term is entirely appropriate. (Miller 1998b: 18–19, emphasis added)

Both artefacts and practices may 'resist conscious articulation and in a sense be embarrassed by language' because they provide an interface with the unconscious (Miller 1987: 100). Material objects, in particular, have an especially 'close relation to emotions, feelings and basic orientations to the world' (107). Indeed, it may be that language suffers from a fundamental inability to deal adequately with objects in everyday interaction. The materiality of artefacts is therefore of crucial importance, since it is this which allows them to act as a bridge, not only between the mental and physical worlds, but also 'between consciousness and the unconscious' (99). Further, 'the physicality of the artefact lends itself to the work of praxis – that is, cultural construction through action rather than just conceptualization' (129). In other words, their very materiality enables artefacts to provide us with the kind of 'psychic scaffolding' suggested above, and to support the embodied habitual cultural competence which can be thought of as a kind of cultural proprioception. The materiality of the artefactual environment, as an essential characteristic and consequence of the dialectical processes of objectification, theoretically secures the artefact's constitutive character, as an essential antidote to approaches which treat artefacts 'as a mere reflection of social relations, that is a "human mirror"' (112).

It is the materiality of the object world which gives cultural form its stability and perceptibility (Miller 1987; McCracken 1988). Indeed, as McCracken puts it: 'material culture makes culture material' (1988: 31). Material objects render cultural categories substantial and tangible: 'they are a vital, visible record of cultural meaning that is otherwise intangible'. Indeed, 'they have a "performative" function . . . insofar as they give cultural meaning a concreteness for the individual that it would not otherwise have' (74).

Ownership as Objectification

What is being developed here is a model of our relationship to our belongings in the broadest possible sense, including our membership of communities and our relationship to knowledge and experience, rather than simply to the objects which we have a legal right to call our possessions. Indeed, the term 'belongings' – almost but not quite synonymous with 'possessions' – resonates with this sense of an ongoing, mutually constitutive relationship. It is not just that our possessions belong to us, but also that we, in a sense, belong to them. We also speak of belonging to communities, organizations and even cultures, although we tend not to reverse this relationship and speak of how such entities belong to us in return (although this is an important aspect of our relationship to them, which tends to be made explicit when such communities are threatened in some way). Such constructive relationships of belonging do, however, illustrate important domains of objectification – we are constructed as socialized human subjects by our belongings in the broadest sense.

Ownership in the narrow sense of property rights may now be seen to be a particular contemporary form of objectification, and is one which tends to collapse broad and heterogeneous forms of relating to the objects we own into a limited economic paradigm. I am suggesting instead that ownership should rather be seen as a multimodal and complex relationship which is continuous with, on the one hand, the developmental origins of ownership as described by Winnicott (and in particular the role of mothers and other care-givers in introducing the social and cultural environment to the individual), and, on the other hand, objectification as those sociocultural processes through which that environment is created through collective human activity. It is these continuities, and the materiality of the object world – the objectness of objects – which enables material culture to provide us with a psychic scaffolding for the self, in relation to which we have a kind of cultural proprioception.

The relationship of ownership may be further elaborated by considering the dynamic processes by which the 'extended self' (Belk 1988) is constructed, maintained and developed, in relation to its social, cultural and material environment. The extended self 'stretches beyond the boundaries of the physical body to include material objects' (Dittmar 1992: 47) and includes not just external objects and personal possessions, 'but also includes persons, places, and group possessions as well as such possessions as body parts and vital organs' (Belk 1988: 140). One might readily add to this list such intangible possessions as knowledges and memberships of organizations and other communities. This is a view of the self as an embodied entity, materially embedded within its culturally produced environment – 'competent in its spaces and times', to echo Glennie and Thrift's phrase (1996: 41).

Home and the objects within it are important elements of the extended self. But while the physical home and its objects form part of the extended self of each individual household member, it is clear that each one of them has their own subjective relationship to the building and the things it contains. While there may be one household, there will inevitably be multiple 'homes' within it (Csikzentmihayli and Rochberg-Halton 1981: 138). The extended self is formed both of the material and immaterial objects one 'owns', but can only be fully understood relationally – that is, in terms of the subjective relationship that exists between owner and possessions. The model of ownership proposed here gives centrality to the relationship formed through ongoing practices of interaction between the owner and the object owned, and it therefore allows for the objects we possess to act on us, and transform us in turn, by becoming part of our extended self. There is thus a profound relationality of self and possessions: the form of ownership proposed here is a mutual belonging. This relationship of ownership is, further, a profoundly embodied one, which is built up between the human subject and the materiality of its external environment, body to body.

Belk's notion of the self extended by its belongings also reflects Winnicott's assertion that there might be a space between the 'inner' life of the individual and the 'outer', objective, reality – an interface with complex topology between the two, rather than a definite boundary. The extended self is, on the contrary, a notion of the self as the interface between the body and the world, a post-Cartesian understanding of the human subject in relation to the social and cultural environment. Rather than seeing subjects and objects as bounded and monadic natural entities interacting in Newtonian fashion, the contemporary view of the subject–object relation may be better envisaged as a dynamic interface with complex topology. As Bourdieu has suggested, the constitution of everyday life in practice is based in the 'dialectic of the internalization of externality and the externalization of internality' (1977: 72).

If physical objects are crucial in mediating the intermediate area between the subjective and that which is objectively perceived, then the origin of the relationship of ownership is perhaps in those 'first not-me possessions' (Winnicott 1971: 96), the transitional objects that are not part of the infant's body yet are not fully recognized as belonging to external reality. Within 'potential space', the gradually evolving and expanding interface between the inner life of the individual and his or her everyday interaction with the external world, reality is in a profound sense both created and found at the same time. Indeed it makes no sense to try to distinguish between creating both self and object and finding them. Within the transitional zone between the 'mine' and the 'not-mine', Winnicott asks us not to (because it makes no sense to) challenge the individual: 'did you find that, or did you create it?' The individual can only develop new skills and experiences, and assimilate new possessions, by extending on what she or he has already incorporated. The activities of ownership are therefore the experience and skills of finding/creating new possessions, at the interface between the 'mine' and the 'not-mine'. It is this duality which allows for both structure (finding) and agency (creating) in social and cultural life – for everyday life to be simultaneously both found and created (Silverstone 1994: 164).

Belk analyses the processes through which objects are incorporated into the extended self, or in other words, come into a relationship of ownership with us. First, an object may become incorporated into the extended self 'through appropriating or controlling the object for our own personal use' (Belk 1988: 150). This may include the appropriation to the self of intangible objects (such as knowledges) or 'non-ownable' objects (such as public property or objects that are 'legally' owned by others):

> We can appropriate by overcoming, conquering, or mastering them. For instance, a mountain climber in reaching a peak has asserted control of the mountain and the panorama it affords. Similarly, it is only through learning to ride a first bicycle, manipulating a new computer system, driving a first car, or successfully negotiating rapids in a new kayak that these objects really become part of the extended self. This is an important point, for it provides an explanation of how nondurable products or services and public property or events may become viewed as possessions and thereby potentially contribute to a sense of self. (Belk 1988: 150).

Objects may be incorporated into the extended self through a variety of other means. By giving possessions to others, for example, such objects retain an association to the giver while taking on a new relationship of possession. This may thereby, cement the relationship between giver and receiver – often one between close friends or loved ones – and extend the identity of the giver to include the receiver and vice versa (cf. Mauss 1990). Material objects or abstract ideas may become part of the extended self of their creator, or of other people who come to know the object: 'our intimate knowledge of a community, store, or book makes them not only "ours" but also part of the self' (Belk 1988: 151).

As was stressed in chapter 1, the notion of ownership as it is developed within this book – of personal property as those objects with which one has a genuinely self-productive relationship – is a broad one, and not to be conflated with a more legalistic notion of private property as those objects (and only those) over which legal rights may be asserted. Such descriptions of the nature of ownership beg the question of how an object gets to become a 'property'. For Simmel (1990), possession is not so much a right of action over an object, but is constituted in action itself.

Possession is an activity, not an attribute. The possession of things

> does not appear as movement but as a stationary and, as it were, substantial condition . . . In contrast with such a notion, I believe that one must also characterize possession as an action if one wished to grasp the whole depth and breadth of its meaning. The habit of considering possession as something passively accepted, as the unconditionally complying object which, to the extent that it is really possession, does not require any activity on our part, is false . . . Ownership that is not to some extent activity is a mere abstraction . . . Property as a reality – even though not as a conceptual abstraction – presupposes, as a necessary corollary, action on the part of the proprietor. Static possession exists only in the imaginary aftermath of the processes that precede it, and in the imaginary anticipation of future enjoyment or use. If one disregards these processes which one falsely considers to be only secondary, then nothing remains of the concept of property. (303–6)

Possession as an activity, then, is not about property as rights rather than things, but is about the ongoing relationship between the owner and the object that is manifested in a variety of kinds of practices and activities as well as actions over objects. This relationship would often be one that is socially recognized, leading to the possibility that the relationship would convey the right of certain kinds of action over the object (and generally also certain responsibilities towards the object). It is clear that the nature of socially recognized kinds of ownership are culturally highly specific, however, and the nature of ownership may indeed be highly contested, with different individuals or groups asserting a claim to either the same or a different kind of ownership. That competing claims may arise from different kinds of ownership, and the extent to which they can lead to conflict, is well illustrated by ongoing debates in Australia about the compatibility of Native Title and forms of land title of colonial origin.

Consumption as Objectification

As consumers, we initially encounter commodities as 'alien', non-owned, objects. Social processes of commodification reinforce the abstraction and generality of consumer goods, so that when shopping we are confronted with a 'vast alienated world of products completely distanced from the world of production' (Miller 1987: 190). These are objects which appear to us as pristine, never-owned objects, which have been so completely abstracted from the conditions of their production that they appear to have been almost magically created. However, commodification processes such as advertising present goods to us as potentially personalizable in an abstract and idealized way (Carrier 1990), often constructing the image of a generalized 'potential owner' for such goods. This is explored with respect to technological commodities in more detail in chapter 3.

While the term alienation tends to have a negative connotation in contemporary use, this emerged only with the Marxian version of Hegel's dialectic. According to Lukács (1975), alienation for Hegel arises as follows: social institutions and forms appear to individuals as existing outside of them and constraining their actions. But this seemingly autonomous and objective social reality in fact arises from collective human activity. The actions of human individuals are therefore capable of generating objective social form which is perceived as existing outside of and independently of the individual. It is this separation that is the essence of alienation. *Entausserung*, the word Hegel used, is sometimes translated as 'estrangement'. Alienation may thus be seen as simply a recognition of the objective nature, when seen from the point of view of the individual, of social and cultural form.

This alienation within the commodity form may be overcome through the transformation of the abstract generic item at the shopping mall into the concrete and particular item which we own at home: 'consumption as work may be defined as that which translates the object from an alienable to an inalienable condition; that is, from being a symbol of estrangement and price value to being an artefact invested with particular inseparable connotations' (Miller 1987: 190). It is through processes of appropriation that the abstracted generalized commodity is converted into a particular personal 'owned' one. This of necessity takes place at the level of the particular, through everyday praxis and activities, rather than at the level of the representations and discourses of the cultural environment where we are presented with commodities as generalized and abstract.

The 'work' of consumption involves a range of strategies of appropriation and integration of the commodity into the everyday life of the consumer. Even before acquiring or considering acquiring a home computer, individuals and households are always already inextricably embedded within broader social processes and are involved in a number of what might be called 'projects' of objectification, part of the advancement of which is the acquisition of a computer. The participants in the present study, for example, negotiate the often conflicting paths of such diverse life projects as a career, personal development, education, hobbies and community commitments, bringing up children and home-building. For many of them, the home computer plays a part within a number of these diverse areas of their lives. Its acquisition is never an isolated act, and its integration into the lives of these individuals and their households is often complex and multifaceted.

The establishment of a relationship of ownership can be a long and complex process, especially in relation to complex commodities, such as the home computer. This process is described by Miller as one 'in which the consumer works upon the object and recontextualizes it, until it is often no longer recognisable as having any relation to the world of the abstract' (1987: 190). Through this process, the depersonalized generic mass-produced artefact becomes, over a period of time, a personalized, singular or particular, *owned* one. It may be that the object itself is transformed through these processes of recontextualization, through physical processes of appropriation and symbolic action.

There is scope for the consumer to appropriate and symbolically recontextualize goods and use them to create themselves in their own image – to bring them into the extended self. But this potential is, in general, bound up in pre-existing hierarchies and structures of social constraint and agency, since the flow of meaning tends to move from the direction of designers, producers and advertisers towards consumers (McCracken 1988: 71). The potential for symbolic recontextualization of objects is invoked through what McCracken refers to as 'symbolic action': 'a kind of social action devoted to the manipulation of the cultural meaning for purposes of collective and individual communication and categorization'. Symbolic action gives 'an opportunity to affirm, evoke, assign, or revise the conventional symbols and meanings of the cultural order' (1988: 84).

It is through such symbolic action – establishing symbolically the right to claim the good as one's own – that the consumer is able to appropriate to her- or himself the meanings which the advertisers and manufacturers have inscribed within the commodity. 'This process of claiming is not the simple assertion of territoriality through ownership. It is also an attempt to draw from the object the qualities that it has been given by the marketing forces of the world of goods' (McCracken 1988: 85). McCracken outlines some of the kinds of symbolic action (termed also 'rituals') which may be performed on goods. These include exchange rituals (for example, where the recipient of a gift is also the intended recipient of the symbolic properties of the gift), possession rituals (such as 'cleaning, discussing, comparing, reflecting, showing off, and even photographing' new possessions (85)), grooming rituals (which are needed for maintenance of symbolic ownership) and divestment rituals (which effect the erasure of previous symbolic links, for example with prior owners, or when preparing to relinquish ownership of the object). Possession rituals are particularly important, because it is these that 'allow the consumer to lay claim and assume a kind of ownership of the meaning of his or her consumer goods' (85). A description of such possession rituals with respect to the ownership of home personal computers forms a significant component of the empirical analysis of this book. Most importantly, however, in the case of technological objects like the computer, the use of the object must be added to McCracken's list of kinds of possession activities.

Conclusion

Objectification, as it has been described in this chapter, is the theoretical thread linking home-building, ownership and technology within this book. Material culture, it is suggested, mediates between the physical and mental worlds, between consciousness and the unconscious, and between the concrete, local and particular present and imagined alternative states or abstract and general entities which cannot be directly perceived. Our possessions may be able to act as 'anchors' or 'scaffolding' for the present self, as place-holders which help us maintain ontological security in everyday life by staying in place to give us our place, and also as 'bridges' or 'handles', giving access to a developmental potential for the self. If the home computer is imagined as a 'bridge' or 'handle' of some sort, then the point of commitment to this route is the point of greatest emotional intensity, and involves both possible threats to ontological security in taking in this 'alien' object and excitement and hope at the challenge.

Because of its concreteness, material culture makes stable and visible the categories of culture, and makes social experience meaningful. However, their logics may not be readily available to conscious articulation and interrogation. Through processes of objectification, contradictions and paradoxes can be made liveable, both at the level of broad public discourse and representation (such as that complex referred to as technological ambiguity) and at the mundane level of everyday life (such as the salesman who can be trusted because he isn't really a salesman).

While there is scope, then, for self-transformation, the self cannot be shaped simply through active conscious direction, since these changes take place through processes of everyday life and interaction which involve the mutual shaping of the subject and its objects. The embodied character of social and cultural experience means that it is not necessarily available to conscious reflection: social and cultural categories appear 'natural' where in fact they are learned, or inculcated through praxis and mimetic processes of everyday life. Personal goals, in particular, are not natural, but are shaped within and resonate with broader societal structures. Individuals have the flexibility to pursue or not to pursue such common paths, but even when they do follow them, they do so through interaction with cultural materials and within social institutions which are not of the individual's making, and which exist independently of them. The outcome of these processes is intrinsically unpredictable, and it is therefore not simply a question of appropriating the desired qualities of the cultural environment to the self and being transformed in the process.

The Information
Appliance

The notion of objectification encompasses the socially constructed nature of artefacts (such as technologies) but because of the materiality of such objects and the momentum of institutionalized social practices, they escape social control in any simple sense. While it has become commonplace in academic writing to view sociotechnical systems as socially shaped or constructed, it remains the case that, from the point of view of individuals, these are developments which seem to take place outside of their (or any other individual's) control, and to which they may only respond and adapt. Such thinking is generally dismissed in contemporary social studies of technology as 'technologically determinist'. But although 'technologically determinist' thinking has been largely superseded in academic writing, it still holds widespread currency in popular public discourses around technology. It is characterized, at the extremes, by a similar mixture of utopianism and dystopianism as have followed earlier innovations, such as the telephone and television (Bryant 1988; Spigel 1992). The ideological hegemony of such technologically determinist discourses has been noted by a number of authors (Slack 1984; Webster and Robins 1986; Postman 1993).

As Skinner argues, for social scientists interested in social and cultural developments in relation to technological change, it should not be enough to 'ritually reject technological determinism and assert the social nature of technology' (1992: 347). For, as Noble points out:

Of course, technology does seem to take on a life of its own, when we remain ignorant of the actual process and blindly surrender ourselves to it, or when we act from narrowly prescribed technical ends. And the path of technological development does resemble a unilinear course, when we

47

yield to the hegemony of those who oversee it. And, last, technology does appear to have its own impact upon our lives, when we fail to recognize the human choices, intentions, and compulsions that lie behind it. *Because of its very concreteness, people tend to confront technology as an irreducible brute fact, a given, a first cause, rather than as hardened history, frozen fragments of human and social endeavour.* (1984: xiii, emphasis added)

Rather than simply reasserting the socially constructed nature of technological systems, the question is raised here of how it is that these pieces of 'hardened history' are able to come to have a life of their own. It is not, however, simply a question of being able overthrow a particular sociotechnical hegemony once ignorance of its processes has been overcome. Although technological systems may seem, because of their concrete material efficacy, to form a privileged cultural domain, the position taken within this book is that the seeming inevitability of technological progression is a particular consequence of those broader social processes referred to as objectification.

Faith in the inevitability of progress – surely one of the fundamental axioms of contemporary western society – largely seems to confirm these as desirable developments. It is clear, however – as warnings of the apocalyptic collapse of banking, air traffic control and other critical computer systems as a result of the 'Millennium bug' or Y2K problem illustrated – that the seemingly hegemonic public discourses of the 'information society' are articulated in complex ways with a dystopian undercurrent. At the level of communities and nations, this results in a dynamic tension between discourses of excitement and anxiety about the future, which Miller and Slater describe in relation to Trinidad (although similar rhetorics may be found throughout the world) as a 'notable oscillation between excitement and anxiety' (2000: 19).

This 'technological ambiguity' (Staudenmaier 1995) is reflected in a pervasive sense of the inevitability of the deepening penetration of information technology into everyday life, both within and outside the domestic sphere. It generates a sense for many consumers that these are changes which they must keep up with or be left behind, but that there is simultaneously both promise and anxiety in these novel technologies. It is therefore not simply a question of striking a 'rational' balance between the irrationalities of utopian fantasy and dystopian fear in relation to technological change. The mix of emotions associated with technological ambiguity is found not only at the level of public discourse, but also at the level of individual responses to new technology. The individual and the household become a site of contestation of these discourses in relation to the practices of everyday life (Allon 1998).

Here is Peter Richards describing the justification for the family's first computer purchase, an Amstrad bought in 1990:

> We felt there was an increasing need for the kids to be computer literate, and we also saw a need for them to be able to type up basic things like letters or assignments . . . At that point the primary schools were just starting to build up their computers too, and we thought what's the point of learning them at school if you can't do it at home. Another factor, just thinking back, most of my work use was on mainframes, so I also felt the need to upgrade my own skills. I could see that PCs were becoming more important, but I didn't work directly with them . . . I could see that having basic DOS skills would be a useful thing. And also, I thought that if I needed to learn that, then my children would need to learn it more than me.

The Richards's reasoning is paralleled in the accounts of many of the participant households. Typically, instrumentalist logics – that they are able to do certain things with the computer and that it will have certain effects on their lives – are integrated with expressive or affective discourses – about not wanting to be left behind by rapid sociotechnical change, or achieving a sense of personal empowerment through mastery of the technology.

Major social shifts such as globalization and changes in the nature of work, education or leisure form the cultural context within which consumers purchase and use their computers. Although these global-level structures of objectification are, in reality, social processes and products, they appear to have their own autonomy and seem to be external 'givens' to which we must respond. For home computer purchasers, there is often a sense that these are changes which must be kept up with or risk being left behind. The link with the changing nature of media, communications and work means that this is a pressure which is particularly acutely felt by parents as proxies for their children, and is keenly felt as a responsibility to provide them with access to these cultural materials. Yet just as there is fear and risk of failure in these technologies, there is also both promise and hope for the future.

While, on the one hand, computer technology embodies these broad cultural associations, they have become, on the other, commonplace items of domestic technology. The 1990s have seen the reshaping of computer technology and its forms of representation to align it with other domestic forms and commodities. In contrast to its previous business and educational roles, it finds its 'natural' place within the home.

Necessarily, then, the activity of acquisition of a novel possession involves an interaction with global, generic and abstract structures at an everyday practical level, that is, at the level of the local, particular and concrete. Consumers engage and interact with these broader structures of objectification through practices of consumption, as a process taking place over a (possibly extended) period of time, and which involves the household mobilizing its commodity knowledge and perhaps also its social network.

Changing Representations of Home Computing

The first computers which could be owned by individuals were self-assembly microcomputer kits which became publicly available in the mid-1970s. These came with no preprogrammed software and appealed exclusively to electronics hobbyists. In 1977 Apple launched the Apple II, which was followed by machine from other producers including IBM and Commodore. By the mid-1980s more sophisticated microcomputers (such as the Commodore 64 and the Apple IIE) were available for purchase by consumers. These came closer to reproducing the functionality of the personal computers which by this time were widely used in business and educational organizations, supplementing the dominant multi-user mainframe computers which had been in common use in large institutions since the 1960s (Haddon 1988; Press 1993). Personal computers became inexpensive enough to be a realistic acquisition for a household, and in the late 1980s developments in the technology and its marketing led to a shift in the portrayal and use of the home computer. Home computing became more of a family activity and less one concentrated in the hands of the (typically male) hobbyist (Haddon 1988).

The 1990s saw the integration of computer technology into broad-ranging domestic commodity markets, and the emergence of an image of the computer as a novel kind of domestic appliance. The image in figure 2 appeared in July 1994 as the main illustration of an Apple computer advertisement. The computer in this image is located squarely as a domestic appliance, through the visual parallel which seems to be drawn between the computer and a microwave oven, and through an explicit comparison made with both the microwave and the VCR in

It has 101 household uses
but it doesn't slice, dice or julienne.

Figure 2 The information appliance: 'It has 101 household uses but it doesn't slice, dice or julienne'. © Apple Computer Australia. Reproduced with permission.

the text which accompanies the image. The text implies that if you already have a VCR and a microwave, then you really need a home computer too: 'Personal computers are quickly becoming as popular in homes as microwave ovens and VCRs.' The range of household functions potentially undertaken by the personal computer is indicated by the text's subheadings: 'give your kids an edge in school', 'organise your household', 'improve your home business', 'make more of your spare time'. The home computer is portrayed as a novel kind of domestic appliance – an 'information appliance' – which, it is implied, will soon become indispensable to the contemporary home. (Although the use of the term 'information appliance' to refer to the domestic use of information technology appears to go back at least as far as 1978 at the Apple corporation (Norman 1998), the symbolic reconstruction described in this chapter took place during the 1990s.)

This advertisement is similar to many of its contemporaries in showing the computer as easy to use, and time- and labour-saving. But a range of contradictory meanings around home computing can be isolated in the advertisement, not because they are addressed directly but because they are implicit in their denial. The eggs and flour around the keyboard and on the bench top, for example, suggest that contemporary computers are robust and can be treated like other household objects – they are not fragile pieces of complex machinery. Computing is not an isolated, individual activity, a possible threat to family cohesion. On the contrary, it is suggested, computing can be a joint leisure activity, a way of spending 'quality time' together as a family. The computer pictured is peripheral to the activity that the father and daughter are engaged in, able in fact to enhance rather than threaten family solidarity. It is portrayed as a passive assistant: the role invoked for information technology is that of servant to the human master, implicitly defusing cultural anxieties about a loss of human control over technology. Finally, there is the gendering of this information appliance: many contemporary computer advertisements, including this one, portray girls using the computer in a positive light, contradicting the possible assertion that they are just 'toys for the boys'. Although there is no adult female household member portrayed in this advertisement, it seems, like many others, to direct its address to mothers and wives in their roles as household managers and as the ones with primary responsibility for the day-to-day care of children.

Domesticating the Information Appliance

Advertising representations of consumer goods give us not just an image of a physical object, but also portray a set of meanings that construct the consumer as well as the product and its appropriate uses. We might therefore expect the discursive site of contemporary home computer advertising and promotion to display aspects of the shared understanding of producers and consumers and to reflect the concerns and priorities of both.

The social processes through which consumer goods are given meaning within processes of production and marketing, and understood by consumers within contexts of consumption form a complex dialectic, as part of the processes of objectification which were described in the last chapter. In its most abstract and general statement, objectification describes those sociocultural processes through which human activity results in the concrete and abstract structures of the social world (including mass-produced commodities, media content and representations), which then form the raw material for all individual and collective self-expression and construction of subjectivity. These processes are irreducibly diachronic: present cultural forms and social processes at each point in time are built on what has gone before. Consumers' understandings of novel goods, then, can only be based on what they already know and understand (du Gay, Hall, Janes, Mackay and Negus 1997: 24), although this knowledge may be based not on direct experience, but on an imagined expectation (Campbell 1992: 61).

The complex social processes through which technological commodities – with which many consumers have had little experience prior to purchase – are integrated into the everyday life of households, have been collectively termed *domestication*:

> Domestication is a process both of taming the wild and cultivating the tame. It is where nature becomes culture. One can think of domestication too, as both a process by which we make things our own, subject to our control, imprinted by, and expressive of, our identities; and as a principle of mass consumption in which products are prepared in the public fora of the market. In a sense the commodity is already domesticated, and it is in this 'anticipation of domesticity' which the commodity embodies that we must understand the context of our own domesticity and of the role of television in creating and sustaining it. (Silverstone 1994: 174)

This concern with the innovation process as an interconnected whole – through which novel goods are created within social contexts of production, but must be symbolically positioned within the marketplace in ways which match the understandings of consumers – is reflected in the *design/domestication interface* (Silverstone and Haddon 1996). The design/domestication interface effectively provides a bridge for the artefact between the worlds of production and everyday contexts of consumption, and consists of collaborative work on the object which is initiated by the object's producers and is taken over and continued by its consumers.

Domestication and design are articulated by way of processes of commodification. In particular, the artefact's likely place in the home is anticipated and built into the design of the object itself and incorporated in representations of the artefact (such as in advertising). Silverstone and Haddon refer to these processes as 'pre-domestication', since they reserve the term domestication proper for post-purchase processes of incorporation of the commodity into the household: 'domestication is anticipated in design and design is completed in domestication' (1996: 49). These articulating processes act as a symbolic bridge between the artefact's context of production and the context of its consumption.

Once the artefact is brought into the domestic space, design gives way to what these authors understand as domestication itself, the processes through which the object is incorporated into the everyday life of the household. These processes, which may be long-term and complex in themselves, are the means through which the abstract and generic item of the marketplace is converted into the particular 'owned' one in its context of use.

Central to the reconstruction of the personal computer as an information appliance for the home, then, is the presentation in home computer advertising and other promotional material of a *domesticated* image of the computer, in this sense of a cultural process which bridges the context of production of a commodity and its context of consumption. The computer is reshaped to the symbolic, aesthetic and functional parameters of the commodity culture of the contemporary western household, thereby losing some of its associations with its prior main contexts of business and educational institutions.

This is a process which largely took place during the 1990s. By the late 1980s, the identification of the personal computer as a consumer electronics item (charted by Haddon 1988) was strengthened by the broadening of its distribution base. It became possible to purchase personal computers in department stores and electrical goods chains selling consumer electronics items ('brown' as well as 'white' goods), and computer equipment started appearing in home-delivered advertising catalogues alongside VCRs, televisions and even microwave ovens. Consumers with little first-hand technical experience might be expected to be more willing to consider buying a computer from one of these stores rather than from a specialist computer retailer, where there is a common perception that the sales people speak in a jargon-laden foreign language. Figure 3 presents an image of shopping for a computer which likens it to shopping at the supermarket.

The Computerized Lifestyle

This evolution in the way that personal computers for the home have been represented in advertising – essentially constructing a domesticated image of the computer – is paralleled by changes in the way that computers are represented in more news-oriented (rather than promotional) media.

A number of Australian computing magazines aimed at the home computer user emerged in the mid-1990s, following a number of similar

Figure 3 Buying a computer at the supermarket? © *Computer Living*. Reproduced with permission.

releases in the United States and elsewhere. The incorporation of computer-related material in the mainstream family magazines, and the appearance on newsagents' shelves of images such as that featured on the April 1996 cover of *Computer Living* (figure 4) (which features Geoff Jansz, a well-known Australian television chef) serve to offer consumers a highly domesticated image of the home computer, showing these technologies as well-integrated into the contemporary domestic lifestyle.

The integration of home computing into the rapidly expanding 'lifestyle' media market is also illustrated by the pull-out 'advertorial' section in *Better Homes and Gardens* magazine in its September 1996 issue. Entitled 'Home technology: how your home computer can help you', this publication appeared particularly to be aimed at persuading non-computer owners to move into owning this technology, and suggested that some people might still be holding back because they were not sure what the computer would do for them:

Figure 4 The computer as a domestic appliance. © *Computer Living.* Reproduced with permission.

if you don't already have a computer, you are probably part of a large group which is planning to buy one . . . It's especially hard to choose the right model when you're still unsure what you will do with your home computer. A home computer can be used to access the Internet, to play games, and to teach yourself a foreign language. You can write a letter, or a book, design a personalised Christmas card or a poster for your home business. It can schedule your appointments and help balance your home accounts. (*Better Homes and Gardens*, September 1996: 196)

This sixteen-page pull-out includes articles on 'making a home for your computer' (setting up the computer in a permanent position and giving advice on furniture), 'what to look for when buying a PC', 'making an income from the home computer', 'home banking and balancing personal finances', 'getting connected' to the Internet, a section on home automation, and 'things you never knew you could do on a computer'. This latter article included suggestions which integrated well with the more general *Better Homes and Gardens* content: gardening, craft, cooking, home video editing, and obtaining entertainment and travel information. In a similar move, the February 1996 issue of the *Australian Women's Weekly* (a monthly publication) included an eight-page beginner's guide entitled 'Switch on to computers' and giving advice on computer purchase, a 'quick guide to the Net', and a glossary of common computer terms ('a guide to the jargon').

At the end of June 1997, the *Sydney Morning Herald* marked this shift in the meaning of the home computer by ending its regular Tuesday eight-page 'Computers and Communications' section after fourteen years, and replacing it with a Tuesday 'I.T.' section, 'aimed at users of information technology in small to medium sized enterprises' (*Sydney Morning Herald*, Tuesday 24 June 1997: 1c) and a Saturday colour pull-out, 'Icon', subtitled 'Computers and technology for the rest of us'. Explicitly designed to provide coverage of information technology for the *Herald*'s consumer readership, which often only buys the paper on the weekends, the twenty-page tabloid, four-colour throughout, format of this publication is similar to other 'lifestyle' format pull-outs appearing in the *SMH*'s sister publication *Sun Herald* on Sundays. As with the *Better Homes and Gardens* and *Australian Women's Weekly* pull-outs, the Internet is included as an integral component of this domesticated image of the computer. 'Icon' is paralleled by content on the *Sydney Morning Herald*'s website (which may be found at http://www.smh.com.au), and the initial launch of the section included a special offer of five free hours of service with the One.Net ISP.

These broad-ranging forms of cultural representation for domestic computer technologies and media in combination construct a powerful normative image of the technologies, their appropriate functions and the cultural values they are associated with. Many of the representations seem to appeal directly to a population which has internalized the need to achieve for themselves and for their children and the importance of the application of technological and economic resources to this project. As such they form part of the broader cultural currency of advertising and other public discourses about commodities and about how personal goals can be achieved through consumption. A range of values is constructed and circulates within this normative domain of discourse, culturally contextualizing the experience of consumers. As we will see, many of the values represented in the advertising materials discussed here can also be found within the interview material collected from the study participants (most strikingly, those concerned with the link between home computing and educational achievement for children), even though the particular advertising materials examined here may never have been seen by the participants in the study themselves.

In the case of personal computers, it is commonly believed that a computer at home is an advantage to children in their education, and conversely, that the absence of a computer in the home disadvantages them. Many advertisements play on this belief. The following slogan for Interactive Electronic Publishing's software products Teddy's Big Day (for one- to four-year-olds) and Teddy's Hide'n'seek (for three- to seven-year-olds), for example, appeared in *Family PC*:

> In 25 years when your kid is pulling 200K a year after graduating top of the class at Harvard and you're lucky enough to catch her on the cell phone, you might want to remind her where it all started. (*Family PC*, November/December 1994: 30)

As the proportion of households with computers increases, the pressure on parents to conform also increases. Other advertisements resonate with parental guilt about perhaps not doing as much for their children as they might. Interaction with the computer is a substitute for interaction with parents, and is preferable to TV, games or hanging around at the shopping mall. Some of this advertising taps into parental anxieties about juvenile delinquency and children 'going off the rails' in a way which would be quite intimidating if it did not seem to be at least partly tongue-in-cheek. A December 1994 advertisement for a geography software package, which appeared in the US *HomePC* magazine, showed two smiling teenage girls working with textbooks and a laptop, with the slogan 'Jenny and Sara explored France and Japan with World Discovery. They didn't go to the mall today.' Similarly, a 1995 advertisement for Olivetti computers used the slogan 'Don't let your child's first biology lesson be behind the bicycle sheds', contrasting monochrome images of a schoolyard with a full colour image of a father and son looking at educational biology software on the computer.

In many cases 'educational' computer software is favourably compared with playing games: one piece of music software uses the slogan 'marking time or killing time', juxtaposing one of their own screen shots with one of a 'street fighting' computer game. Other computer software advertisements take advantage of parental concerns about the harmful effects of too much television: computer use is presented as interactive and therefore better. The television, as 'babysitter in a box', is contrasted with computer use – 'creativity in a box'.

Indeed, the concepts of education and entertainment tend to become conflated around computer use, indicated in the use of the term 'edutainment'. There is a widespread belief that even game-playing is computer use and thus beneficial for children, assisting them to acquire generalized 'computer literacy' skills. This conceptual slippage works in the other direction too: many of us believe that our recreational pursuits should be good for us. As Murdock, Hartmann and Gray point out, promotional discourses around home computing have presented home computing as 'a form of rational recreation, in which domestic space becomes an extension of the classroom and the office, and the user practices "useful" skills' (1992: 153).

A further strategy in the process of domesticating information technology products for household consumption is that of using brands which are associated with children's toys and educational products (such as Disney, Time Warner, Crayola, Fisher-Price, Virgin) to produce computer software products. Many of these brand names have associations of quality in children's commodities and some are also positively associated with educational soundness (such as Sesame Street and Fisher-Price). This product placement strategy also functions to legitimize products for which many parents may have no pre-existing 'brand awareness' and defuse the intimidation that people without prior experience with these technologies might feel towards shopping for such products. The inclusion of characters such as the Flintstones, Scooby Doo and so on in computer software products, the now common practice of including a software product in the marketing product array which accompanies major movie releases and the rapid turnover in these products encourages a continuing investment in software products on the part of households. The involvement of these cultural industries with their broad-ranging entertainment and educational interests is part of an ongoing process of integrating computer and software production into these interests, organized along the same lines.

From Information Superhighway to Information Utility

By the late 1990s, the symbolic reshaping of the home computer described here saw it transformed into the model of a domestic information appliance. While retaining both the legacy of its history as a business and educational tool and the computer's powerful symbolic resonance with futurity, the home computer's contemporary pattern of representations also resonates with those of other household

Figure 5 The information appliance: a cross between a computer and a vacuum cleaner? © Apple Computer Australia. Reproduced with permission.

technologies such as the television, VCR, CD player and even the microwave oven.

Apple's iMac computer (released in 1998) represents a further aesthetic development for the personal computer. Figure 5 shows an iMac marketing image which makes it look rather like a vacuum cleaner; indeed, this is a view of the iMac taken from above, as if it were sitting on the floor and the viewer is looking down on it. Throughout the 1990s, a number of largely unsuccessful attempts were made by computer manufacturers to market computers with the look and feel of consumer electronics items – in charcoal grey or matt black finishes, and with styling more like CD players and VCRs than the more usual 'boxy beige' casing. One such computer was the Olivetti Envision, released in late 1995, which was matt black and looked rather like a VCR with floppy disk and CD-ROM drives. This computer connected to the television as monitor, and was controlled with a remote control and cordless keyboard. Another example was the Acer Aspire line, released at about the same time, which included models in dark emerald green and charcoal grey. These models were designed to make the home computer conform to the traditional differentiation of household goods into 'white' and 'brown' goods, but their lack of commercial success suggests that consumers were not willing to accept this recategorization of the computer as a home media and entertainment device. For consumers, perhaps, the significantly higher cost of computers as compared to televisions, CD players, VCRs and other consumer electronics items meant that the computer needed to be clearly associated with more serious uses than mere entertainment. The home computer therefore needed to retain its 'boxy beige' office equipment appearance.

The success of the designers of Apple's iMac, then, seems perhaps to have been in moving beyond the 'brown goods'/'white goods' dichotomy. The iMac not only challenges this distinction, but does so by moving into symbolic dimensions occupied by objects of personal consumption, such as food (the original colours of the iMac had the names of fruit), and appealing to more individualized and bodily pleasures than was previously the case for computer advertising. As du Gay et al. point out, mobile technologies such as the Walkman already had a history of symbolic association with youth, activity, leisure and health (1997: 38), and even appeals to erotic pleasures (32). These associations are now extended to the computer as an object to be owned personally rather than shared as an appliance. The appeal is less to the instrumental rationalization than to the aesthetic, and less to the kitchen appliance than to the beach: the slogan 'Surfer's Paradise' is used in a 1999 promotion for the iMac. The iBook laptop computer takes this process one step further, making it a kind of personalized 'information accessory' (along with WAP-enabled mobile phones and personal digital assistants). Its feminized styling calls up associations with the purse powder compact and the clutch purse, and its 'sorbet and cream' colouring looks like nothing so much, in Australia at least, as a popular kind of ice cream block. This trend may indicate that the battle to naturalize the personal computer's place in the home has, at the turn of the millennium, largely been won.

The process which I have been describing as one of the domestication of the personal computer as an information appliance for the home has been paralleled in the way the Internet has been represented during the latter half of the 1990s, when the World Wide Web can be seen as a domestication of earlier perceptions of the Internet as an 'information superhighway'. The 'information superhighway', as a metaphor for what is now in common usage simply referred to as the Internet, was very widespread, at a point just before the emergence of the Web as the dominant Internet modality (see Gates 1995, for example). By the turn of the millennium the term seems to have largely fallen out of use.

In the mid-1990s the Internet was widely talked about and understood as an innovation which would have profound effects on everyday life. The World Wide Web at that point was simply, however, just one type of service within the larger constellation of FTP (file transfer protocol), Gopher, WAIS (wide area information system) and Usenet services (among others). The cultural and commercial potential of the Internet as a new mass medium, which seemingly exploded within a few short years, was still unexplored. The 'highway' seemed appropriate as a metaphor for this potential: the new electronic infrastructure would facilitate getting from one (digital) place to another, but it was not clear what would be there once one arrived.

Along with the emergence of representations of the computer as a kind of information appliance for the home, the late 1990s saw the parallel development of a more domesticated metaphor for the Internet than that of the highway. Indeed, Adrian (1995) points out that the information superhighway as a metaphorical representation of the global information network is itself a domestication of the widely circulating notion of cyberspace, which originated in the 'cyberpunk' fiction of authors such as William Gibson. Cyberspace is a scary place, populated by spiky haired hackers, where no-one is in control. The superhighway metaphor suggests a more user-friendly, familiar place, a place rather closer to home.

It was in 1996 that World Wide Web URLs started regularly appearing with print and television advertising for a wide range of business services: banks, real estate, movies and so on. Television and print advertising of Internet service providers became commonplace by the end of 1996 and early 1997. The 1996 marketing for an IPC 'Family Magic' Pentium computer included the slogan: 'Now, Cyberspace is just another place in your family room'. The information superhighway is, in fact, perhaps now better thought of as a kind of 'information utility' for the home, which is increasingly convergent with other communications services for the home such as the telephone and broadcast media.

Indeed, the concept of the 'information utility' was referred to as far back as 1992 by John Young, a former CEO of Hewlett Packard. It would be: 'a public infrastructure as widespread as electricity, an intelligent network of networks stacked with services, such as intelligent directories, the Library of Congress online, the expertise of the world's best

Figure 6 The information utility (detail from an Apple advertising brochure). 'Now, cyberspace is just another place in your family room.' © Apple Computer Australia. Reproduced with permission.

doctors'. Extending the electricity analogy, the information appliance 'will plug into the information utility as easily as a lamp into an outlet ... It'll be intuitive; users can plug into the information utility and get to work without ever reading a manual' (Young 1992: 57). Figure 6, taken from a recent promotional brochure for Apple's iMac computer, demonstrates how close we may already be to this vision of the information utility.

The information utility brings directly into the home an information service unlike any that has been seen before, and transforms the home computer from an isolated software 'player' (Haddon 1988), to the true information (and communications) appliance. While the Internet certainly contains intelligent directories and access to the world's best libraries, museums and galleries, it also enables interpersonal communication on an unprecedented scale, through email, ICQ ('I seek you', see www.icq.com), IRC (Internet Relay Chat) and so on. Further, it brings commercial services into the home in novel and until recently unanticipated ways. It is generally expected that, over time, the Internet and e-commerce will transform the nature of consumption, but it is always the case that cultural forms, including technological innovations, may be taken up in unanticipated and creative ways by consumers (Miller 1987).

It is perhaps early days to make predictions about how e-commerce and other new technologies of consumption will transform the activities of consumers, since it is clear that, at the time of writing in 2001, e-commerce is still in its infancy. Throughout the world, the Internet is rapidly picking up new users, transmission capacity and services. Western industrialized countries like the United States and Australia can still count only on approximately 50 per cent of their populations being online at home, the most likely site for e-commerce. (In the USA the 50 per cent marker is estimated to have been exceeded by the end of 2000, in Australia by the end of 2001 (ABS 2001a: 3).)

The proportion of households with Internet access is expanding rapidly, however. As Internet use becomes a more established part of the everyday life of householders (as we can see already happening), e-commerce will also become something that consumers feel more comfortable engaging in. It is also perhaps likely that the uptake in Internet shopping will be quicker in places where there is an established culture of catalogue buying, as in the USA. It is clear, too, that in Australia at least, the home is rapidly becoming the most important site for Internet access. In Australia, more people now access the Internet from home than from any other site, including the workplace (ABS 2001a: 7). There is evidence that the longer consumers are on the Internet, the more likely they are to shop online, and spend more money when they do. In the twelve months to November 2000, only 10 per cent of Australian adults purchased or ordered goods or services over the Internet, but this was an increase of 66 per cent over the previous twelve months (ABS 2001a: 11). Books, magazines and music were the most popular items bought.

When it seems like everyone else must be doing their shopping online, consumers are more likely to try it. Figure 7 shows the cover of an advertising brochure for Shopfast, a Sydney-based online supermarket, which in May 2001 registered its 100,000th customer, in a city with around 1 million Internet-using households. ('Bananas in Pyjamas' is a locally produced pre-school children's program.) Like the Apple '101

Figure 7 Buy your bananas in pyjamas. © Shopfast. Reproduced with permission.

household uses' advertisement shown in figure 2, the Shopfast marketing also addresses its appeal to the mother as home manager. Shopfast also mounted a 2001 Mother's Day promotion suggesting a free Shopfast registration as a gift for Mother. E-commerce businesses are finding that they need to use non-Internet channels such as television and print advertising for building brand awareness. In the case of Shopfast, this includes distinctive delivery truck signage.

The increasing profile of e-commerce players on traditional media channels is clearly also, however, an important conditioning influence for consumers who are not already online, or who have not so far ventured into online shopping. The stress and anxiety which may be experienced by consumers who are exploring such unfamiliar territory was, however, well illustrated by the Manfredotti case study in chapter 1. Consumers want to feel safe and in control and will therefore behave in ways which reduce the risk and uncertainty in such investments (of time and household activity, as well as in economic terms). When

Shopfast launched a television advertising campaign in mid-2001, the resulting increase in demand for their services severely strained the company's capacity to maintain the standard of their service for both new and existing customers. But while the increase was clearly precipitated by the advertising campaign, many of the new customers indicated that their reason for taking up the service was that it had been recommended to them by friends and family. The relationship between the strategies of commodity producers and those of consumers is the subject of the next chapter.

Conclusion

During the 1990s the home computer became integrated into the broad media and consumer structures of objectification within which western urban households are embedded. Since consumers' understandings of novel goods are based on what they already know, understand and can imagine for themselves, experiential and discursive bridges must be provided for the artefact between the worlds of production and everyday contexts of consumption. The domestication of the home computer, then, has involved reshaping it to the symbolic, aesthetic and functional parameters of contemporary domestic commodity culture. Domestication is therefore a process by which disparate structures of objectification are brought into alignment. Novel commodities are reshaped to harmonize with existing culturally familiar ones, reassuring consumers that their existing cultural competencies will be adequate for the new cultural terrain.

four

Acquiring a Handle on
the Future

The complex of utopian and dystopian imaginaries which has been referred to as technological ambiguity is translated into hopes and fears at the level of individuals: the sense that technological change is inevitable at the level of broad public discourses is felt at the level of the household as parental responsibility for providing ready access to these technologies for children. The meanings and values around home computing which circulate in public discourse are reflected in consumers' own discourse and understandings of their experience, most notably in the link between education and the need for children to acquire computer literacy skills. The home computer is associated with the perceived parental obligation to provide an optimal developmental environment for their children and with contemporary faith in the application of technological and economic resources to such projects. Since children are not culturally autonomous, parents take on the responsibility for providing them with access to media of objectification, and the developmental process involves the acquisition of cultural competences such as those involved in contemporary consumption processes.

Most people I interviewed for this study, even those without workplace experience of computers, maintain a general sense of trends in information technology development. Apart from workplace experience, the most important source of information about technological developments for consumers is the broadcast media, particularly television, newspapers and magazines. Discourses about the Internet, in particular, have gained wide currency on television and in other media over recent years. The mass media have a pivotal role in generating both a general awareness of IT developments and a particular knowledge of current computer technology. We will see later, however, that these abstract representations must be 'reality checked' against what people see in the shops and advertised locally, against advice and information gathered by asking friends, relatives, acquaintances and retail outlet sales staff, and juxtaposed with workplace and educational experience.

A Handle on the Future

Participating in Technological Progress

Consumers' expectations are textured by the circulation of the domesticated images of the computer as a convenient and useful 'information appliance' we saw in the last chapter. However, the association of computers with futurity and the apparent inevitability of technological progression also provide a powerful sense that these are changes that they must participate in or they will be excluded, in a sense, from contemporary culture itself (Haddon 1992: 83). There is both promise and fear in these technologies, and they therefore hold out not just the threat of being left behind but also the promise of privileged access to the future through them.

Consumer goods can 'become a bridge to displaced meaning and an idealized version of life as it should be lived' (McCracken 1988: 110). Indeed, one of the engines of consumption in modern society is that which regularly declares 'certain purchases obsolete (when they can no longer serve as bridges) and demands the purchase of new goods' (115). This effect is particularly strong in the case of new technologies where the rapidity of technological development results in very short product life cycles and a sense that computer technology is very rapidly outdated.

> There is a real sense of not wanting to be left behind, in an intellectual, technological way, not in the sense of wanting to have it because the Joneses have got it, but in the sense of not wanting to feel left out of the technological advances. And also the fear of – if I didn't go along with this computer business and so on I'd have to admit I was getting too old to do it, and there's a terrible fear, in my mind, of being old, and not being able to do things. (Irene Farrell)

For Irene Farrell, the inevitability of technosocial progress is linked to the inevitability of the ageing process itself. Her fear of not being able to keep up with technological change is essentially a fear of becoming too old to remain fully engaged in everyday cultural life.

Conversely, there is excitement and fascination for Irene in the technology. Although it certainly seems to be important to people that a computer will do certain things and that they can acquire a home computer if they need a tool which will perform these functions, computers are also highly evocative cultural artefacts. For many people there is a fascination with the computer as a thing in itself, as a symbol of futurity. As Jessica Lane put it, 'I'm very aware that computers are the way of the future, for kids too, and so I wanted to have that technology in the house.'

This expressive element is generally modulated through more instrumentalized logics, such as the children's education or the adults' own employment prospects. But for many of the participants in the study there was a degree of urgency in their acquisition of a computer – a sense that these technologies are changing so rapidly that it is possible to be left behind unless an effort is made to keep abreast of developments.

For older people like Irene Farrell, in particular, keeping pace with changing technology is an integral part of keeping up with a rapidly changing world, and of staving off the ageing process by staying physically and mentally active. One of the other retirees in the study, Ruth Bourke, referred to her computer as like having 'a handle on the future':

> It makes me feel as though I've got a handle on the future . . . I'm no longer engaged in day-to-day work, so this makes me feel as though I'm still in the workaday world in a way. That I can keep up with the technology – oh, I'm not into toys for toys' sake – but I do like to know what's happening in the world, and I don't like to feel that I've been left behind.

This age group is of particular interest in showing how information technology is pressed into service in personal projects of self-development. In an empirical study of the use of a range of domestic information and communications technologies by people at or near retirement age, Haddon and Silverstone suggest that these technologies can 'enhance and improve the quality of life of the elderly, through increases in the control of the physical and symbolic environment that they are believed to be able to provide' (1996: 155). It is clear that for Irene Farrell and Ruth Bourke, the computer gives just such a sense of control over a rapidly changing cultural environment. Indeed, as Miller and Slater note, with nuclear families increasingly widely dispersed around the world, the use of these technologies (particularly email and other forms of Internet communication) can keep 'the new physical separation but in some other respects can keep [older people] in the heart of family life' (2000: 58).

Richard Brown, a retired fitter and turner who is now in his seventies, became interested in computers in his sixties after his retirement. He refers to the cultural association of information technology with futurity. Computers are part of a long trajectory of technological change that he has taken a keen interest in following throughout his life:

> I've been a science fiction fan since 1932. I read *Analog*, which is science fiction and fact, so I keep up to date on scientific advances . . . Television was only developed in the year I was born, 1923 . . . The development I've seen in my lifetime: up until the war we only had two plastics, celluloid and bakelite, and now we're surrounded by plastics.

For Doug Fowler (an unemployed man in his thirties), too, a large part of the attraction of computers is their association with science fiction and representations of the future. Doug calls himself a 'futurist':

> Computers have been a passion of mine ever since I knew that computers were around. To me it's part of technology and I'm interested in technology, science, so it was just one thing that I could have. It was my access to technology . . . I am a science fiction fanatic . . . and you read stories with computers, so to own a computer is my way of being in science fiction.

It may well be that it is the very novelty of these technologies – having had such a profound impact during recent living memory – which make them the medium *par excellence* for imagining the future at this particular contemporary moment (Miller and Slater 2000: 14). In the not too distant future they may become more mundane and taken for granted, but for people now in their thirties, forties and fifties (and not just at or near retirement age), these technologies have come to symbolize the future and represent an important medium of engagement with a complex and rapidly changing world. For Gail Shaw, in her late thirties, it seems that while younger people have not had to make an effort to acquire familiarity with computer technology, it is often necessary for people of her generation to make a conscious effort to come to terms with it:

It feels like younger people are much more computer literate. I feel like it's a way of leaving a generation behind in some ways. I do feel that quite strongly, I think that's probably part of the thing for me about getting my head around it . . . Because it's not that I have an incredible *fear* of ageing or being left behind, but I don't want that to happen, like I want to feel like I'm actually participating.

The pace of technological development leaves consumers feeling that it must be responded to in some way, particularly by parents on behalf of children, who are not culturally autonomous but are dependent on their parents to provide them with access to media of objectification. There is often a heavy sense of parental responsibility for providing children with as many life opportunities as can reasonably be achieved. As we saw in the Manfredotti case study in chapter 1, not wanting to be left behind was an important motivating factor – not for Laura and Max themselves, but certainly on behalf of the children. Danielle Singleton also says that she doesn't feel the need to keep up with the technology for herself, but was concerned for her son:

I don't mind being left behind with reference to technology. It wasn't that . . . I was probably more aware that Ian my son might be left behind . . . It was probably more my concerns for him and an awareness that it would be useful for him to have some familiarity with the machine but from my point of view it was just simply convenient and very much a pragmatic thing.

Indeed, for Danielle, as is clearly the case for many parents, a home computer is a necessity as far as children are concerned: 'I actually think it's a necessity for a child growing up as well, nowadays. If you want them to participate in the culture that's around them.'

For many people their workforce experience is enough to keep them from feeling that they might be left behind. Charlotte Thompson bought her computer because she was interested in computers and wanted to go further with them than was possible through work. Chris Talbot has a similar interest:

No, I don't feel that [a feeling of being left behind] because I have it at work. I'm exposed to it all day and I don't feel like – sometimes I would like to have one at home to experiment with, software that I don't have at work or that is there but I don't know very well . . . I would like to know a lot more about computers.

The sense that it is necessary to make an effort to keep up with the changing technologies is not a universal one, however. For some people information technologies have become a commonplace part of their lives and the possibility of being left behind does not arise for them. The technology has become incorporated into the extended self and is no longer in question, and is therefore no longer seen as an area of self-lack needing to be developed. As we saw above, for Richard Brown computers are part of a long trajectory of technological change that he has taken a keen interest in following over many decades. For young people too, such technologies may have become such an unquestioned part of their lives that there is not a sense of urgency about keeping up. Regine Vassallo is in her early twenties, and says that 'there have always been computers in my house'. For other people, a computer has become naturalized as an almost-expected acquisition, like the VCR and microwave oven did in the 1980s. 'Everybody seems to have one these days, don't they?' said Elizabeth Martin and, as Felicity Attard put it: 'I think it was just that it was time to buy a computer.'

For some people, their home computer was almost an accidental acquisition, and it is also possible for it to play a very minor role in the lives of the people who own them. Janet Fuller bought an old IBM-compatible machine from her work colleague Hilary Lacey, initially intending to give it to her godson, but then deciding to keep it for herself. I asked Janet whether she had any interest at all in being at the forefront of technological change: 'Oh, god no. Far from it, I would rather go bush walking.' Janet says that she can't imagine ever updating it or getting a new one: she did think about it but, as she says, 'I thought, no, I would rather have the money to do other things, to travel. I mean, it costs a *lot* of money to buy a new computer.' The major projects of objectification in Janet's life tend to be ones which do not involve computer use. She contrasts the computer purchase with her purchase of a 'beautiful' stereo system: 'I use it all the time, I'm really into music, and I did a lot of comparison shopping and it was completely the opposite to with the computer.'

The Chapman household is another example of a household which had no explicit intention, at the time of acquisition at least, to acquire a home computer. They 'willingly agreed to accept' the Apple IIE the Farrells no longer needed early in 1996, in exchange for a 'good' bottle of red wine. This gives an assessment of the economic value of the computer to both the households, and indicates an item which was of more utility to the Farrells than the computer had become. The willingness to accept must, however, be a positive intention in itself, since there has to be an allocation of the household's temporal and spatial resources to the acquisition, even if the financial investment is small. For the Chapmans, particularly Paul Chapman, this is their children: 'We were interested in having it to increase the kids' familiarity with that technology, because they use Apple Macs at school. So they have a little bit there and this was a way of extending it . . . Familiarity with the keyboard, and to overcome any technophobia that they might otherwise feel.'

The desire for the children to acquire computer literacy skills is not sufficiently strong at this point to overcome other household priorities for the allocation of their financial resources. But for this family, as for many others, the parents want the younger children to have home access to a better computer by the time they are in high school.

Home Computers Contributing to Employment and Education

Complementing the computer's symbolic associations with futurity and technosocial progress, an important instrumental aspect of the home computer as a form of objectification is as an important technology of work and education. Parental hopes for children's future career prospects tend to be one of the most powerful motivators for home computer purchases. As we saw in the discussion of the Manfredotti household, there is a powerful and emotionally charged motivational context for computer acquisition, often manifested as a sense of obligation to purchase. Parents buy computers 'in much the same spirit as they might earlier have bought a set of encyclopaedias' (Murdock, Hartmann and Gray 1992: 154).

While adults tend to specify particular concrete benefits and uses in explaining their home computer acquisition, the hope that a home computer will be a benefit for children tends to be expressed in more generalized and abstract terms, often in terms of 'computer literacy':

> Yes, I think [computer literacy] is important. I think most of the employment areas I see them being interested in working in, computer literacy will have some bearing or have some importance. Matthew, for example, worked a bit earlier in the year for [a fast food chain], and I think that convinced him that he didn't want to work with his hands like that. (Peter Richards)

For many parents it is a question of providing their children with the opportunity to follow their own ambitions, and providing them with the resources to ensure that they have flexibility in their career options. This means that they need to gain computer skills, since it is universally believed that computers are going to be at least as important in the workplaces of the future as they are today. Many parents believe that unless their children have a computer at home they are at a disadvantage relative to their peers who do (Noble 1986). This becomes more important as the children move through their schooling, and is particularly important for children when they reach secondary school.

Chris Talbot's computer is an old one which her husband brought home for her (because he knew that she wanted a computer) when his employer was upgrading equipment. I asked if part of the motivation for the acquisition was so that the children (a son aged seven and a daughter aged three) could have access to a computer at home:

> That was minor, because they would use it more at school than they'd use it here and they've got more educational games at school than what we have here. I don't think that was a priority. When he gets older I would like to get a more sophisticated computer. I would like him to be very computer literate . . . Not this age no but very shortly yes.

Sylvia Cooper offers a slightly different point of view – that of social or peer group pressure. It is not so much that children will be left behind without home access to a computer, but that they might feel socially excluded: 'It's more a status type of thing . . . their education is not going to be affected, but it's that image thing. It's just how people feel about themselves I think. That horrible feeling everyone else knows what's happening except me.'

It was suggested in chapter 2 that these parental roles in introducing the social and cultural environment to the child are an intrinsic part of the individual's development from complete dependence to relative autonomy (Winnicott 1971). It is not just a question of providing children with opportunities to develop the skills they will need to ensure their future options, but also of providing them with the cultural resources to establish and maintain social status within their peer group. Such attention to creating the material conditions for children's development is not limited to parents. Grandparents can play a role in this process too, as illustrated by the case of Jessica Lane, the single parent whose father bought the computer for her and her son.

A number of the study participants had bought their home computers principally because of their own, rather than children's, study or further education. Sylvia Cooper had previously gone through a tertiary vocational education course by using equipment available at her local neighbourhood centre, but bought a computer when she started a university course. Both Hilary Lacey and her partner Margaret Paine also bought computers (separately) soon after starting university courses.

A home computer contributes to adults' engagement in the world of employment, as well as education, on a number of different levels: at the abstract level of idealized hopes and fears for the future, on the general but concrete level of developing a familiarity with personal computers ('computer literacy'), in the development of particular work-related skills (such as wordprocessing, database or information retrieval skills), and in their ability to be able to bring work home from their employment based elsewhere or establish a small business from home (Haddon and Silverstone 1993).

The Turner family bought their first home computer in 1990 when Thomas Turner established a home office from which he could do freelance architectural work. Jessica Lane was also freelancing from home, and after she had handwritten one research consultancy report she decided that she was 'never, ever, going to do that again' and that she needed a computer in order to be able to take on such tasks.

Although the ability to work from home often forms part of the justification for a home computer purchase, such plans or vague intentions to work from home do not always come to fruition. Elizabeth Martin bought a Macintosh Performa after she was widowed, and thought she might do some work from home but had 'never got around to it'. Many of the study participants had, however, bought a home computer in order to bring work home. For many adults, across a range of professional and semi-professional occupations, a home computer is justified by giving them flexibility in the use of their work time. Having a home computer is more convenient and 'family-friendly' than spending longer at work or bringing a work computer home. Charlotte Thompson also feels that it is less stressful to bring the work home, rather than do it in the office: 'I had decided it was more relaxing to be able to do some stuff at home away from the distractions of work'.

For women who take a significant break away from the workforce (or who remain only partially engaged in the workforce) while raising their children, this has a significant impact on their development of self through employment. Work technology is changing rapidly and even a short break away from the workforce can make it difficult for women to re-enter employment on the same basis on which they left it. A home computer is often an important element in the preparation for a return to employment.

For two of the women in the study, the use of a computer at home formed an integral part of their updating of employment-related skills. Sarah Richards, who had been out of the workforce for 16 years, achieved this partly by persuading her husband to bring home a Macintosh computer from work which she could learn to use, to supplement her IBM-compatible skills gained on the home computer. Ann Harrison had recently changed jobs within the local government organization she worked for, after having worked for a number of years in an office without computers. Her employer had closed down this section and was in the process of redeploying its staff. In her late forties, she faced the (for her) daunting prospect of having to develop a new set of skills in order to be able to adapt to a new working environment: 'It seemed like for decades things were done the same way but things are changing so rapidly now ... People our age and a little bit older you think "what about my job?"' Ann had been making an effort to develop wordprocessing skills on their home computer, and she and her husband Laurence had enrolled in a Microsoft Excel course.

Other people in the study had more technically ambitious plans to upgrade their employment skills, or to start computer-related businesses. Carlos Martinez for example, was undertaking a course in developing computer-based training materials, with an ambition to develop and market (via the Internet) multimedia courseware products. Sue Kozlowski and Phillip Healey, who were both employed only on a casual basis after having been unemployed for a period of time, were hoping to move into working directly with computers. Their home equipment consisted of a network of four computers, including one Sun Sparcstation – a minicomputer that is not normally found in homes – running the Linux (a public domain version of Unix) operating system. Shortly after our interview, Sue was successful in gaining a position as a Unix systems administrator, interestingly on the basis of the systems administration experience she had gained on her home equipment.

As we have seen, the computer's symbolic association with futurity allows it to objectify an ongoing engagement with a rapidly changing world – to act as 'a handle on the future'. Further, the integration of information technology into the cultural domains of employment and education means that the home computer is able to act as a strong point of articulation between the domestic domain and these larger spheres. However, it does so via its incorporation into the domestic domain of the present, and it makes its transition into the home through processes of consumption.

Acquiring a Home Computer

Deciding to Acquire a Home Computer

A home computer purchase is itself a process of engagement with the broad social and cultural context of consumer institutions and practices. Rather than a single isolated act, it may take place over an extended period of time, since the acquisition of a home computer is often the culmination of a long process of research and planning. The Bartlett family is perhaps at one extreme – they considered buying a home computer for about five years before finally buying one. For others, the purchase itself is more like an accidental response to a fortuitous set of circumstances, such as a financial windfall.

The acquisition is, for most households, a major expense which must be balanced against other possible expenditures. The computer's priority relative to other purchases will depend in part on whether it is seen as a necessity which must be budgeted for (for example where an adult household member considers that they need one for work), as an investment (perhaps as an important contribution to the children's education) or as a recreational pursuit or hobby item (which essentially must be acquired from 'disposable' income).

Where the computer is seen as a 'hobby' item, which family member it is who is interested in acquiring one will also make a difference as to where a computer comes in the priority list, and how much money can be spent on it. Kirkup (1992: 271) contrasts male hobbies, which generally involve the purchase of expensive accessories, with female hobbies, which are often based around creative craft activities and involve little financial outlay. In the Talbot household, for example, it is Chris who would like to own a computer:

> I've always wanted a computer but it's never been a financial priority for us . . . I do plan at some time in the future to get one but there has always been higher priorities, the house, paying off the house or fixing something. I think it would be more of a luxury than a necessity for us. That's why it has been put off.

The computer they currently have was bought by Chris's husband as a Christmas gift for her, from his employer who was getting rid of outdated equipment.

There may be differential access between individual household members to the financial resources of the household, and prioritizing of possible uses of the household's resources often involves explicit negotiation (Pahl 1990; Vogler and Pahl 1994; Haddon 1992: 84). During our interview, the Richards good-naturedly ribbed each other about whether the blinds (Sarah's higher priority) should come before a computer upgrade (Peter's choice). Doug Fowler (who is unemployed) finds it difficult to convince his wife that resources should be put into the computer. It has only cost Doug about $100 so far: 'Things like upgrading the motherboard, upgrading the RAM chips, Sound Blaster, they can wait. She knows that I want to upgrade the hard disk and she's agreed to that.'

Sometimes factors other than the availability of financial resources may precipitate a purchase. The intense social pressure on parents to buy a computer is particularly important in precipitating a computer purchase as the children get older, especially when they reach secondary school. Other study participants bought computers at the point at which someone had started to undertake a higher education program (this was the case for the Cooper household, and for Hilary Lacey and Margaret Paine). Losing access to computers through work may also precipitate a computer purchase. This was the catalyst in the purchases of Helen Samuels (who was made redundant) and Ruth Bourke (who bought a computer on her retirement). Ruth had wanted to buy a computer for several years, but other major expenses had always intervened, particularly weddings:

> I would have bought a computer years before, if I hadn't had to keep funding weddings. [laughing] Oh, there's been one more wedding since . . . Well I thought about buying a computer, then Graham decided to get married, and I really did think I would buy a computer and Robert got married in England, so I had to go to England . . . So for about ten years I've played around with the idea.

My discussions with the Turner family were instrumental in precipitating their purchase of a new computer, which occurred between my first and second visits to interview them. At the first interview Sally and Thomas gave several reasons for wanting a new computer, such as more attractive educational games for the children and a modem for access to the Internet. As Sally said then: 'I would like to by the time Jonathan's in high school – I think it would be really useful for him to have access to that information for assignments.' Between then and my second visit a month later, the family had bought a new Macintosh. I asked whether they felt that my discussions with them had any influence on the purchase: 'I think it was an impetus, in some ways . . . I would say that your visit did focus our thinking about getting a new computer, and the discussion that we went into, about all the reasons for upgrading.'

With a purchase like a computer, the size of the investment is greater than many households will have available at one time. The Turner household had financed their new computer by borrowing money from Sally's father. For the Richards, the easy availability of cheap finance for the purchase (through a low interest special offer) was a factor in precipitating their computer purchase. Both Elizabeth Martin's and the Cooper household's computers were bought on a 'six months interest free' deal with a department store credit card. The Coopers' computer also came with twelve months' hotline support from IBM and a small portable television. Such deals seem to be a common (and successful) way that the market acts to make the decision as simple as possible for the consumer. The social processes which Silverstone and Haddon (1996) refer to as the design/domestication interface include a range of such strategies which are designed to facilitate the acquisition. 'Sweetener' strategies, such as low cost finance options, or a 'free gift' element like the Coopers' portable television, are clearly effective. For some of the study households, the act of purchase was itself precipitated by such an offer, after a sometimes considerable period of considering and researching the purchase.

There is variability in people's willingness to go into debt for a computer purchase. As Lunt and Livingstone (1992) point out, consumers in general will only borrow money for the purchase of goods which are judged to be necessities or investments (although credit card purchases are an exception to this generalization). The actual purchase may therefore be prompted by a sum of money becoming available that is surplus to the household's normal income stream. Under the Australian taxation system, tax instalments deducted by the employer are calculated to result in an overpayment of tax, which is refunded in a lump sum after the end of the taxation year, on submission of a taxation return to the Australian Tax Office. This is often a sizeable amount of money. The Coopers paid off the debt for their computer with their tax refund cheque. Similarly, Hilary Lacey bought her first new computer when her tax refund arrived. Retirement may also be a time when there is access to a lump sum of money. Irene Farrell's financial adviser told them that there was little point in hanging on to a number of small investments, so they cashed these in and spent the money on the computer, rather than reinvesting the sum.

Some of the study participants had saved to buy their computers (including Margaret Paine, Jim Christou, Felicity Attard and the Manfredottis), and it was also possible for the purchase to be precipitated by some chance or periodic event in the consumer's own life (rather than an offer on the part of the computer manufacturers and sellers). Marjorie Brennan, for example, had been considering buying a second-hand computer when she saw a notice displayed with one for sale. Similarly, Janet Fuller bought her computer only because her work colleague, Hilary Lacey, was offering it for sale.

It is clear, then, that for major purchases which fall outside the normal provisioning level of expenditure of the household, households are able to deploy a range of strategies to direct their resources in various directions, as they are prioritized by and negotiated between the household members. It is not so much a question of households being able to afford, or not being able to afford, a home computer of a certain value (say, a new model as opposed to a second-hand one). It is not that this is an objective state of affairs within an instrumentalized discourse about the financial resources that the household has at its disposal, a point which Miller (1998b) makes in discussing the ideology of thrift. Thrift, as a normative discursive framework about shopping, is more about objectifying the relationship of mutual dependence and equity between household members in relation to the household's resources, than it is about saving money in any instrumental sense.

Indeed, it is clear that the purchase of a home computer is part of the ongoing investment required by home-building. Often the initial computer acquisition is followed up by subsequent acquisitions of software, additional hardware and perhaps eventually a new and more up-to-date computer. Children will often pressure their parents to buy or upgrade, motivated by the desire to play games they have seen at their friends' houses or in magazines. This is unlikely, however, to be the main deciding factor in a purchase, although it may be cited as 'one reason' among others for upgrading (by the Richards and Martinez households, for example).

Technological developments result in a continually changing expectation about what a home computer should be able to do. Computers which continue to be able to perform the same tasks they have always done will eventually come to be perceived as 'slow' and with only limited capacity. Although in the workplace it may be acceptable to replace computers every three years or so, it seems common for home computer owners to cite an expectation of their computer lasting 'about five years' before they will replace it. This seems to be a compromise between the business experience and consumers' comparisons with other domestic appliances, which tend to last rather longer than five years.

The acquisition of a home computer clearly does not, then, guarantee a sense of keeping up indefinitely. This has particularly been true since the mid-1990s around the Internet. Even the study participants who did not have Internet access on their home computer or through work or study felt that this was something they would eventually have to come to terms with. The Coopers have considered installing a modem on their home computer: 'I still have that feeling with the Internet, and that this is how we're going to get our information and if I don't know how to access it I am not going to have the information.' At the time of our interview they were still unwilling to make the commitment, largely because of uncertainty about the ongoing costs involved:

> I think the thing that holds us back is that we're still not sure whether we will end up with this whopping big bill. We want to look into that or maybe wait and see other people that have got it. I think that is a money issue that's holding us back from running out and getting a modem. (Sylvia Cooper)

During the late 1990s it became common practice to include a modem as a standard component of new home computers. Often an introductory package with an Internet Service Provider is included in the package, and ISPs are increasingly offering 'unlimited usage' options for a flat monthly fee. These developments have undoubtedly contributed to the rapid rise in the take up of Internet-capable home computers by reducing the financial risk involved. The transformation of the Internet from information superhighway into the information utility has also meant that many people have moved between cynicism about its utility to dedicated Internet users in an astonishingly short time. Claire Matheson, for example, told me: 'The information superhighway implies that you have a modem, otherwise you don't have access to it. It also implies a very expensive telephone bill. Both those things I'm not interested in . . . What do you get off it? It's just a more expensive toy again.' Within two years of making this statement, however, Claire was not only connected to the Internet but had published her own web page giving information and support to tinnitus sufferers.

Consumers clearly have a complex engagement with the world of goods, constructed in relation to discourses circulating about the kinds of goods available and their uses and symbolic associations, and involving imagined expectations about how such objects would fit into their everyday life and activities. Future possibilities are imaginatively investigated in the present, and may be acted on in response to a range of precipitating events and conditions. Consumption decisions take place within a complex context which involves not just a simple intention on the part of the purchaser. There is often a need for the consumer to negotiate with others who share in the household's resources. On the commercial sector's part, there are many strategies for encouraging the acquisition, an area of commercial activity which seems to have undergone a rapid expansion in recent years.

Once the decision has been taken, activities of acquisition are undertaken. Contemporary consumers draw on an established repertoire of knowledges and cultural competences when contemplating the acquisition of a consumer good (Glennie and Thrift 1992; Gottdiener 1995). The size of the investment in the computer and the risk inherent in branching out into new cultural territory means that for the consumer who is inexperienced and lacks knowledge of a particular segment of the market, this is often a stressful and anxiety-provoking experience. As Laura Manfredotti put it, she was 'nervous and feeling like an idiot' because she 'didn't know anything'. The establishment of a situation of trust in the process itself (which often also means trust in the institutions and individuals one is dealing with) is therefore an important prerequisite to the consumer's commitment to the purchase.

Engaging with the World of Goods

Consumers of innovative goods like personal computers, particularly those without much prior direct experience with computers, must gather information on which to base a purchase decision even once they have been convinced in general of the need to acquire one. The participants in the present study used a range of strategies in researching their computer acquisition. Many gathered information from magazines and newspapers, from letterbox deliveries of retailers' catalogues, by visiting retailers or trade exhibitions, and through talking to friends, relatives and acquaintances. Margaret Paine had saved to buy the computer and her computer purchase was preceded by a period of keeping an eye on the market and buying when a better than usual deal came along. Ruth Bourke is another participant who had a clear idea of what kind of computer she wanted and was keen to get the best deal she could. Ruth was sure that she wanted to buy a Macintosh, and simply went back to the one retailer until they offered her a deal she was prepared to accept. The computer she wanted to buy came bundled with an ink-jet printer, but Ruth wanted a laser printer, and she bargained with the dealer to trade one for the other:

> I said 'I don't want an $800 ink-jet . . . well, alright, knock $800 off the price', and he did. I just kept going back. I'd go back one day, then I'd go again the next. It just took me about a week to buy it. Until at last they said they would do it at the price I said. The whole thing cost me exactly $4000. And I thought that was an *enormous* sum of money, and for $4000 I should get what I wanted!

For both Ruth and Margaret, knowledge about the market and control over the financial resources to purchase the computer (by not having to borrow), led them into the purchase process from a position of empowerment and control. For others the process of acquisition is involves a number of uncertainties and potentially anxiety-provoking factors. Consumers use a range of strategies to overcome these uncertainties.

Some people buy a particular kind of computer because it is the same as the ones they work with, which makes it simpler for them to work at home. Patricia Collins wanted to buy a Macintosh because of its ease of use and because that is what she was familiar with at work, but also wanted access to IBM-compatible functionality because she felt that this platform was of more relevance to the future employability of her children. She eventually decided on a Macintosh capable of running in DOS-compatible mode in addition to the normal Mac operating mode.

Consumers' sense of control over the acquisition process often relies on a sense of trust in the people who are dealt with as part of the process. John Powell and Hayley Crowther, on the other hand, did not have such previous experience to underpin their purchase decision, and relied heavily on the advice of family and friends. It is important to consumers as they gather information that the social source of that information be trustworthy. In many cases this involves getting advice from friends, relatives and other acquaintances, but generally also entails developing a sense that those people who are involved in the organizations which sell computers can be trusted to give accurate and unbiased information and advice on the purchase.

The idealized model of commodity transactions which sees them as involving the transfer of alienable goods between transactors with no enduring social relationship between them does not do justice to the fundamentally social and cultural nature of commodity exchange processes in the contemporary western world (Gregory 1982). This is manifested in a number of ways. First, there is the sense of trust in the people that consumers are dealing with as they research their purchase, which is often pivotal in determining exactly where they will buy their computer. Second, there is often an expectation that the purchase will initiate an ongoing relationship between the consumer and the retail organization (perhaps in the form of ongoing support services), or in more abstract terms with brand loyalty or a continuing association with the manufacturer of the product (so that some consumers identify themselves as 'Macintosh' people or 'Windows' people). Through the purchase of a commodity, the consumer enters into an ongoing social and cultural relationship. The choice of computer is not based on some instrumentally rationalized calculation, but often comes down to a choice between potential social and cultural relationships.

Although Patricia Collins visited the local outlets of the major chain stores, she settled on buying from a specialist computer retailer because she thought she would get better after-sales service from them, but also because she had a more personalized sense of trust in them:

> I didn't know what sort of backup would be available through [the general appliance retailers]. They do have a service centre there but there again I wasn't too sure what sort of real help they could give if we came across any problems. Which is why I chose [a local computer retailer] because they would give you the backup and repairs and I felt they were more genuine – they will actually do what they say they will do.

For the Bartletts, a personalized sense of trust in the person they were buying from was also important: 'We read a lot of catalogues and went to a lot of shops and all of them were as confusing as the next one and we thought "Well who do you trust? Which one is the better one to get?" We didn't have a clue and that's why we held off for so long.' The Bartletts considered buying a computer for about five years before finally taking the plunge, eventually buying from a dealer who was personally known to Stephen Bartlett. The Coopers, on the other hand, felt that more trustworthy information could be obtained from friends and colleagues who have computers than from sales people who gave contradictory information:

> We talked to a lot of sales people. But we also talked to people who had computers. That was probably more so than talking to sales people. I wasn't distrustful of sales people at first but after talking to a few I started

to wonder if they knew what they were talking about. At first I thought
they knew everything about a computer. (Sylvia Cooper)

The purchase may also involve the establishment of an ongoing
relationship with the producers of the computer as an abstracted entity
(rather than the particular individuals who manufactured the computer). The Richards family, for example, bought their 486 computer
in 1995, after Peter had been looking at catalogues for about two years
and so had a fairly good idea of what kind of computer they could get
and what it would cost. Peter had compared the prices of computers at
a number of outlets, but felt that having a 'name' brand machine,
bought from a reputable company, was important:

> So I'd actually compared what I could get with this minor supplier, and
> the brand names of the computers were unknown to me. There was also
> a new place in [local town], selling extremely cheap computers . . . But
> we did decide that whatever we did we would go with a reputable
> company, where there's some reasonable backup, and a 'name' machine,
> not necessarily IBM, but an IBM-compatible.

They had decided that these factors were important after having a
'bad' experience with their first computer, which they had bought from
a major retail outlet who later stopped selling computers. They had been
unable to buy a printer ribbon without going through the computer's
manufacturer and, as Peter says, 'I suppose we didn't want to get caught
twice':

> I always had a lingering doubt about the first one, because it seemed to
> be out-of-date as soon as we got it. It probably wasn't really quickly, but
> it just seemed really quick. Probably because we didn't use it a real lot
> when we first got it, or even throughout the time we had it and it always
> seemed a bit like a lemon, because it was so slow and there wasn't much
> you could do with it.

As in the case of the Manfredottis, the impression made by the
salesman at a large electrical goods and furniture retailer and Peter's
consequent feeling of trust in the advice he was being given was
important in determining where they bought their computer:

> They were very helpful there, and I found that the salesman there was
> very good. He really seemed to speak with a level of authority, which was

the thing I was impressed with. I went there several times, at different times, and spoke to different sales people, and I'd look around the store and ask the questions. I pretended I didn't know anything, which was pretty close to the truth.

Here again we see the strategy of asking the same questions of a number of different people, to establish a consistent picture. If, as a number of authors have argued, consumption practices may be organized in ways which provide a defence against the inevitable anxieties of life in the contemporary world (Silverstone 1994; Robins 1994), then these strategies on the part of consumers may be seen as means by which their ontological security (in Giddens's sense) is maintained within a novel cultural domain in which they have imperfect knowledge and immature competence.

Peter Richards (like the Manfredottis) finally bought the computer where he found a sales person who seemed to be an 'authoritative' source of information – one who could be trusted – as opposed to the common perception that sales people cannot be trusted without corroborating evidence that the advice they are giving is sound, since it is commonly assumed that their primary motivation will be making the sale. At one store which had recently opened:

they had a couple of sales people in there, one of them looked barely older than my daughter and he looked like he was supposed to be the expert on the subject, and he explained what you were getting for your money, but didn't strike me as being very professional . . . it was that once bitten twice shy feeling. I thought 'at least I've checked this place out'. I only went there once.

The Coopers, with little prior direct experience to base a decision on, bought an IBM because: 'I guess we thought IBM was a name. If machines were IBM-compatible that must have been for a reason. So if everything is IBM-compatible, well why not get IBM. Maybe it's in reality it's not that logical but it seemed it to us' (Sylvia Cooper).

It is not, however, a question of whether such decisions are logical or not, but that they obey different logics to the dominant instrumental, rational model of such decisions. Different brands and different kinds of consumer outlets objectify different values for consumers, and may therefore be seen as quasi-social entities in themselves (Clarke 1998; Lunt and Livingstone 1992). The associations around a brand name or retail organization are built up in complex ways through diverse pathways: advertising, media discourses, workplace experience, conversations and meanings circulating in informal discursive situations. Individuals interact with these abstracted structures, however, in particular and local situations and must negotiate and improvise their specific actions, often in situations where the proximate social other is seen as a representative of these larger and more abstract structures.

Danielle Singleton, for example, describes her attraction to the Apple Macintosh brand and her decision to support a local retailer rather than a big chain as based in such 'ideological' justifications:

> That was the biggest disaster really. I don't think I thought it through well enough. I had this idea that I wanted an Apple Mac because I didn't like IBMs and because Apple Macs were more ideologically sound because of their history of two young left-wing Americans beating the system. I liked all that ideological stuff. It was really that which drove me to get an Apple Mac, nothing much to do with practicalities . . . I bought locally, at the computer shop which has now gone defunct and I'm sure I paid much more than I could have paid if I bought it at [a large chain] . . . I would do a lot more exploration next time.

In addition to this attraction to the symbolic positioning of the Apple brand, Danielle also felt that she should support local retailers, and in return could expect support from them:

> There was very much the idea that there would be local support and that did encourage me to buy from one of those places but the reality was that there wasn't the support I imagined there'd be . . . I was annoyed. I was annoyed with myself more than with them that I had these illusions, these idealistic notions about that and it didn't work out but that's all part of the learning. Next time it would be different.

Danielle's apparent threat that 'next time it would be different' suggests that consumers will tend to act on the basis of past experience of similar purchase decisions as well as on the basis of imagined expectations.

The variety of outlets in which computers are available offers consumers a broad variety of symbolic choices. Large chain stores offer name-brand computers, while computer 'warehouses' offer less expensive computers but are not perceived as being as reliable as businesses (some consumers suggest that such stores have a reputation for not staying in business for very long). Small local PC dealers are viewed as offering more personalized service than larger more anonymous chains (by Carlos Martinez, for example), even though they might be more expensive than the warehouses. Specialist computer resellers, such as the Apple reseller network and university consortium dealers, are also seen as offering a more personalized service with an expectation that after-sales support will be available.

Other sources of computer acquisitions are seen by consumers (and this is part of their attraction) as outside the commodified sphere of computer manufacturing and distribution (Lunt and Livingstone 1992; Clarke 1998). Some study participants avoided the mainstream market by buying their computers second-hand: from work colleagues (Janet Fuller); old ones from work (Chris Talbot); from a friend of a friend (Richard Brown's first computer); or from a flyer put up at work (Marjorie Brennan).

Both Claire Matheson and Hilary Lacey rejected the mainstream retailers in order to buy their computers from individuals who make the computers up cheaply, generally operate from their homes and advertise in the local press and the weekly *Trading Post*. Claire is keen to minimize the cost of her computer purchase, and does not see any value in paying extra for a 'name' brand or to buy from a major retailer:

> And of course I always try to find the cheap way out. I mean we bought the computer cheap. [Claire's youngest son] and I went to Parramatta, had a go through the *Trading Post* to find the addresses. And we found some shoddy ones, and ones that were too expensive, and then we found this one that the fellow put together privately in his home, and it cost me a whole nine hundred dollars.

Hilary Lacey also bought her computer from one of these dealers. She has recommended him to other people, and took her mother to see him when she wanted to buy a computer. Hilary feels that the prices in the major retail outlets are higher than they need to be: 'I had a look. Like not to buy, like when we were there just getting other things, whatever store it happened to be. Yes, I would look around and see what was there but it was outrageous. What a rip off.' Hilary and her partner Margaret, however, identify differently within their relationship to the market-place for such consumer goods. Margaret bought her own computer (at about the same time as Hilary) from one of the mainstream retailers, illustrating that households are not necessarily internally homogeneous with respect to their consumer behaviour, and that joint purchases may therefore be differently negotiated from individual ones.

Consumers, as we have seen, act on the basis of what they know and understand, that is, on the basis of established cultural competences. Consumer strategies for exploring novel cultural terrain, then, must also draw on what the consumer knows and is familiar with, a process which the market itself also assists through the kinds of activities described here. These processes construct practical and symbolic bridges between the domains of production and consumption. The consumer's relationship to the marketplace is thus complex and dynamic, and although it is highly asymmetric there exist possibilities for consumers to negotiate the hegemony of corporate commercial power from a position of control and empowerment.

Software Piracy

> This is where you change my name. Everything I own is pirated. Every piece. (Doug Fowler)

An aspect of home computer use which exemplifies the articulation of the individual to broader cultural processes, and in particular to the commodified world of the mass-produced products of multinational corporations, is that of software 'piracy' (the installation of software which the consumer does not have a legal licence to use). The possibility for software piracy arises because of the convention that software is only licensed to users (generally for use on a single computer only), not sold outright. In other words, the property rights of consumers over the software they buy are significantly different from (and more limited than) those they are generally familiar with. This issue illustrates the complexity and contradictions inherent in consumers' positioning with respect to such commodities and how these are negotiated through discourses and values and through everyday improvised actions and interactions.

Many of the study participants had such software installed on their computers. This is an issue of some delicacy, as all of them were well aware of the illegality of this practice. This knowledge is balanced, however, against the ease with which software can be copied, the cost of software and the general understanding that this is something that 'everybody' does.

Ruth Bourke's neighbour installed a number of programs on her computer: 'I've never tried to use Microsoft Word . . . My next door neighbour put it on for me sometime, I'm not quite sure why, I think he thought he was doing me a good turn.' Ruth is aware of the legal status of such programs, but sees this as something that everybody seems to do:

> It's illegal. And nobody has any qualms about it. And yet, on most other things, I would disapprove wholeheartedly of illegality. It's just that they seem to me, and I think that the reason that everybody feel this way, is that they are so expensive, and people feel that they are overpriced, and that they're being got at.

I asked Ruth whether, if she found Microsoft Word useful, she would consider going out and buying a copy of it: 'Probably – not [laughter]. Well, that man, that Bill Gates fellow, he just turns me off.'

Ruth's reference to Bill Gates as a symbol of corporate wealth and as a representative of the software industry as a whole is discussed further below. It is instructive also though to draw attention to her laughter, which can be read as an indication of the paradoxical status of software piracy. Software piracy is seen as morally wrong and illegal, and at the same time as a normal standard of behaviour. Many of the study participants used laughter or humour as we discussed software piracy, not to resolve this ambiguity, but to indicate that, at a level of abstraction if not of behaviour, it is possible for both these standpoints to be true. Helen Samuels, for example, has no qualms about telling me that she would readily take an illegal copy of a software program which costs around $1000, except that she doesn't know anyone who has it. 'I must admit that all my programs are pirated [laughter], well not all, but, you know, a lot of things. I can't afford to. Express is another one I would love to explore, but I just can't afford the thousand dollars, nor do I know anyone who has it [laughter].' At the time of our interview, Helen was in the process of trying to register a shareware game, which involved communicating with the US-based publisher and arranging to send them the software fee. The only reason she was going to this trouble was because the software had to be registered in order to be able to play the whole of the game.

Hilary Lacey is another study participant who has many illegal copies of programs: 'I've probably got more software than what the computer's worth. I've got heaps of software . . . that I've pilfered [laugh] . . . I will just ask people for it.' Hilary will also pass on software she has acquired to other people:

'Can you get this?' and I will say 'Oh yes, I can get that'. Even if I don't use it I've got it. Like hundreds of dollars, thousands of dollars worth of software I've got at home . . . I don't give a shit. [laugh] I really don't. I don't care . . . I don't have a problem 'accepting' [laugh] software from anywhere, for free.

For Sylvia Cooper, home use of such software is different to work use:

Yes, I do, I do sometimes [worry about it]. Especially if someone else's name is on the logo thing when it comes up. I do but I don't. I would be totally different at work . . . To me that's where the ethical comes into it, organizations should buy, organizations should not swap programs. But it doesn't apply at home. I don't know why. That's really awful isn't it? . . . It's almost like sharing and lending, it just doesn't seem the same. I don't know why. It's almost like, yes, well they bought it I guess they can do what they like with it.

The ambiguity in the status of pirated software is clear here in Sylvia's 'I do but I don't' worry about it, and in her challenge to the researcher to find such an attitude immoral or offensive: 'That's really awful isn't it?'

The practice on the part of software manufacturers under which software is only licensed to consumers, rather than sold outright, contrasts markedly with other domestic commodities with which consumers are familiar. Software licensing is more aligned to the practices of the workplace, where the legal ownership of equipment and other infrastructure remains with the employer, although individuals may be able to appropriate spaces and objects symbolically in order to develop a sense of ownership of their personal working environment (Lupton and Noble 1997). Sylvia Cooper's feeling that if 'they bought it I guess they can do what they like with it' indicates that the common understanding of the nature of property is *not* that of a system of rights, but that of domestic possessions as owned outright. Consumers may be required to formally 'accept' that their rights in relation to the product are limited (by clicking a button as part of the installation process, or by virtue of having broken the seal on the packaging), and that they should not give copies of the software to others. But this does not fundamentally change the perception that the software 'belongs' in its entirety to the consumer who has purchased it.

In some cases, the study participants had installed illegal copies of software on their home computers by bringing home the installation disks from work, and such practices seem to be seen as similar in nature to other petty office pilfering, such as taking office stationery home. While this may simply be a case of taking copies for their own personal use of software which they use at work, it may also involve a wider circulation in such software: someone who worked with Thomas Turner, for example, installed software on the Turner family's computer for them.

Doug Fowler installed DOS and Windows onto his home computer from original software disks which his friend brought home from work in order to install the software on his own home machine. Using the original disks to install the software means that Doug's own name appears on the startup screen, rather than that of the original owner of the software. Doug describes himself as the 'end of the chain' – he gets software from his friends and his father, but does not give software to anyone else. This is not, however, because he wouldn't if he was in a position to, but rather because does not have access to copies of software that his other contacts do not already have. Doug doesn't consider the kind of swapping of software that he (and the other people in the study) engage in as piracy:

> I think that people like myself are really not pirates. It's the people out there who have seven or eight computers and are punching disks in all the time to make copies to sell. That's the piracy . . . the disks never leave my possession nine times out of ten and if they do they are only within a select group, and really, my select group is like two people. It's not done for commercial profit. It's done between myself and my friends.

The notion of 'piracy', it seems, carries with it something of the flavour of a kind of Robin Hood activity which robs the (corporate) rich to give to the (consumer) poor. Similarly, Hilary Lacey's term 'pilfering' to refer to software piracy calls up images of a kind of 'Artful Dodger'-ish activity. This notion of software piracy as a romantic and transgressive activity of the underdog (as the consumer undoubtedly is when contrasted with the commercial interests which produce software) perhaps also retains a hint of the original hacker ethic – which held that all computer tools should be free (Rheingold 1994) – and which still continues in the circulation of public domain and shareware programs, and in the 'open source' movement.

These illegal software distribution networks may also be likened to a 'black' or alternative economy which runs parallel to the official, commercial economy, and which operates along the lines of barter and gift exchange through personalized transactions which cement social bonds through complicity, rather than impersonal commercial exchange. Within these networks, heterogeneous goods circulate, and the social credit for a copy of a software application may eventually be repaid with something completely different:

> it not only helps my friend because he gets what he originally wanted and at the same time gets me a tick on the favour list so that maybe somewhere down the line I can call that favour back up and it might not have to do with computers but a favour for me. (Doug Fowler)

As Doug Fowler puts it: 'It's like an underground. You scratch my back, I'll scratch your back, just don't tell anybody.' These informal chains of distribution, as a kind of 'underground' to the regular commercial economy of software distribution, act as a form of resistance to the corporate wealth and power of the multinational manufacturers.

Doug has acquired some software from his father, who refused to give him the illegal copy of Excel he asked for, but gave him instead another program which he was no longer using:

> I wanted to get a copy of Excel for Bev . . . I knew my father had a copy of it so I rang my father up and said . . . 'is there a possibility of me borrowing [the disks] to download to my computer?' And he said 'No, that's pirating' [laugh]. I said 'That's okay I understand, no problems' and he said 'But I do have some other stuff that I've got. You can have those because they're mine and I don't use them. They're not on my system and I know I have the right to use them.' So I got those which were totally useless, but he's a stickler for if he buys programs he only uses that program.

Another such 'stickler' is Carlos Martinez who, as a technology professional, feels that the expense of software purchasing is part of his 'tools of the trade':

> It's not a practice I would be involved in . . . I know some people that are, sort of, offering their software to other people – 'I've got this one here, have it'. I wouldn't have a hand in that, I'm very conservative about this stuff . . . And especially since some of the people aren't really poor, and they still want it for free. That I think is just not on. It shouldn't be. If you can afford it, you should buy it.

Carlos sees this as a problem which may eventually affect him personally, since he would like to develop computer-based training products: 'It is a concern for me, because if I want to produce something, how can I protect it?' Jim Christou is another computer professional who has done programming himself. He has no pirated software on his computer other than shareware software that he has not paid the licence fee for. Jim traces this attitude to his own experience as a programmer: 'I guess I'm a programmer myself, so I know how I'd feel, when I write something, if someone did that.'

It is not just a choice of whether to spend the money to buy the software or not. For many people the perception that the cost of software programs is inflated and does not represent good value is a common reason given for pirating them. Consumers see software copying as a legitimate activity given the rapid commercial rise of the software industry. Microsoft, for example, had by 1995 expanded to an organization with 17,000 employees and annual sales of US$6 billion per annum, from its foundation in 1975 by Bill Gates and Paul Allen (Gates 1995: 18). Part of this expansion, as consumers are well aware, is achieved through short product life spans: software programs are often superseded by revised versions after one or two years.

Laurence Harrison's attitude seems to be one that is quite common among people who regularly and actively pirate software (as opposed to those people who have software installed on their computers by well-meaning friends and colleagues, but who do not instigate this behaviour). Laurence does not buy software at all, and expects that this attitude would be quite common. If software were cheaper, he says, more people would buy original versions:

> Prices are very high for what is a very mass-produced product, there are hundreds of thousands of copies of Windows so they must be making a lot of money, since it only has to get programmed the once. Bill Gates has become a mega-millionaire – America's richest man – if he'd slashed his prices by half he would still be very, very rich and could even have been richer.

The common use of Bill Gates as a metonym for the software industry as a whole is illustrated again here. Thomas Turner also likened software piracy to not 'putting money into Bill Gates's pockets'. If, as we saw above in the discussion of home computer acquisition strategies, abstract and depersonalized institutions may be seen by consumers as quasi-social entities with their own brand 'personalities', the identification of the person of Bill Gates with the powers of corporate wealth of the software industry as a whole may be seen as a means of personalizing and de-abstracting what are otherwise highly alienated and generalized entities. The demonization of Bill Gates is therefore also a demonization of the whole software industry, as represented by the software giant Microsoft.

The symbolic relationship between Gates, Microsoft and the computer industry as a whole is rooted in the history of the development of personal computer hardware and software, via the role that Microsoft and its operating system products (MS-DOS and Windows) have played in this development, and the part Gates personally has played as both leader and figurehead of Microsoft. In no other computer company has the founder and head of the organization been so closely identified with the organization as a whole (Apple's Steve Jobs may come in at a very distant second place). Gates is often, therefore, felt to be single-handedly responsible for his company's success, which may help to explain the kind of personal demonization which has been described briefly here. The large number of anti-Gates web sites is a further indication of the level of this demonization.

In the case of computer hardware purchasing this personalization may also take the form of a positive identification with the producing institution – the brand loyalty of Apple computer buyers is perhaps exemplary here. Software piracy, on the other hand, might indeed be seen as a kind of anti-consumption – a resistance to and refusal to be involved in the marketplace relationship between consumer and producer, with its attendant asymmetric power relations. Danielle Singleton's preference for Apple computers because of their 'garage industry' origins, and for supporting local retailers, which we saw above, is perhaps less overtly anti-consumerist than outright software piracy, but still seems to be underpinned by a desire to localize the globalizing power of consumption.

In a country like Australia, Microsoft and Bill Gates are often also seen as representative of the dominance of US interests in the information technology industry, and in cultural production more generally. The antagonism to Microsoft may also therefore be symptomatic of a need to preserve localized products as forms of resistance to this perception of US cultural imperialism:

I mean, OK, we're some dot in the arse end of the universe as far as Microsoft's concerned, but to actually go to the trouble of, with Dangerous Creatures, to have a guide, an Australian guide, who takes you through the Australian bush – that man has an English accent [laughter]. Enough said. Why would you go to the trouble of trying to pretend there's something there without going to that little bit of extra trouble to put on an Australian voice? (Helen Samuels)

If a sense of ownership over objects which start life as mass-produced commodities involves overcoming the inevitable alienation of these forms – inevitable because this is intrinsic to the processes of objectification – then the degree to which they resist incorporation into particular contexts of use may arise, in part, because they were created in culturally very different contexts. Some objects will therefore, because of the characteristics of their design and production, retain a quality of 'alienness'. (This alienness may also be an aspect of their attraction to consumers, as the consumption of 'exotic' goods and services attests).

Gail Shaw compared software piracy to the illegal copying of recorded music, and suggested that where products are personally identified with struggling artists, rather than highly successful businesses, then piracy can no longer take on the character of anti-consumerist resistance. Gail says that they had illegal copies of software on the computer at one stage, but had got rid of them, and makes a comparison between copying software and copying music CDs onto cassette:

> I think it is interesting, just buying a new CD the other day, and thinking about taping it for someone else, and then reading . . . their plea to 'no, please don't do this'. And I was thinking it was almost as if it was about how connected you feel to the artists in some ways, how much you value what they're doing, whether you feel like they're marginalized. If you really feel like they're raking it in, you're less likely to not do it.

A similar sense of personal relationship with and regard for the producers of software is often associated with non-commercial software, such as shareware or public domain software. The programmers who create these products are often highly regarded within the community of their registered users. Joy Lester has paid the registration fee for a number of shareware products, and appreciates the personalized nature of the relationship: 'I usually pay for my American software. I like getting the little things from America, like when I registered Tetris. And StuffIt, I registered StuffIt. I don't know what made me get like that. And some of them, you get nice little funny things in the mail. So I just like that.'

Such processes of personalization or localization, I would suggest, may operate as a kind of anti-alienating force within the processes of objectification, as an aspect of the social processes involved in the design/domestication interface. It is necessary and intrinsic to late capitalism that such experiential bridges are provided, through which abstract and intangible entities (such as transnational corporations) may be made real and intelligible for consumers. It may even be that this is one of the cultural functions of celebrity in the contemporary globalizing world, and therefore the reason for the symbolic role of the person of Bill Gates and other key individuals within the corporate landscape. The fascination with the most mundane details of the everyday lives of celebrities serves to connect together – to articulate – the lives of individuals with broad and abstract cultural processes.

Conclusion

The acquisition of a home computer is a process taking place over a (sometimes extended) period of time, which must be prioritized (as necessity or luxury) and negotiated between household members. Consumers draw on an established repertoire of knowledge and cultural competence, which can to some extent be transferred to novel cultural territory. This may include tapping into the social networks of the household and reducing stress and anxiety in the process through following comfort, familiarity and trust in individuals, institutions and situations. Consumers learn from their experiences in unfamiliar situations and through them develop new skills, competences and dispositions (such as brand preferences). Associations around a brand name or commercial organization objectify different values for consumers, and some of the available choices for consumers may be seen as a form of resistance to the forces of big business and the mainstream market.

While changes in technology over the lifetime of some of the older individuals in the study are striking, the rapidity of these changes and the rate at which they are naturalized into everyday life is also evident in the young, who may have no memory of a home without a computer, in much the same way as those of us who were born into the age of television have no memory of everyday life without this technology. It is clear that the self is in a continuous process of being made and remade, and people's interactions with such cultural objects form an important medium by which this occurs. For many people, then, whose life course has been marked by profound technological change, continuing to keep up with new technologies is able to provide a particularly powerful medium of self-transformation.

Symbolically potent cultural objects like the home computer may therefore be able to act as 'bridges' to an imaginary future. The use of such metaphors – 'bridges' and 'handles' – suggests the relationality of these cultural forms: they may be tools which enable us perform particular concrete tasks, but they are also capable of giving access to and control over broader cultural domains. Where such objects have been incorporated into the extended self and are therefore not in question as part of the self, they no longer need to act as 'handles' or 'bridges', in the sense of providing a path between the present self and an imagined alternative state. These objects perhaps do then have a role, however, in 'anchoring' the present self – providing a kind of psychic scaffolding by staying in their places to give us our place (in Romanyshyn's terms).

Computing in the Domestic Pattern of Life

During the interview I conducted with Patricia Collins, her daughter Caroline was playing a game of Tetris on the computer while her brother Sean and his friend played Nintendo together (figure 8). On this particular occasion, Caroline had got to the computer first, otherwise Sean and his friend would have been playing on the computer instead.

A home computer must find its place within individual and joint patterns of activity within the household. In the Collins household, Caroline's use of the computer is generally a solo occurrence: when her friends come over, they generally do not engage in computer-based activities. For Sean, however, using the computer when his friends come to visit is common, and the computer (along with similar ones his friends own) forms an important area of activity:

Figure 8 The Collins's computer is located in a downstairs family room.

One wet weekend a little while ago he and his friends spent hours down there together going through all of the stuff we had and all of the stuff someone brought over with them and they walked away with little square eyes. Once upon a time it used to be the things in the toy box that they hadn't played with for a long time. (Patricia Collins)

As we have seen, a home computer acquisition is an important element in contemporary home-building practices in the western world, particularly for households with children and adults in professional and semi-professional occupations. Home-building is about collectively constructing the household as a structure in space and time, made up of material objects and established patterns of activity, as well as ideas, meanings and values. Although it is created by its members, it exists outside of them but not independently of them. And although home generally supports and enables the everyday life of its inhabitants, their actions and activities are also constrained by it. It is, indeed an objectification of its members in the sense developed in chapter 2.

A significant appropriation of the technology into the daily life of the household may require a continuing and substantial investment of time and energy on the part of the user, and not just a financial investment (Caron, Giroux and Douzou 1989; Hirsch 1992; Murdock, Hartmann and Gray 1992; Wheelock 1992). A home computer is brought into a domestic context which is already organized around structures and hierarchies of age, gender and other specific roles, with pre-existing patterns of interaction and activity, and which already contains a large number of objects and other technologies. These structures provide the household's existing patterns of activity with a considerable momentum.

The household is thus a complex structure which sustains, often nurtures, but generally constrains the behaviour of its members, and technologies take on an important role in constructing and maintaining these structures (Silverstone and Hirsch 1992). Further, the household cannot be thought of in isolation from the economic, political and cultural structures within which the household is embedded, including the need for engagement in processes of consumption to maintain the household's infrastructure.

The integration of domestic information and communication technologies into the everyday life of the household is a dynamic complex process, grounded in the concrete specificity of particular people, times, places and practices of everyday life. The household is both an economic and a cultural unit in which the respective material position of each sets profound limits on the opportunities available for consumption and self-expression, but within these limits and in important ways perhaps transcending them, households are able to define for themselves a private/public moral, emotional, cognitive, evaluative and aesthetic environment – *a pattern of life* – on which they depend for their survival as much as on any economic security. (Silverstone, Hirsch and Morley 1991: 223, emphasis added)

Domestic information and communications technologies, then, are not only of interest at the level of everyday experience and daily life, but also raise questions about the household's articulation into broader regimes of cultural value and social order. The computer brings with it a range of meanings and values, including its links with the sense of the future and its associations with, on the one hand, leisure and entertainment, particularly through computer game-playing and, on the other, 'serious' uses such as educational and employment-related functions. These associations are mobilized by consumers in developing their understanding of their evolving use of the computer. In order, however, for the computer to become an established part of the household it must find its place within the pre-existing structures of value and activity within the home, the household's 'pattern of life'.

In this chapter, who uses the computer and what it is used for are explored. In order to come to an understanding of how it is that household members are able to develop a personalized relationship of ownership with both the home computer and the home in its entirety, subsequent chapters will develop the computer's role in the changing temporalities of the household, in negotiating interpersonal and social relationships, as well as age- and gender-based roles.

Education and Work

Educational uses of the home computer are important at all age levels, including for adults. Pre-school children use the computer for drawing and playing with pre-school software which has an 'educational' or developmental focus. John Powell and Hayley Crowther's two-year-old daughter Jennifer, for example, uses The Playroom as a way of introducing her to mouse and keyboard skills. For primary school children, the emphasis moves (apart from playing games) to informally supporting their school work: writing stories, typing out spelling lists. Once children get to high school they tend to start using the computer more formally to support their school work, to complete assignments, for example. Danielle Singleton comments, for example, that her son 'started using the computer much more this year', particularly for writing up his school projects 'because he's just entered high school'. On the other hand, in some households with high-school aged children, the parents report that the children rarely use the computer for school work. The Cooper children, for example, only use the computer for playing games, not school work, and Patricia Collins's children's use is also mainly game-playing.

Many of the adults in the study were involved in formal higher education. For these people the home computer generally played an important role in supporting their educational program, which was often a major factor in their acquisition of the computer. At a minimum, adults involved in higher education used their computers for word-processing assignments and theses. Others used them to organize and analyse information for postgraduate research projects (Marjorie Brennan and Thomas Turner), or used the Internet to research assignments (Hilary Lacey, Helen Samuels). Regine Vassallo, who is an undergraduate majoring in Computer Science, used her computer for a range of assignment tasks, including programming and database development, and Carlos Martinez used his for undertaking computer-based training assignment tasks.

For many adults a home computer is implicated in the relationship between work and home. Many home computers are used extensively by the employed adults within the study households (particularly those who are employed in professional positions) to support their employment activities. Some used their home computers for working from home on a freelance, consultancy or self-employed basis (Thomas Turner, Jessica Lane and Danielle Singleton had all done this at one time), or for bringing work home from their formal employment.

Nippert-Eng (1995) describes how the boundary between work and home is one which must be actively managed, through the development of strategies and techniques which may serve to strengthen the differentiation between the two and keep them separated, or which may, for other householders, be used to blur these boundaries. Where a home computer is used for employment-related purposes, the boundary is already to some extent blurred by the existence of the computer in the home. Strategies for keeping work and home life separated, then, may include temporal or spatial segregation of work-at-home activities from other computer-based activities. Organizational routines which link the external workplace and home computing activities may also be established, for example so that files may be transferred and shared between work and home computers.

Sometimes an employer-owned computer may be available to be brought home when it is needed for employment-related tasks. When there is this kind of easy access to a work computer, it may mean that the individual does not feel the need to buy a computer for personal use. Helen Samuels, for example, only bought her own computer when she was facing redundancy and the loss of access to a dedicated employer-provided laptop. Ruth Bourke bought her computer on her retirement, since she was used to having access to computers at work. Access to a work computer for personal uses may also justify or precipitate a purchase. Charlotte Thompson bought her own computer because it was more convenient to have a computer at work and one at home, and just move disks between these locations rather than regularly have to transport the whole computer.

Home computers and work computers are in many ways in competition for the activities of their users. The Richards's first computer, an Amstrad, fell into disuse as a consequence of Peter Richards bringing home a Macintosh from work, and this eventually led the family to buy a new computer. Similarly, for the last four years the Parsons' home computer has been used only for playing games – if there is work to be done at home Virginia will bring a work laptop home. Often the computers people have access to at work are more up-to-date and powerful than the ones they have at home, and this influences the amount of use the home computer gets and what it is used for. Janet Fuller, for example, hardly uses the home computer she bought second-hand from Hilary Lacey, and tends to use a computer she has access to at work for personal uses rather than the home one:

> To be honest I don't use it very much at all . . . When I first had it I used it quite a lot and I bought all the books to go with it and everything but we've got a computer at work and I tend to use that more because it's a better one. We're on the Internet and that's really addictive so whenever I come to work I use the computer but the one at home I rarely use. It just sits there.

Indeed, Janet had become a very keen user of the Internet at work and at the time of our interview was in the habit of using any spare time between seeing clients at the community health centre she works for on the Internet. Having access to these facilities means that she doesn't feel the need to have access to them at home: 'I think that's what it is too because it's such a good computer here. I guess if I had a great computer at home I would probably go home and do that.'

When an employer-owned computer is readily available to be brought home, it may also come to be used there for personal activities, and this may sometimes involve other members of the household in addition to the one who has a work-related reason for using it. Working from home and, in particular, bringing a work computer home may, then, be seen as an encroachment on the spaces and times of home by externally based work. However, having been inserted into the domestic space, the employer-owned computer may in turn be colonized by the activities of home, and members of the household may come to see the work computer as one which they all have a relationship of ownership with.

The Chapman family's construction of a proprietary interest in the computer which Paul Chapman brings home from work illustrates this point. Paul frequently brings his work computer, an up-to-date Macintosh, home from the high school he works in as a senior teacher, particularly on weekends and during the school holidays. During the Christmas holidays, not long before my interview with them, Paul had the work computer at home for a six week period. While this computer is at home, the rest of the family use it too: as Paul puts it, 'if it's here, they will fight for the use of it'. The eldest child in the family, Martin, is in the second year of a university nursing course, and has often asked his father to bring the computer home specifically so that he can complete an assignment:

> The reason that the machine came home was because I had so much work to do, and I needed the machine at home to do the work. So that's how it initially started, and then I noticed that it gradually became something that the family relied on happening, so I had Martin saying 'Can you bring the computer home because I've got an assignment?' (Paul Chapman)

The family does own a computer (or they would not have been selected to participate in the study), but it is an older Apple IIE computer. This computer is now located in Martin's room (and is shown in figure 11), so that he can wordprocess his assignments on this computer, rather than being reliant on the one Paul brings home.

The family (who assert symbolic ownership over the computer) and the school (its 'legal' owner) each construct a relationship of ownership with the work computer. However, its pattern of moving between work and home, and the appropriation of parts of the hard disk by the family members for their own personal uses, complicates these relationships. When the work computer is taken back to the school, its hard disk still contains personal material belonging to the family, such as 'Sunday School stuff, resumes and job applications'. It is located there in Paul's office, and while it is available for use by other staff members (because a laser printer is attached to it) – Maureen's workplace use of this computer may still be seen as rather proprietorial: 'Paul and I used to work together, so if I wanted to use the computer, even though there was one in our staff room I used to whiz up and use the Mac that I was most familiar with, which is Paul's' (Maureen Chapman).

This computer is therefore still seen as partly belonging to the family, even when it is at work. As Maureen says, 'I wouldn't dream of putting our personal stuff on a faculty computer' (such as the one in the staff room). But it is not seen as problematic that the computer still contains the family's personal material when it is at school, since it is located in Paul's office and is seen as 'his' computer.

This case also illustrates the substitutability of such artefacts: because the Chapmans have ready access to an up-to-date work computer which Paul regularly brings home, this has meant that there is little pressure on them to buy their own computer. Employees are often able to construct a personal ownership relationship with their workplace computers, through strategies of appropriation and personalization. One of the participants in Noble and Lupton's study said of his work computer: 'technically it is not mine but it feels like it is' (1998: 810). In the Chapman case, this workplace relationship is constructed partly through the family's private use of the computer, and through the encroachment of home activities into the spaces and times of work.

As these examples show, the boundary between home and work is often a complex interface, rather than a barrier which keeps these domains separated. Further, this boundary is constantly in the process of being constructed and reconstructed, as a process of negotiation between the activities and objects of one domain and that of the other. Both objects and meanings flow across this interface: in particular, the strong association between information technology and contemporary workplace administrative practices, coupled with the insertion of work-mode activities into the home environment, means that the home computer is often drafted into a range of household management tasks.

As individuals acquire familiarity with a range of computer functions in the workplace, these may be translated into the automation of activities previously carried out manually (Christmas mailing list databases and wordprocessed 'family newsletters', for example). Gail

Shaw used the appropriate phrase 'life administration' to cover the range of wordprocessing, database, spreadsheet and accounting functions now undertaken on the home computer by many householders.

All of the study households had used their home computers for personal correspondence, and many had also recorded household information in databases or spreadsheets. Danielle Singleton has found that she has simply been recording more and more information on the computer: 'I've got an address and phone number and fax section . . . I'm probably making much more use of it now than I did even a few months ago just for little details like that'.

Transferring some kinds of activity to the home computer may allow them to be taken to a new level of importance. Peter Richards, John Powell and Margaret Paine are all using the computer to manage their household finances. Margaret, for example, now keeps all her household and personal financial accounts on the computer, and updates them ('fastidiously') at least once per fortnight. Up until the time of our interview, she had been maintaining this information on a spreadsheet, but was beginning to gather information about specialized accounting software. Even before buying the computer and implementing this financial monitoring system, Margaret would categorize and monitor her spending using a manual system, although not with the same level of detail as she currently does. 'I've always had budgets, and that's why I wanted the computer to keep track of different categories but I've got much more into it now with the computer. I do have a sense of more control.'

If the home computer – as information appliance – allows and even encourages an increasing sense that everyday domestic life needs to be professionally managed or administered, then its availability also makes possible an increasing professionalization of the community-based activities which householders may be engaged in. Increasingly, these personal activities are supported by the Internet, in the form of email correspondence in maintaining contact with family and friends, publication of personal web pages and the use of the Internet to gather information and for the emergent e-commerce functions. The use of the Internet is covered in greater detail below.

Many of the study participants use their home computers in their voluntary and community work: Ruth Bourke, for example, uses her computer in support of her activities as secretary of the local branch of the University of the Third Age (a community-based educational organization for people over fifty-five years old). Other participants used their computers in support of a range of community activities and areas of voluntary work: in family and local historical research, sporting clubs, occasional childcare organizations, neighbourhood centres, church groups, school Parents and Citizens organizations, and school canteen work.

This process of professionalization across a range of domains of everyday life, and the involvement of information technology in this process, is related to the contemporary trend in which even our leisure and recreational activities are subjected to such processes of rationalization (Haddon 1988).

Play

Game-playing

Game-playing is often the principal use of the computer as far as children are concerned. Children's game-playing tends to be related to their playing of games on dedicated machines such as Playstation and Nintendo consoles. Many of the participant households had such equipment in addition to their computers. In the Manfredotti household, for example, the children tended to play games on the dedicated consoles rather than the computer, because of the limited games available on the computer, but would use the computer if the games console was already in use.

Game-playing as a joint, rather than single-player, activity occurs in many of the households, both by family members and when friends come to visit. As an activity where greater size and weight may not necessarily give the advantage, computer game-playing seems to be able to provide a joint activity for siblings greatly different in age, or for parents and children to play together. Joint game-playing also occurs between adults, and adults also play dedicated games machines. All these permutations provide further inflections of the seemingly natural category of 'game-playing' as a leisure activity. It may have the purpose of encouraging social interaction within the family or be an escape from it, or may be a way of avoiding work or a way of making the user more relaxed and therefore more productive.

Adult game-playing, in particular, can be seen to be a heterogeneous category of activity, rather than a simple form of leisure or entertainment. Some study participants frequently play a computer game whilst simultaneously doing something else, either computer-based or non-computer-based. Peter Richards, for example, plays Solitaire on the computer while talking to his mother during their weekly phone calls, while Claire Matheson has her cup of tea in one hand and plays a game with the other while she watches the news. Katherine Scarborough sometimes plays Solitaire at 2 a.m. because she goes through cycles of insomnia. Merilyn Bartlett, the mother of four sons, says that she 'very rarely gets time to sit down and just have switch off veg time'. However, she manages occasionally to escape from the demands of her family to the relative isolation of their extension to use the home computer and get 'three-quarters of an hour of peace and quiet' to herself. Murdock et al. (1992: 158) also note that computer use may allow older teenagers to win space and privacy within the household.

Interspersing work sessions on the computer with 'game breaks' seems to be a common occurrence. While Claire Matheson was preparing the Annual Report for the eisteddfod she is involved with: 'I was alternating between Patience and the General Report, I just kept switching from one to the other, which is jolly good! . . . So I'd write another paragraph, then I'd go back to Patience, and then I'd get another inspiration and put another paragraph in [laughter].'

Larry Lester also plays a couple of games of Solitaire just before getting down to his work sessions on the computer. Since these games are essentially a five- or ten-minute intermission within a larger task, it is not really accurate to describe them as a separate activity, but rather as a particular inflection of that other activity.

Adults will often emphasize that they play computer games because it is a relaxing way to wind down from the stresses of the day:

> I like Patience, I do like that. It's very quiet, it's very restful and I just find it relaxes me but I don't like the other games at all, especially the noisy ones . . . I find it a great switch off because nothing penetrates. I just lose myself in that . . . Especially if things are a bit stressed or I've been particularly busy at work. I find it difficult to go home and just switch off. And I'm not a television person in that sense. I'll put it on and watch the news but some nights I don't put it on at all. (Katherine Scarborough)

While the home computer is therefore a domestic technology which tends to blur the distinction between 'work' and 'play', this generally takes the form of what Haddon (1988) has termed 'rational recreation': the notion that even leisure activities must serve some instrumental purpose. Computer game playing is legitimized for adults, for example, because it is important to have relaxing activities which reduce stress because this is bad for one's long-term health.

However, one common kind of computing activity which forms a large proportion of their use of the computer for some of the study participants is precisely that of a pastime which serves no overtly rational purpose. I asked Claire Matheson whether the computer, for her, is a kind of toy: 'It is a toy, to a large extent. But then I'm the kind of person, I've done crossword puzzles since I was six. I always do crossword puzzles, I like crosswords. It's just another way of puzzling.' The computer is an activity for which many people enjoy the 'problem solving' aspects of its use, and which for some people is one of the major pleasures in this activity. Turkle refers to this as the pleasure of 'cognitive play' (1985: 184), an appeal which is both intellectual and aesthetic. The respondents in Turkle's study of computer hobbyists spoke of 'the elegance of using computer techniques to solve problems' and of 'the beauty of understanding a system at many levels of complexity', and described their interaction with the computer as 'mind stretching' (184).

Doug Fowler is another such user, whose principal activity might perhaps be best described as 'tinkering' with the computer. His computer has been cobbled together from parts donated by friends and others bought very cheaply, and it doesn't always function smoothly. He gets great enjoyment, however, from solving such operational problems: 'I get frustrated . . . but it's fun to get it fixed.' At one point he had moved his computer ('less than thirty feet') and it no longer worked. His detailed explanation of the problem not only gave some indication of the amount of time and effort he put into working out what had gone wrong and fixing it, but also of the excitement and pleasure he derived from working on the problem and the sense of achievement and of his own expertise as someone capable of working with the computer at this level. Such pleasures are undermined for Doug in that the computer is largely seen as his 'toy' (both by him and by his wife Bev, even though she sometimes uses the computer for school canteen accounting purposes). The ambiguities and tensions around this computer's place within the household are illustrated by the computer's 'floating' non-location within the household space, which is discussed in greater detail in chapter 10.

For Doug and for several of the other study participants – particularly Laurence Harrison, Richard Brown and Claire Matheson – their computer use is a kind of hobby, a pleasurable but essentially directionless way to fill spare time. Of these people, only Laurence is in full-time employment. Doug is unemployed, Richard is retired and Claire is semi-retired and they therefore all have time on a day-to-day basis which is largely at their disposal. Although the range of activities involved might separately be able to be classified as game playing, systems administration or consulting CD-ROMs (such as the Encarta encyclopaedia or trawling through the contents of shareware CDs which come attached to magazines), this use of time has a different quality when it is an end in itself than when it is a means to some other end (such as playing a game to switch off at the end of a busy day, or consulting the Encarta for research). This kind of 'tinkering' or hobbyist use of the computer is therefore an important domain of home computer use which is largely made invisible by the constructions of home computer utility which circulate in public discourse. These constructions tend to result in such pleasurable but directionless activities being seen as time-'wasting', as will be seen in the next chapter in the discussion of the 'proper' uses of time.

For many users, tinkering with the computer is also a way of learning about it or of finding out how it works. One of the participants in Noble and Lupton's study, for example, argued that such 'playful' uses of the computer were essential to understanding the possibilities of the technology for work (1998: 811). For Laurence Harrison, experimentation with his home computer allowed him to spend time investigating how to do things, since he would not be able to find the time to do this at work. Regine Vassallo had spent the morning before I arrived to interview her 'playing with sounds', partly as a recreational activity, but partly to find out more about how to do new things with sound. And when Hilary Lacey bought her computer: 'I would wipe everything off and format the hard drive and, you know, where it says "don't do this", I did it because I just wanted to see whether I could put everything back on again and start from scratch.'

When I spoke with Claire Matheson, she had three computers in the house and her main computing activity could certainly be called 'playing', in the sense of a directionless activity done essentially for the pleasure of the activity itself. Although she does play games, most of her computing activity is not game-playing. She spends quite a lot of time exploring the contents of inexpensive CD-ROMs attached to magazines, and loves the challenge of a problem to solve, such as the time she had bought a shareware disk at a computer show which contained a virus, or installing her own CD-ROM drive.

A musician, Claire at one point during the interview referred to her computer in passing as 'the instrument'. Interestingly, other people I have interviewed who are interested in computing as an activity pleasurable for its own sake report that one of the activities they have less time for now that they have a computer is playing a musical instrument. This observation places a different slant on the sense of the term 'playing' as applied to computer use. When Turkle and Papert (1990: 152) ask 'if the computer is a tool, and of course it is, is it more like a hammer or more like a harpsichord?' they are asserting the need for a new set of intellectual and emotional values to be associated with the computer, in opposition to the dominant rationalist paradigm for computing. Perhaps what Claire's example shows is that their analogy might be taken even further: for some people the computer is able to function as an expressive medium in much the same way as the playing of a musical instrument or of working in another creative medium.

Programming, for example, which was one of the principal uses of home computers in the 1980s, is now uncommon. Those people who do program, however, speak of the pleasures of cognitive play and problem solving in debugging their programs. In part, at least, this is because these early microcomputers had little pre-packaged software available for them, in contrast to the current generation of home computers. Haddon (1988) has charted the emergence during the mid-1980s of the home personal computer as a software 'player' and the subsequent lessening of the importance of user programming of computers. The computers available to contemporary consumers require a far greater level of knowledge and investment of time to program them to do anything even remotely as interesting as the pre-packaged software that is available for them (because of the need to integrate a user-written program into the graphical user interface operating systems of these computers). Further, the earlier generation of microcomputers came with the BASIC programming language built in, while users who wish to learn to program more recent models must acquire and install a programming language package.

Claire Matheson, for example, who originally became interested in computing through programming the Commodore as a pastime, still does occasionally write programs for that machine. She has bought books on DOS programming, but found that she couldn't 'get into it'. The only other study participants who have ventured into programming their home PC are Jim Christou (who works as a computer programmer), Regine Vassallo (who is undertaking an undergraduate computer studies course), and Carlos Martinez (who teaches electronics in Australia's TAFE (Tertiary and Further Education) sector and who is currently undertaking studies in computer-based training software with a view to eventually creating multimedia training products).

Uses of the Internet

The Internet extends the functionality of the home computer beyond that of professionalizing household information management functions or support for work and education, into the realm of communications device and media receiver. This aspect of home computer activity is rapidly becoming more important, and it remains to be seen in the coming years to what extent this domain of functionality will supplant other uses of the home computer, just as the 'software player' concept has superseded that of the home computer as a user-programmable device.

Internet access is rapidly becoming normalized as an almost mandatory component of home computer use. It is clear from the experience of participants in the study that consumers who in the mid-1990s could see no reason to have Internet access, and were concerned that it would be very expensive or that their children would be exposed to unsuitable material and interactions, were within a very short space of time surrounded by URLs appearing in television advertising, in magazines and newspaper, on billboards and the sides of buses. This ubiquity of the Internet – which seemed to be precipitated almost instantaneously by the development and commercialization of the World Wide Web – normalized and domesticated it as an information utility to the point where many consumers could hardly recall what their earlier reservations had been based on. Many of the participants in the present study who expressed little or no interest in the Internet when I first spoke to them in 1996 and 1997, were online in follow up contacts within a year or two.

In November 2000, 37 per cent of Australian households had home Internet access (which represents two-thirds of the Australian households with a home computer). The proportion of households with Internet access is higher in households where there are children under eighteen: almost half of these households have Internet access (ABS 2001b: 3). The Australian Bureau of Statistics study of home Internet use also supports the suggestion that older people are an important and growing demographic for home computer use, both because of the possibilities for Internet communication in maintaining family ties and because the ability to keep up with technological change may be associated with staying fully engaged in social life. Although the ABS found a 9 per cent increase in the proportion of adults using a computer (at any site) during the period 1998–2000, they found a 38 per cent increase in the proportion of adults aged between 55 and 64 who used a computer (ABS 2001a: 17). Communication is clearly an important category of use for both this age group and the young: the proportion of Australian adults who used the Internet for email or chat was highest among those aged 65 years or over, and among 18–24 year olds (ABS 2001a: 17).

Most adults in the ABS study were using the Internet to gather various kinds of information: relating to work or study, to goods and services, to government information and services (such as information relating to the new taxation system introduced by the Australian federal government in 2000), or to technical information and shareware. This reflects the dominant uses of the Internet for the people in the current study: communications (email and chat) and information gathering (for both adults and children) appear to be the core uses of the Internet at the present time. None of the study participants had used the Internet for any kind of commercial transaction.

There is evidence from the ABS study, however, that e-commerce and Internet transactions started to take off during 2000, particularly among some demographic categories such as those on high incomes and those with a higher education qualification. The proportion of adults paying bills or transferring funds via the Internet rose from 1 per cent in 1998 to 9 per cent in 2000. In 2000, 15 per cent of Australian Internet users ordered or purchased goods and services online. Higher proportions were found among those with high incomes, and among people with university level qualifications. It appears that, particularly among educated 'baby boomers' and younger people on above average incomes, these forms of interacting with commercial and governmental institutions are rapidly becoming naturalized (Centre for International Economics 2001).

It is clear, however, that the Internet is not one but many technologies – for communication, information gathering and increasingly for commercial transactions – and will therefore mean different things to different groups of people. The Internet is not a monolithic medium, but rather is 'a range of practices, software and hardware technologies, modes of representation and interaction that may or may not be interrelated by participants, machines or programs (indeed they may not all take place at a computer)' (Miller and Slater 2000: 14). People do not so much use 'the Internet' as assemble various technical possibilities that add up to 'their' Internet. As Miller and Slater's study of the Internet in Trinidad clearly also demonstrates, what the Internet is to people in a particular time and place may not be the same thing as elsewhere, and is, in addition, changing rapidly. While much of the existing literature on the Internet concentrates on MUDs (Multiple User Domain or Dungeon) and MOOs (MUD, Object Oriented), bulletin boards and 'flaming', the Internet now seems largely to be about websites, communication via email and chat, and the emerging importance of e-commerce.

Inevitably, differences of local culture will be reflected in the form and emphasis of the use of this ostensibly 'global' medium. In Trinidad, for example, 'chat as a medium has been used to re-create a very particular mode of interaction and socialization full of banter and innuendoes that for many people is the quintessence of being Trinidadian; yet this hardly played any role in email communications' (Miller and Slater 2000: 15). Forms of sociality with an existence prior to the arrival of the Internet are recreated in novel ways.

In Australia, where sport is an important area of local interest, traditional forms of appreciation have found themselves transformed for the new electronic environment. Sports tipping is traditionally a common workplace activity, in which participants compete to achieve the best performance over a season in predicting the outcomes of weekly sports matches (often across a range of sports). It generally requires a minimum number of people to be involved and someone to take charge of organizing the activity (circulating information about match fixtures and outcomes, keeping track of the cumulative performance of the participants and so on). An April 2001 Nielsen//Netratings press release describes strong growth in online traffic to sports tipping websites, driven by the channelling of users between competing sports portal sites (Nielsen//Netratings 2001b). Taking this activity online means that people can be involved who would not otherwise be able to take part. These sports tipping sites have inserted themselves into pre-existing cultural circuits linking sporting events, television broadcasting and newspaper reports on sporting events, and people's interactions with sports news and information in homes and workplaces, transforming these circuits in the process. The flow of people between particular Internet sites is itself a complex social and cultural process, through which people's attention and activity is technologically channelled, delivering audiences to particular events, users to one search engine rather than another and so on.

Internet Communication

Email communication is rapidly becoming an essential part of the daily routine of many people. If Hilary Lacey is not working, she will collect her email 'probably half a dozen times a day'. If she's working, it will be 'in the morning and when I get home and maybe very late at night because it comes from all over the world so you are getting different times from where it is coming'. She subscribes and is active on a number of email discussion lists, largely related to issues of queer sexuality and feminism.

Regine Vassallo prefers the immediacy of Internet chat communication over email, for socializing with her friends. The Internet is one of Regine Vassallo's major uses for her home computer, and is her principal mode of communication with friends, even those who live locally, including her boyfriend:

> It's my stereo system at the moment . . . I play some games but mostly I use the Internet and I'm quite a big devotee of IRC, Internet Relay Chat. It's a social medium for me I have a lot of friends I talk to via the computer . . . It sounds really nerdy but I suppose it's one way of communicating.

Her boyfriend lives in a different telephone zone, so a phone call to him is more expensive than chatting online. In the evenings they both tend to be online at the same time anyway and will chat to each other then. While much of the public attention to Internet chat has tended to focus on interactions between strangers online (particularly those resulting in romantic relationships, or on the perils of children interacting with dangerous strangers), Regine is similar to the young people in Miller and Slater's study of Internet use in Trinidad, and uses Internet chat primarily to communicate with people she knows and also sees 'in the flesh': 'Mostly IRC is the only way I'll actually get to them. I do a lot of "hey where are you, where will you be this weekend?" and organize meeting people. Or just chat to people who I haven't seen for a long time.'

While none of the children in the present study were using Internet chat, Miller and Slater observe the use of IRC and ICQ as extensions of playground gossip and interaction among school children:

> ICQ seemed to have replaced the telephone as the privileged medium for continuing school conversations after school, letting each other know about or commenting on events that day, in the privacy of their one-to-one chat . . . Many pupils used an IRC-based chat room where they tended to congregate online, especially on Friday nights continuing through into the morning hours while the parents were asleep. (2000: 76)

Regine herself only frequents a particular channel, which is used by people she knows who live locally. IRC 'channels' can be thought of as a kind of virtual meeting space, but unlike MUDs and MOOS, which tend to be fantasy spaces of interaction disengaged from the realities of everyday life, the kind of channel used by Regine is more like a real but spatially distributed space of interaction. Teenagers 'hanging out' at the local mall may feel that, while they may meet people they have not met before, they are nonetheless meeting someone who is already part of their community. In the same way, Regine says both 'I don't really meet anybody new through IRC' and 'you make friends'. Regine knows several people who have formed romantic liaisons through IRC, which she describes as a 'huge phenomenon', although she herself has 'never met a man through IRC'.

It is clear that for some people, Internet chat spaces can be places to meet people one would never have the opportunity to become acquainted with in person, and to make new friends who might be anywhere in the world. While the predominance of sexualized banter in Internet chat interaction is often commented on (Miller and Slater 2000: 63), there is also a sense of the possibilities online for a kind of virtual tourism, and for the building of 'pen-pal' kinds of relationship, where the interest is in meeting people from different countries and learning about places quite different from home.

Hilary Lacey, her partner Margaret Paine and Janet Fuller work together at a youth health and counselling centre. At the time of the study, a number of the staff members there were going through a period of intense involvement in IRC chat. Hilary had been instrumental in introducing the other staff members to IRC, and had been encouraging Margaret to get involved, but with little success:

> Hilary's been keen to get me on the IRC chat and I've been resisting her for ages. She's taught other women here IRC chat and they are totally obsessed with it . . . There's been this whole burgeoning culture happen at [the centre] with women on the IRC chat. What's interesting is that a lot of those women never had any computer interest or skills at all and there they are, Hilary shows them and . . . in five minutes they know how to do it and you go back an hour later and they're still there. And it's just the IRC that they're into. [EL: What particular channels?] 'Netsex' they get into that. Our work is about sexuality so it's not unusual I suppose. They love it.

Janet Fuller was one of the individuals who had become particularly intensely involved in IRC at work. She herself referred to IRC as 'addictive' and at the time of the study was 'chatting' during all the time she was at work and didn't have clients to see. Her home computer, on the other hand, got very little use:

> I probably haven't used [my home computer] for about three weeks, very rarely. Whereas at work it's a different thing, I use it every time I come to work but that's because it's much better . . . On Saturday if I don't have any clients I will just be in there as much as I can, maybe two hours if there's no clients.

Part of Margaret Paine's own resistance to spending time on IRC relates to a lack of interest in interacting with strangers. She could imagine, however, developing an interest if people she knew, particularly friends and family in New Zealand, were contactable online, and would even contemplate chatting to strangers if they were New Zealanders:

> I'm a counsellor, I chat to people all day long so why would I want to chat to people on a computer? However, I would really like it if people overseas were connected that I know . . . I know that if my family were on it I would certainly use it because they're people that I'd want to talk to. If I was going to use it I would find something that was in New Zealand that I could hook into for reasons like keeping me up to date with politics and other things. I would be prepared to talk to strangers if they were in New Zealand.

Indeed, the emerging importance of the Internet to diasporic communities, as a place of interaction and to enact national identities, is becoming well recognized. In the case of the Trinidadian diaspora: 'the Internet, specifically email – allows the kind of mundane, constant and taken-for-granted daily contact that enables Trinidadians once again to live in families of the kind they see as natural, to be involved in active parenting and mutual support, despite the diasporic conditions that had earlier been making this impossible' (Miller and Slater 2000: 11). Miller and Slater observe that, compared to other Caribbean immigrants, Trinidadians tend not to form local communities in the UK (2000: 95). The Internet gives individuals an ability to retain a strong sense of national identity and engagement in culture of origin, without necessarily having to construct this in relation to a local diasporic community.

In a Canadian study of Internet use within a public library, Curry (2000) found that 41 per cent of Internet chat was at non-English language host sites. Public libraries may be extending their traditional role as public information service sites for people who may not have Internet access at home, work or educational institutions. Just as Miller and Slater observe that the one almost ubiquitous feature of Internet use among the Trinidadian diaspora was reading the Trinidadian newspapers online (2000: 94), this public library study found that library patrons made extensive use of the Internet to access news sites, often in languages other than English, and also used the library for email and other forms of web-based communication.

The Internet as Information Utility

It is clear that the Internet, as information utility, is transforming the relationship between the public and traditional sources of information. It is likely that public libraries, for example, will increasingly need to find new clients and develop value-added services as their traditional role in information gathering is supplanted by the use of the Internet at home for accessing all kinds of information: health and medicine, arts and literature, politics and law, hobbies, jobs, entertainment, sports, personal finance and investment, television and films, performing and fine arts, computer support and instruction, education, cars and real estate, spirituality and so on.

For children with Internet access, the Web is often seen now as the first and only port of call for information: 'there has been an enormous embrace of the Internet as a study tool and children are encouraged to use it as a homework tool (indeed children from a prestige girls school informed us that they will only research topics they can pursue over the net, regarding books as redundant)' (Miller and Slater 2000: 45).

An increasingly important aspect of the Internet as information source, however, relates to its integration into broader media structures, as we have already seen in the example of sports tipping in Australia. The Internet is playing a progressively more central role in all forms of popular culture, and in expanding the possibilities for people to engage with popular cultural forms, particularly among the young. For example, Popstarsonline.net, the website supporting the UK 'Popstars' television show, in February 2001 achieved the biggest UK audience for a TV show's website since the 'Big Brother' phenomenon of July 2000 (Nielsen//Netratings 2001a). Reality TV shows are a hugely successful television phenomenon, but one which is also drawing viewers online to catch the latest news and gossip, find background information about contestants and to take part in chat and discussion.

An online component is also becoming essential for other forms of cultural production, including literature and cinema. Two-thirds of February 2001 visitors to Warner Brothers' site (warnerbros.com) were visiting pages on the upcoming Harry Potter movie, and the average time spent on the site was thirteen minutes, longer than for any other entertainment website within the ratings period (Nielsen//Netratings 2001a). The Harry Potter movie site invites users to register as pupils at Hogwarts School of Wizardry and Witchcraft, and develops a sense of community that encourages users to explore further and stay longer. This example suggests that, as far as the audience is concerned, the balance between the consumption of content online and that through other media will tend to be very variable.

These hybrid media forms, combining online and offline events, sometimes on a global scale (as in the case of the 2000 Olympic games in Sydney), are an essentially new phenomenon. By allowing the audience to engage more closely in the event, in real-time, (and perhaps even allowing the audience to influence the course of the event itself, as 'Big Brother' does), these forms blur the boundaries between the Internet and other media, and between the event as spectacle and the event as participatory activity (Lally 1999).

While the World Wide Web, as a vast searchable library, is clearly the principal mode through which the Internet fulfils its role as information utility, the use of email lists on particular specialist topics is also an important source of information. Hilary Lacey subscribes to a number of lists relating to her interest in queer studies and feminism, and finds them both a good resource and a source of interesting discussion and debate, which she enjoys engaging in.

Marjorie Brennan, however, expressed some concern about the question of the authority of information found on the Internet:

> The only thing that concerned with the Internet was no references . . . I like a library for that sort of stuff . . . I suppose it is like having a library in your own home, . . . but it's more of an informal process. When you go into a library and you're searching it seems as if you are searching in a more credible way. You are looking at publications. When I go into a library I know that the information that I'm going to get is of quality.

As the Internet matures, it is likely that users will be able to make increasingly sophisticated judgements about the differentiated kinds of information that are available. One important way in which the Internet is transforming the relationship between people and information sources is in access to news. The Internet makes a much broader range of materials accessible than has previously been possible. This is particularly of interest and importance to diasporic individuals and communities (Miller and Slater 2000). In the Burnaby public library study (Curry 2000), 8 per cent of total usage was of electronic news media and magazine web sites (paralleling the traditional use of public libraries for these services). Less than half of the news sites accessed were in English, however, and the public library is therefore providing access to its clients which would not have been accessible locally in any other media format. While this study is a quantitative analysis of the web sites accessed from a public library, and is not able to give any direct insight into the place of public access Internet in the lives of the people who used the library, it is nevertheless able to provide tantalizing glimpses, such as the observation that an Albanian news site was read at the same time every day from the same terminal.

The Internet and Creative Cultural Production

One of the most important aspects of the Internet is its emerging role as a democratic medium for personal expression and individual creative cultural production. Jim Christou publishes an electronic guide to science fiction and fantasy on cable and free-to-air television, and an information guide to cable television providers which he posts to a newsgroup and puts on his web page. He started doing them for his own interest:

> I mainly did those just for myself, like I do a sci-fi compilation, go through the TV guide just to see what's on there and also do a pay-TV information compilation going through all the different carriers, working out what they will do and for how much. Now I basically did those just for my own benefit, to start with. Then I was getting questions from people on the Internet, 'what's going on, no-one knows anything' which is why I started posting them there.

Jim's compilations have developed quite a following, and he gets 'fan mail' and emails of appreciation from people who read them.

A website or electronic newsletter, of the type Jim produces, is clearly an important contemporary means by which individuals can develop a kind of fame, by producing symbolic goods which achieve value and circulate within new kinds of online community (Miller and Slater 2000: 20). Jim is certainly conscious of having a privileged position with the Internet community focused around the Usenet newsgroup he posts to and the people who visit his website:

> I guess that's another reason why I do all these compilations, to try to be part of that community. Being someone important in some way I suppose. But like I wouldn't want to be in the public eye, I wouldn't want to be on TV or radio or anything like that. I don't want to be, sort of, seen or anything. [But] I don't use any pseudonyms or anything, I don't mind giving my name. [EL: And it's an area in which you're seen as an expert?] Yeah, it feels good. Like if anyone wants any pay TV questions answered they'll just ask me.

Websites as forms of cultural production have already differentiated into a large number of genres. The personal websites of people like Jim Christou will never achieve the same degree of cultural prominence as the major commercial sites. However, Miller and Slater argue that 'websites are an expansion in space and time of their creators' (2000: 20), and that the aesthetic of the medium is designed as a trap to attract and bring appropriate others into the circulation of symbolic exchange. The possibilities for creatively constructing an object through personal activities of self-expression which can reach a global audience have previously only been available to individuals whose creative work (in art, literature, television, film and so on) could find patronage or commercial backing. It appears that, for a growing number of people, the Internet will provide a medium of personal objectification of a completely unprecedented importance and nature.

Conclusion

The local and particular home is articulated into and constituted through broader social and cultural structures, and information technologies have an increasingly important role in mediating this interrelationship in the contemporary western world. Building this technology into the domestic context transforms both the symbolic qualities of the technology (the process of domestication), and also transforms to some degree the domestic context itself. The computerized home becomes more workplace-like, as some of the dominant cultural meanings and associations of the computer are imported into the domestic setting: home 'offices' are set up, teleworking becomes possible, and domestic activities and community work take on some of the character of office administration.

For some households, such as the Coopers, the computer remains a luxury, but one that they wouldn't want to be without: 'I think we can work around it, I wouldn't like to, but I do think it's a luxury'. Over time, however, in many households the computer builds itself so thoroughly into the everyday routines of the household that they couldn't imagine life without it. As Hilary Lacey puts it, 'nothing is necessary, I suppose, but, yes, it's become a way of life'. Jim Christou feels, too, that he 'pretty much couldn't live without it'. Katherine Scarborough experienced first hand when her computer was stolen in a burglary how stressful life would be without her computer:

> I was without one for nearly two months while this one came in because it was on order and while the insurance gave me the money and all that sort of stuff. It took about two months so I was at that time without one, which I found quite stressful actually because it is part of my life.

Temporal Rhythms of the Computerized Home

Over time, the home computer is integrated into the household's patterns of everyday life and activity through its incorporation into the activities and routines of everyday living, into its temporal structures and hierarchies of interpersonal power, its established roles and ways of interacting. Eventually, the computer is transformed from a commodity into an object which is owned. As the computer finds its place within the pattern of activity of home life, some kinds of activity are privileged: some uses of the computer are 'proper' uses (both of the computer and of time), while others are not worthwhile or may even be time-wasting. This process of valorization is, however, complex and multifaceted: game playing might be seen as time-wasting when there are other tasks which need to be done, but can also be a 'rational' recreational activity when used to unwind after a long day at work.

Douglas (1991) refers to the home's structure in time as its 'time rhythms', institutionalized responses to past events in anticipation of future ones. Home as a temporal structure is made up of a number of different kinds of temporal cycle. At the level of daily activity, the temporal patterning of the everyday routines of the household may remain stable over an extended period of time: meal times occur at regular times, and there are routine times for sleeping, working and leisure. At longer time scales are the cyclical patterns of working weeks and weekends, school terms and university semesters, summers and winters. At even longer time scales the temporal patterning of the household is structured by life-cycle changes: bringing up children, career development, ageing and retirement.

When the Computer Was New

> Yes, there was a novelty effect and there was a fear. Like really wanting to find out what this computer was all about but really scared that we could muck it all up too. When we first got it we spent weekends like staying up to 3 o'clock in the morning, and getting up the next day and going straight back to it . . . We use it more now for real work but when it was new there was just a lot of investigating. (Sylvia Cooper)

Although for many people their employment or educationally related experience prepares them to some extent for what owning their own computer will be like, for others who have no such experience it is a case of their imagination meeting reality. A new computer is often secondary only to a new home or a car as a substantial purchase of a consumer good, and there is often a pronounced 'novelty effect' accompanying the initial period of ownership. This novelty effect, which may effectively be a way of testing or exploring the potential for the new acquisition to build itself into the everyday activities of the household, is often characterized by a sense of excitement among the household members, which may be accompanied, as in the Cooper household, with a sense of fear. The phenomenon of technological ambiguity, then, with a sense of excitement about the possibilities but also of the risks associated with exploring new cultural terrain, is often most intense during the period just before purchase, and while the computer is new. There is scope for failure, but also for significant gains in an expanded potential for the self.

For households acquiring their first computer, its arrival is often a significant event. Initial use of the computer is typically heavy, involving household members who may later play little part in the computer's use. This 'novelty effect' differs in length and intensity between households and in what happens afterwards, when the novelty 'wears off'. Sometimes one main user emerges after an initial period, or there may be a gradual diminishing in the extent to which household members use the computer. In other cases it builds up over time.

The initial period, when having a computer within the home is a great novelty to the members of the household, is often characterized also by a pattern of exploratory use of the computer – finding out what it can do. People often try doing things with the computer during this time that they never use the computer for again, and, like the Cooper family, they may use the computer until very late at night. Individual household members may also stay up to use the computer after the rest of the family has gone to bed.

The sense of novelty is not only associated with the purchase of new equipment: Janet Fuller (whose computer was bought second-hand from her work colleague Hilary Lacey) played games on it every evening when the computer was first bought, and then as she puts it 'the novelty wore off'. For Janet this happened after two weeks, and in general the sense of novelty tends to last for a few weeks or up to a couple of months. Some computer owners, however, suggest that for them there will always be something of that sense of novelty left. This tends, however, to be symbolically attached to the technology itself, rather than the particular computer owned. Doug Fowler, for example, suggests that for him, the novelty of computers will never wear off.

For the children in the Chapman household the computer was quite a novelty when it was first acquired, even though it was quite an old model. 'Wet days during the holidays . . . when we'd first got it, they'd be on it as long as they could get away with it. Like they'd be quite happy to stay there all day with a break for lunch.' Maureen Chapman adds, however, 'But now, it would be about an hour a fortnight, wouldn't it? Between the lot of them.' More generally, because of the flexibility of the computer as a technology, it is possible for the sense of novelty to be sparked again with the acquisition of new software or a new computer game, if Paul brings home a different software package from school, for example.

Marjorie Brennan remembers being quite excited when she brought her new computer home, and recalls that there was also excitement among her close-knit local community:

> I was quite excited that I had it. I think it's still something of that left. Because I don't know all the full capabilities and I'm learning all the time . . . I think the excitement was in the street too . . . There is a single woman a few doors down: she's also got a computer but we're the only ones with a computer so for the neighbourhood it was quite exciting. Everyone appeared and at that time the kids could play games and things like that. It was a real draw card because they did have computers at school but they hadn't really seen a computer in the home.

A community nurse, Marjorie feels closely linked to the community and is very much aware that most of her neighbours with children are low-income families who would probably be unable to afford a computer of their own. Marjorie therefore allows other people within the neighbourhood to use her computer, for example children completing school assignments or adults preparing resumés and job applications. This use of Marjorie's computer by other people within her social network supplements those examples given in the discussion of computer acquisition processes of how the home computer is tied into the broader social networks of the household.

Where the computer is acquired primarily for work-related reasons, the sense of novelty may relate, not so much to the computer itself as a whole, but to certain of its functions, such as computer games:

> No. There wasn't [a sense of novelty], it was bought purely as a functional workstation. There was a bit of novelty with some of the games initially perhaps but that goes through phases. In terms of the overall use of the computer, no, in fact I think I slowly built up using it more over time . . . It's probably been a slow progression of dependence [and] realization of its potential over the course of time. (Danielle Singleton)

Once the novelty of having a new computer wears off, the nature and level of its use generally changes, becoming more purposeful, and falling into a more sustained pattern:

> I think they just accept that it's there now . . . I think the nature of its use has changed . . . They spent a fair bit of time [when the computer was new] using it more as a toy, whereas since then the use is more, as well as using it for those purposes, it's more used for assignments, wordprocessing, tables, spreadsheets. (Peter Richards)

In some cases the amount of use that the computer gets in the initial intense period of novelty is never matched again. Over a longer period, there may be a tendency for the amount of use the computer gets to reduce, while in other cases usage builds up. Ruth Bourke is one person who finds that she is using her computer more as time goes on, because of finding more uses for it, as is Margaret Paine: 'I use it more than I used to in the beginning. It's become much more part of my life than it used to be.'

For other people, however, the pattern has been to use the computer less as time has gone by. Hayley Crowther, who has a two-year-old daughter, has found that the demands of her daughter are incompatible with computer use as an activity: 'I did use it more when we first got it . . . [but] I've found, sort of as Jennifer's got more demanding, and I've got into a routine where if she goes to sleep then I'll study rather than use the computer. I use it less and less.'

The child's routine of sleeping at particular times of day – a temporal rhythm which itself will evolve over time – therefore structures Hayley's time, and the routine which has emerged for her during these times does not include spending time using the computer. The nature of computing as an activity – requiring the user to sit in one spot for a period of time, and often also needing concentrated attention to the task at hand – means that, although it fits well with these sleep times, Hayley has other things she prefers to do with the strictly limited time she has for activities which are compatible with the demands of childcare. This example, then, gives one indication of the gendering of the computer within the domestic setting (an issue which is taken up in more detail in chapter 8).

The Changing Temporalities of the Household

The normal daily routines of the study households are structured by adults' working patterns (full or part-time, largely away from home or working at home, dependent on the computer or not), weekends, temporal patterns set by the length of school days and dates of school holidays, university semesters and study periods for adults (Silverstone 1993). At longer time scales the activities within which a home computer is implicated are shaped by the ages of children in the household (moving from primary to high school, and then on to work or further study), and by adults' changing work commitments and patterns (women returning to the workforce, changing from home-working to out-of-home work).

For Claire Matheson, computer use forms an important component of her daily routine:

> My procedure actually is, I get up in the morning, I switch on the computer, I get my cup of tea and I have my breakfast in one hand and with the other hand I play jigsaws [on the 486], or Mah Jong on that one [the Commodore]. And I'm there for lunch, and dinner, and afternoon tea and whatnot . . . I want something I can do with one hand. I don't want two hands on a keyboard, it has to be done with one hand, so I can have my cup of tea in the other one.

As an 'information appliance', the computer may be similar to an appliance like the fridge, which is left on all the time, or may be like the vacuum cleaner, which is only used for particular tasks and then is put away. It may also be like the television, which in some households is switched on and left on irrespective of whether anyone is watching it, or may be strictly required to be shut down and switched off when not in use. In the contemporary workplace, and particularly since the advent of email, many personal computers are left switched on, even when the user is engaged in some non-computer-based task. By contrast, if a home computer is left on it tends to be because someone is planning to go back to it. In households with children there are often explicit rules about this (see chapter 7 for further detail on this point). The amount and temporal patterning of computer use is, however, very variable. In some households, the computer is more or less on all day, while in others it is switched on for a particular task and then switched off again. As we saw in chapter 1, in the Manfredotti household the weekday pattern is different from that at weekends. In the Bartlett household, similarly, the computer is used much more at the weekend and during school holidays, to the degree that it is simply left on all day during these periods: 'Our nine-year-old usually scoots out at about 8 o'clock in the morning on weekends and holidays and things. Before school it won't go on, but leisure time it will go on about 8 o'clock in the morning and will be on all day until 9 or 10 o'clock at night' (Merilyn Bartlett).

Margaret Paine leaves the computer on to remind her that that's what she should be doing: 'if I wander away at least it's a reminder that I should be sitting at that computer'. Katherine Scarborough also tends to leave the computer on at the weekends, rather than switching it on and off as needed:

> If it's at the weekend, and I'm home, it would probably be on most of the day and I would go back and forwards. And I would think 'I might start a letter to someone' and I'll do a bit. I'll play a few games. If I've got work to do I might do a couple of hours work but generally, yes, it would be on all day. I would just keep going back and forwards.

For adults' work and study, computer use conforms to their patterns of work, and may vary according to changing work commitments. Thomas Turner, for example, no longer uses the computer for freelance work: 'A couple of years ago I spent six months working a lot from home and that was when it was on eight hours a day, five days a week . . . Whereas the six months before then it was hardly on at all.'

In many households, the pattern of use of the computer varies according to the temporal pattern of work or study commitments. Jessica Lane works at home on Fridays so uses the computer then, although it was bought when she was working from home full-time. For both Thomas Turner and Jessica Lane, as in many other cases, the amount and type of use of the computer has changed markedly over the time the computer has been within the household. Margaret Paine's computer, for example, would be on every night during semester and probably also most of the weekend. Out of semester she uses it only when she does her personal financial management or writes letters to family overseas.

Often work or study deadlines will determine a pattern of use: 'I start really using the computer at night, and it varies, it depends on what work I have to do. One day I worked on the computer for 16 hours, non-stop, almost no eating . . . But other days I would use it for an hour or so' (Carlos Martinez).

Sometimes other things happening in a person's life distract attention away from activities involving the computer. Katherine Scarborough, for example, had not been using her computer much because of problems within the family:

> I've got some family problems with my mother and my sister is not very well and so I really haven't done very much with it and I also have been working a lot. I guess I go home pretty tired and I'm getting home late . . . so I'm not using it very much at the moment.

While it may seem that the amount of time in the day is essentially limited, it is sometimes possible to gain a sense of making more time in the day available. When Danielle Singleton has a deadline to meet, for example, she will get up at 5.00 a.m. to do some work before her son gets up. The quiet time before the 'real' start of the day can seem like finding extra time over and above the normal twenty-four hour allocation. Joy Lester finds time for her creative writing on Sundays, when she might spend the whole day in bed with her laptop.

Particularly in a place like Australia, the Internet appears to be responsible for an increasing awareness of the temporal distortions of global time zones. 'Live' events in other parts of the world but accessible over the Internet often take place in the middle of the night in other parts of the world. Paradoxically, these technologies both make people more aware of the relativity of such 'natural' diurnal rhythms, but also allow people to 'time shift' activities out of their 'natural' times. Email allows a rapid turnaround in communications interaction, but without the necessity for concern with time zones which accompanies telephone communication. Hilary Lacey says that she often checks her email both last thing at night and first thing in the morning, because 'you've got stuff coming in from all over the world'.

These examples illustrate that individual temporal structures map onto a variety of environmental temporalities, to some extent constraining what kinds of activities can be conducted at which times. But it is also clear that there is room to manoeuvre and to manipulate these imposed temporal rhythms, and that technologies play an increasingly important role in making this possible within domestic time and space.

It is also worth remarking on how the subjective sense of time passing may be mediated by the use of technologies, either in terms of time appearing to pass quickly, or slowly. Some kinds of computer activity absorb all the attention, and the subjective sense of the passage of time is suppressed. That time seems to pass quickly when one is enjoying an activity, but slowly when one is not is a common observation. The effect is particularly strong for activities that intensely engage the attention, such as computer games and concentration on computer-based work:

> When I'm working at home I'll find that I've got to be very careful. If I'm doing it for a client I've got to be very careful to actually note the time when I start because I will just work away and work away and look up and think 'Oh my God, four hours have gone by' . . . That happens more so at home than it does at work. There's always interruptions at work that keep you focused on, I guess, most of the time approximately what time it is. (Katherine Scarborough)

In chapter 2 it was suggested that the space of the extended self – the interactive relational interface between the self and the external world, including those technologies and other objects we interact with – can be identified with potential space in Winnicott's terms. While in many kinds of activity the self is relatively disengaged, for a deeply engrossing activity it is as if the self expands to encompass the activity and the sense of separation from the objects or technologies involved.

'Proper' Uses of Time

The high cultural value attached to information technology is symbolically available to be transferred to those functions which are constructed as appropriate uses within public discourses. As Murdock et al. put it in relation to societal concerns about computer games: 'beneath these debates [lies] the familiar Victorian concern with the "proper" use of leisure, and the continual clashes between contrasted definitions of rational recreation, trivial pursuits and dangerous pleasures' (1992: 157).

These contradictions play out in complex ways within the domestic sphere, and result in value differentials between different kinds of computing activities.

The study households would generally be similar to those surveyed by Elliot & Shanahan Research for Apple in September 1995:

> There is a hierarchy of perceived worth or value for the various uses of the home computer. Income-generating adult work at home tops the list, followed by children's school assignments, projects and research. Next comes household administration, children's creative efforts, and discovery experiences, such as the exploration of CD-ROMs and sophisticated software, followed by educational or 'good' games, then, lastly, 'silly' or violent games. (Apple Computer Australia 1996: 13)

Within households this hierarchy may be institutionalized in explicit rules ('homework comes before games') and conventions ('the person whose homework deadline comes first has first turn'), but is also open to negotiation (adults can stay up later than children so the homework can sometimes come before the adult income-generating work) and to the established play of interpersonal power ('I always defer to my children', says Helen Samuels).

The appropriateness of different uses of time is an issue for regulation within the moral economy of the household. Some kinds of activity have higher moral value, and are therefore encouraged, while others are seen as less desirable and to be limited, either by self-regulation or by the imposition of parental authority. Many people feel that they must resist the desire to spend more time playing games, and they feel guilty about spending time on this activity. Carlos Martinez stopped playing games because he felt it was time-wasting: 'I used to play games, and I noticed that I was wasting too much time on the games. So I decided to stop playing games.' Jim Christou felt that he had 'wasted' his three weeks' holiday by watching television instead of doing things with his new computer: 'I've pretty much wasted my three weeks, watching TV a lot. I've probably used [the computer] more, because I wasn't at work to use the work computer, to get email and stuff, but I guess in general, probably, not too much more.'

On the other hand, playing games is of value if it is done for relaxation or for 'de-stressing' at the end of the working day or a busy week. Doing nothing, or doing something which would otherwise be discouraged, may not necessarily be seen as a waste of time:

> Actually, it's good for a diversion, like I would often sit in front of the television and watch a program to relax at the end of the day, like after everyone else has collapsed in bed, but I also find that playing a computer game can also be used to relax, for a diversion rather. (Peter Richards)

Value judgements about the use of the computer based on rationalist criteria are widely applied by computer users in both discussing and negotiating their use of the computer and that of other members of their household. However, this moral scheme presupposes a certain scarcity of time for both this and other competing activities. Although it seems almost unacceptable to admit it under contemporary western conditions of modernity, it still seems that some people do have 'spare time' at their disposal. The potential of this technology to provide a pastime – in the sense of an activity which pleasantly passes the time, simply because time is there to be passed – is explored by some of the people in the study:

> It does take time to sit down and go through all this, with thousands of programs on the one disk [CD-ROMS which come with magazines]. So, if you're a busy mum and you're going to work, it's a time thing. I happen to have lots of time available . . . I'd rather do this than the housework! [laughter] (Claire Matheson)

Claire clearly does not find it difficult to resist the prescription that housework, as 'useful' activity, is morally superior and therefore would be a more legitimate use of the time she has available ('lots of time') rather than 'playing around' on the computer. However, her recognition that this might be seen as a somewhat transgressive choice is indicated by her laughter at the comparison, and specifically that I as the interviewer might think so – in other words, this is something that 'we both know'.

Claire seems to be able to spend her time as she personally pleases, without being plagued by the guilt that Elizabeth Martin felt in a similar situation after she had bought her granddaughter (whom she is raising) a Gameboy. (Again, Elizabeth's laughter during the interview indicates that this is behaviour which 'we both know' is somewhat absurd.)

> She's got a Gameboy that she plays. If she can get it off me [laughs]. When I first bought it I was putting new batteries in it every day because I wasn't working. So she would go to school and by ten I couldn't stand it any longer so I'm in the bedroom getting the Gameboy out. Then I think,

'Oh God, it's three o'clock, she'll be home soon. I had better put some fresh batteries in, so she doesn't know that I've been playing it all day.'

Elizabeth estimates that this pattern lasted for about three months before she had had 'too much of a good thing' and the novelty of the activity wore off. Like Claire Matheson, Elizabeth sees housework as an unpleasant task which should come before computer use, but often doesn't. She feels guilty about using the computer while there are other things she thinks she should be doing. On the other hand, television watching can be justified as relaxation, especially since she can get up during the advertising breaks and do a few things:

> While I'm watching telly I will do the washing. While the ads are on I will get up and I will dust or I can get up and get tea going or something or do lunch so at least I'm doing the jobs I'm supposed to be doing while I'm watching TV but when I'm in there with the computer I don't come out for anything. I will literally be busting to go to the loo, I am desperate to get out of there and I will tend to shut down before I come out because I know if I don't shut down I will just go back to it.

Conclusion

This chapter and the previous chapter have described how the computer comes to be integrated into the household's 'pattern of life', manifested in routines of activity and temporal rhythms. But although these structure the everyday life of the household members, this pattern is not rigid but is able to respond both to external factors and to the changing needs of its members. The introduction of a complex cultural object, such as a home computer, into this context initiates an intricate process of negotiation between the household as a structure of objectification and the multidimensional characteristics of the technology as a cultural form comprising structures of meaning, value and functionality. While the emphasis up until this point has been on how the home computer is incorporated into the household as a collective entity, each individual household member constructs their own subjective relationship of ownership to the objects and spaces of the household. In other words, the home is differentially incorporated into the extended self of each of its inhabitants.

Negotiations of Ownership

In the existing literature drawing on the notion of objectification in investigating how we come to own mass-produced objects, this process has in general been seen as one of appropriation and symbolic recontextualization. The relational notion of ownership which is developed in this book extends the conception of ownership as appropriation in a number of key ways. First, ownership is seen as a process and as an activity. Second, we have seen that the processes by which such objects are appropriated are in fact part of larger projects of home-building, and are in fact directed towards the production of the home as an objectification of its members. Finally, the relationship of ownership is one of mutual belonging: the complexity of interrelationships between people and objects means that we do not simply appropriate them, but that they also 'appropriate' each other, and (individually and collectively) they 'appropriate' us in turn. In this and subsequent chapters, the complex and multifaceted negotiations between the individuals who inhabit a household and the objects with which they attempt to make themselves at home in it are explored.

Households are generally the collective constructions of a number of individuals, and it must be recognized that they are places of conflict and negotiation. As Douglas (1991) points out, homes work by imposing control over their inhabitants, including explicit or implicit rules and conventions developed over time in order to make them equitable, structured spaces for living. Although, if successfully constructed, the home is a space of ontological security, it is not a space of personal freedom:

> [It] has a lot of authority as its disposal, but it is not authoritarian or centralized . . . It is extremely coercive, but the coercion is anonymous, the control is generalized. The pattern of rules continually reforms itself, becomes more comprehensive and restrictive, and continually suffers breaches, fission, loss at the fringes . . . It is hierarchical, but it is not centralized. (306)

Home works by imposing control over its inhabitants, including explicit or implicit rules and conventions developed over time in order to make the home an equitable, structured space for living. Yet this is not a space of personal freedom: 'even its most altruistic and successful versions exert a tyrannous control over mind and body' (303), and over space and time, bodies and objects:

> Apart from its tyranny over times, the home tyrannizes over tastes. In the name of friendly uniformity, the menus tend to be designed not to satisfy food preferences but to avoid food hates. One person's rooted dislike or medical prohibition results in certain foods being totally eliminated even if they are everyone else's favourite food, so in the regular menu everyone gets what they are indifferent to, and no one ever gets their favourite dish. (303–4)

While in some households there is one individual who is definitively recognized as the owner of the home computer, either by explicit consensus or as an emergent outcome of subtle long-term processes and patterns of use, householders must often also negotiate shared access to or ownership of the home computer. This may involve formal negotiation, but since much of everyday domestic life is habitually routine, often the shifting balance of relationships around the home computer arises implicitly. An explicit assertion of the joint ownership of the computer on the part of one household member may sit in opposition to someone else's sense that they would like the computer to be theirs alone, and this may be the source of explicit dispute and negotiation, or implicit tensions. As children develop expertise on the computer, they may eventually surpass their parents, thus shifting the balance of power between them, and establishing an area of authority for the young person.

Negotiations which take place around the computer, it seems, tend to reflect the broader need for the individuals within a household to manage both their shared access to the household's joint resources, and also the household's embedding within the broader social networks and structures in which it takes part. The processes and strategies described may be seen as reflective of the general household repertoire of techniques of managing their living together.

Constructing the Relationship of Ownership

Who Does the Computer Belong To?

In some households there is one individual who is definitively recognized as the owner of the home computer, while in others ownership is more complex. In the Brown household, the computer is clearly recognized as belonging to Richard, although his wife also sometimes uses it. Similarly, in the Lester household the computer is seen as belonging to Joy, although Larry uses it frequently. This kind of ownership, which might be thought of as a kind of consensus about whom the computer belongs to (as an attribution), generally arises out of the history of the acquisition of the current and any previous computers. A more subtle form of ownership, on the other hand, may arise out of who uses it most, or with who is seen to be responsible for any 'housekeeping' tasks which might need to be done (such as clearing out old files and keeping the hard disk organized and backed up). These more implicit modes of ownership are also involved in the negotiation of relations between household members and how these are constructed through dimensions of age and gender.

In the Martinez household there are two computers, the newer 486 which is located in Carlos's study (from which the children are generally excluded) and the older 386 which is located in the eldest son's room. The 486 is definitively seen as Carlos's, and this is manifested in the limitations which are placed on the children's access to it: 'Well, most of the time it's available. Just on condition that the place doesn't get messy. And I limit the time that they can spend, an hour or an hour and a half. But it's a problem, [in] that they don't really want to use the other one now.'

Carlos has started to think about upgrading to a newer computer, which would mean that the 486 would become available for wider use. Although there has been no change in the way the 486 is used, Carlos is already starting to distance himself from it: 'I tend to think that I own it, but I suppose I'm losing that feeling, because everybody really has the right to use it'. This example indicates that a change in the subjective sense of ownership of the object, a psychological distancing from the object, is often an early stage in the phasing out of the object from ownership, and may be a necessary part of the divestment rituals which precede the end of a relationship of ownership (McCracken 1988: 85).

Some households, such as the Richards household, appear to be able to develop a genuine sense of communal ownership. In others, while the computer 'technically' belongs equally to all household members, some individuals are able to achieve a more proprietorial relationship to the computer than others. The negotiations around these issues of ownership can be very delicate, and discomfort or embarrassment may be experienced when someone oversteps the mark without thinking about it. Although the explicit consensus within the Turner household, for example, is that the computer belongs to the family as a whole, it is clear that there have been times when Thomas has treated the computer as his alone. Thomas has always been the major user of the computer and used it as his work tool when he was working from home. His defensiveness at being challenged about his proprietary behaviour, however, is illustrated by the following exchange, conducted light-heartedly, but with some embarrassment on Thomas' part:

Sally Turner:	He put his name on the licence. You know that 'this computer belongs to', he put his name on there.
Thomas Turner:	Yes, but that's changed now.
ST:	I don't think so.
TT:	Oh, not on the software, you can't change it on the software licence.
ST:	So he has this personal sense of ownership there.
TT:	Not any more [laughter].

The organization of the computer's hard disk – the storage space inside the computer – is also an indication of individual household members' personal appropriation of the computer. While the hard disk on the Thomas computer is nominally organized so that each member of the family has their own folder (to keep their files separated), Thomas has also created a folder called 'Masters' for his university work which is outside all the individual family members' own folders. Sally sees this as proprietorial, but Thomas has an instrumental justification for doing it this way:

ST:	You should have your 'Masters' inside 'Thomas'.
TT:	But it was getting too big, I didn't want to have to double click through 'Thomas' to get into another one, because I was already going through anyway.

In both the Martinez and Turner households, ownership of the computer is reflected in and partially constructed through ownership and use of the space in which the computer is located, an issue which is explored in more detail in chapter 10. In the Turner household, the extent to which the children are able to construct a sense of ownership over the computer, and the obstacles to such a construction, is illustrated by whether they tend to ask permission to use the computer:

> It's probably more that they may phrase it 'can I'? Certainly when we first bought the computer it was very precious and [to Thomas] you were fairly strict about how and where and why the children were using the computer because they were on this precious thing that we had spent all this money on. That's changed and the computer has become more familiar to us and so they may not ask. Generally they would indicate that they need to because they have to get the key to go down there because it's locked. (Sally Turner)

What might be the explicit consensual view about who owns the home computer – who has the right to use it, and what they must do to assert that right – therefore contrasts with rather more subtle differences between household members in the degree to which an individual has developed a personal relationship of ownership with the computer. As we saw in chapter 1, because Angelica is the major user of the computer in the Manfredotti household, Laura feels that she has to tread carefully and not reinforce a sense that Angelica has more proprietorial rights over the computer than the rest of the children.

Such differences in proprietorship may also relate to more generalized structures of interpersonal power within the household, as a 'shifting and fluid field of negotiations, exchanges, counter attacks, investments' (Hawkins 1998: 131). In some households, proprietary behaviour in relation to the computer is a fulcrum for more fundamental tensions and power relations within the household. In the Fowler household, an assertion of the joint ownership of the computer, in opposition to Doug's sense that he would like the computer to be his alone, has been the source of explicit dispute and negotiation:

> We have this major argument. Like, we have a car in the garage, which we've just bought and we decided that Bev should be the one to learn to drive first so it became 'her' car. When I got the computer I said 'This is my computer'. 'No, it's not it's ours'. So there's been a running argument. It is technically mine, it was given to me, but it's the family's. Even though I'm getting hassled because I've set the computer up my way without consultation with anybody but it's our computer. My computer is called Beast, I named it. I set the sounds up, 'I don't like those'. So I've got to change them to suit the rest of the family.

Doug, who is long term unemployed, embodies what Miller and Slater (2000) refer to as the dynamic of expansive realization with respect to these technologies. As we have already seen, Doug sees himself as a 'futurist', and his ownership of a computer is part of becoming the person he always thought he 'really' was. As this example shows, however, an assertion of the claim to become who one wants to be or feels oneself to be is never simple. Everyday domestic life is a dynamic process of improvisation and interpersonal negotiation. Personal relationships to particular objects and activities must be established in relation to other people's possibilities for proprietoriality too.

Helen Samuels's son feels proprietorial about everything in her life, she says, and not just the computer: 'I do tolerate it. Although I get a little bit upset when, having borrowed my car for all three days of his uni, he says "there's no petrol in the car!" "Well . . . " [laughter]. He's used it all week . . . he expects me to provide everything. I've brought that on myself a lot.'

Helen describes this as a tendency to indulge her children, particularly her son, but it is also possible to see this as a mother's complicity in and justification for an unequal domestic power relationship. Although her son does not live with her, he frequently comes to use the computer for his university work, often when his mother is not home. Not only do he and his partner have their own folders on the hard drive, but: 'in fact they've relegated my folder to "z.mum", so that it'll be right on the bottom, so that their stuff's above it'. She is laughing as she tells me this: rather than seeming antagonized by these quite aggressive appropriations, Helen seems almost proud of the precocity of her son. If she is using the computer when he comes over: 'It's "how long are you going to be?" and he'll stand over me', she says, laughing again. If, as I argued in chapter 4, the use of laughter within the interview context may be an indication of deep ambiguities which need not be resolved in the practical context of lived experience, Helen's laughter may be read as an ironic acknowledgement of the contradictions inherent in the asymmetries of power in this, one of the most important relationships in her life, and also of her own role in having shaped these aspects of his personality through her techniques of parenting. Although the behaviour of her son as it is described is clearly appropriative and even exploitative, this is an integral aspect of their relationship. Her laughter is a distancing move, necessary to protect her from being rendered within the context of the interview as the bully's victim and revealing her complicity in this power asymmetry.

These examples illustrate the contradictions and necessary ambivalence of family relationships, and recall Miller's (1998b) description of familial 'love' as a category of social and interpersonal relationship which involves care, concern, obligation, responsibility and habit, but also resentment, frustration and even hatred. Family relationships are therefore complex and contradictory, and must remain largely unexamined in order for them to stably constructed and maintained.

Negotiating Joint Ownership

In households where the computer is in high demand, there is the possibility for conflict over such competing demands. This potential is recognized in most of the households studied, and is handled more or less formally. As we saw, Laura Manfredotti used to allocate time amongst children wanting to use the computer by using the kitchen timer, particularly when the computer was new and was more of a novelty and there were disputes between the children about getting access to the computer. In the Richards household, for example, it is 'pretty well first come first served', although sometimes it is a question of who gets there fastest, particularly among the boys: 'Whatever they're watching on TV will finish, they'll tear out there, "I'm here first".' The eldest daughter, who is in her final year of high school, will often signal her priority: 'She might say immediately before dinner, "Straight after dinner, I'm on the computer", so she'll stake a claim.'

Most of the explicit conflicts in this household are about getting a turn. Conflicts are sometimes resolved by one of the parents stepping in:

> One of us usually steps in and says 'right, who's got what due when, how long is it, how long will it take?' and if they're both due on the same day the youngest one goes first. Because they have to go to bed before the older one. Jessica being the oldest, too, is also somewhat of a night owl, she can last longer in the evening. (Sarah Richards)

In the Bartlett household, with four boys aged between ten and nineteen, the queue for the computer is often two or three deep: 'somebody on the computer, somebody waiting, and somebody else waiting for that'. Merilyn tries to stay out of any disputes, and lets the children sort it out themselves. In the Cooper household, however, the older children feel they have a right to 'pull rank' on the younger ones, but they too feel that they have to give way when their older brother (who lives elsewhere) comes over. As Sylvia Cooper says, 'They complain to me, "Oh Tim's on the computer and he's been playing that game for ages". I think it's an age thing really.'

Conflict around the home computer, then, tends to centre around access to it, but the level of conflict around the computer is in general no different from that around other common activities. In the Martinez household, for example, Carlos estimates that there are more disputes about what to watch on television than there are over access to the computer. While in the Chapman household: '"You've been on long enough." "You touched the keyboard and interfered with what I was doing." But then, that occurs when there's three of them in the swimming pool ... So there can be conflicts, but no more with the computer than with any other activity' (Paul Chapman).

The home computer, as with many other kinds of domestic object, is (except in cases where it is definitively the personal possession of one individual) effectively a shared possession of the household's members. Although computing is often seen as a solitary, even isolating, activity, in many households there are frequently computing activities involving two or more participants. In the Chapman household, for example, it is a common occurrence for two or more of the children to sit together and do things on the computer: 'They'll quite often crowd around, waiting their turn, as a threesome.' The computer also provides activities which can be jointly engaged in by children who are significantly different in age, and one in which greater size and age do not necessarily convey an advantage. As Mitchell observes in her study of video game usage: 'Video games did not automatically ensure the superiority of the older and larger children in the family' (1985: 129). This may be resented, however: in one of the cases in Mitchell's study a younger child's greater skill aroused anger in an older sibling (130). In the Richards household, where the children's ages range between six and seventeen, the children will often play games together:

> They actually do quite a lot of playing together, either with the two-person games or with one playing and one watching. There's a lot of joint enjoyment from one person using it ... Although there is one person who is moving the mouse, it's a joint activity in that the other one will be saying 'Put one here'. Quite often, too, when one person gets out, the other one will swap into the seat and have a go. Particularly with James [the six-year-old], one of the others will sit with him and show him how to do different things. (Peter Richards)

Peter will also sometimes sit with the youngest child, although Sarah does not get involved in the game playing, since as she (laughingly) puts it, she 'can't work the games'. Both Peter and Sarah feel that the computer has provided a facility for joint activity within the family, although they also feel that there is neither more nor less joint activity than there was before the computer. Computer game-playing is, however, viewed as superior to television, since it is 'interactive', reflecting the higher value constructed for these activities in home computer advertising, as seen in chapter 3. As Sarah puts it: 'We'd rather have them doing that than sitting glued to the TV. At least they're using their mind.'

It tends to be fathers rather than mothers who play together with their children on the computer. Wheelock (1992) found that seven fathers as opposed to one mother played on the computer along with their children, although Danielle Singleton (a single mother) sometimes plays draughts or SimCity together with her son. If the children eventually develop greater skills than their parents, the adults may be discouraged from playing after a period of time. This was certainly the case with Peter Richards and his sons, for example, and Mitchell also observes this effect in the participants in her study: 'Most fathers played enthusiastically at first, both with their children and alone. At the beginning they were competing well with the children. Within a few weeks, however, records showed many sons surpassing their fathers in scores, which discouraged the fathers from playing' (Mitchell 1985: 127).

Adults sometimes also play video games together, and Claire Matheson finds that computing is valuable as an activity in common with her youngest son and her grandchildren, whom she might otherwise not have much in common with: 'You can relate to your kids in this area. I never had trouble relating to my son out there. Or any of my kids, 'cause we can talk computers.' She enjoys finding pictures to import into a jigsaw program for her grandchildren when they come to visit.

As children develop expertise on the computer, they may eventually surpass their parents, thus shifting the balance of power between them, and establishing an area of authority for the young person. Within the Martinez household, Carlos and his fifteen-year-old son both have their own recognized areas of expertise around the computers. Although Carlos is the main 'expert' within the household, his expertise has been built up over a number of years with evolving generations of the technology. His son Jonathan has not had this length of time to develop his skills, but Carlos supports and acknowledges the skills that Jonathan has developed in the more recent technology of Windows 95. In a sense, perhaps, Carlos is allowing his son the cultural space to develop his own autonomous expertise, which his father does not encroach upon, as part of the parental role in facilitating the child's development from complete dependence in infancy to relative autonomy (Winnicott 1971). Carlos's overall superiority as the technical expert within the family is essentially unchallenged and, as Carlos puts it, if he needed to find out something he *could* do it himself, but instead he relies on Jonathan to provide expertise: 'In general I know more. But he knows more Windows 95 than I do ... But still I know more about the hardware and he won't be able to catch up with me there.'

Carlos recalls the point at which Jonathan had developed an interest in computers:

> When I first bought the Amiga, he wasn't interested in computers, just the games. When I bought the 386, he was still interested in games, but one day he came home from school and he said 'Daddy, open the computer for me.' At school they had learned about computers and he said, 'I'm interested in computers, can you open it and explain everything about the inside of the computer?' And from then on I didn't have much to do with it, he just found out by himself.

On a recent occasion, Carlos had called on Jonathan's expertise when he was assisting a friend to fix his computer: 'I didn't have to know it, I could just ask him, rather than going to the books.' Carlos feels that Jonathan has an edge over him when it comes to learning new things, but that his own practical expertise, picked up over many years, means that he has some knowledge that Jonathan will not be able to just pick up. Between Carlos and his son, then, a division of labour with respect to computing expertise within the household has emerged gradually over recent years, without this having been an explicit goal of either of them.

The Extended Household

As we saw in chapter 4, the household's social networks are involved in gathering information before a computer is purchased, but this involvement does not end once the computer has been brought home. Murdock et al., for example, found that these networks were of crucial importance on an ongoing basis, since 'those with little or no contact with other users were more likely to have stopped using their machines once the initial novelty had worn off' (1992: 151). The home computer is often also a significant focus of activity for children with their friends, particularly, as in the case of the Collins household, for boys (Haddon 1992: 93; Wheelock 1992: 106).

Sometimes, the relationships that people outside the household have with a particular home computer may even extend to a kind of ownership of the object. It is difficult to regard the household as a bounded unit, with a clear definition on the basis of residence as to who is part of it and who is not, when the issue is one of a generalized sense of ownership over the spaces and objects of the home. Adult children who live elsewhere will often still regard their parents' house as 'home', and treat its objects in a way which indicates that there is still a sense of ownership over them. This may be the case even when an object, such as a home computer, is a recent acquisition for the household. These examples indicate the subtle complexities of ownership seen as an activity, and based in interaction, rather than as simply based on the legal establishment of rights.

Helen Samuels's adult son, who is married with a child and who lives not far from his mother, will often come to her house while she is absent to use the computer, although he also comes at times when she is home. In another example, Katherine Scarborough's daughter frequently visits at the weekend, and has fallen into a habit of playing games on the computer as a regular activity during her time there.

> She'll play for three or four hours sometimes and I've got to interrupt her for lunch . . . She comes over, we chat for a little while to catch up, then the children want to spend a bit of time with Grandma, so we do things, and the next thing, she's away playing computer games, that's her switch off time, because she's got two pre-schoolers. So she uses it every weekend in that way.

Katherine's grandchildren also sometimes play on the computer, and indeed will squabble over access to the computer.

Such joint use of the household's resources is not limited to people who are part of the extended household in the sense of the 'extended family'. Ruth Bourke's neighbours as well as family members come to her house to print things because she has a laser printer: 'All the people in the street who have Macintoshes know that I have a laser printer, I've discovered. "Just want to run my CV off, Ruth, can I use your printer?"'

Marjorie Brennan also allows other people in her neighbourhood access to her computer, particularly children from low-income households where there is no home computer, who use her computer for school assignments. She insists, however, that the computer is only used for such 'serious purposes': 'I say it's not a toy. When I first got the computer I think that because it had the games and that some of the kids were using it as a toy and then I just affirmed that it wasn't a toy and then I stopped the games and now I just use it for if they want to do assignments.'

Neighbours wanting to use the computer must fit in with Marjorie's own work commitments and deadlines. For Marjorie there is an ethical dimension to this community involvement: 'I think that there is an inequality for children at school because of that economic factor, because obviously the people who have got computers at home, the children have so much advantage over the children who haven't. There isn't access to computers after school hours and things like that yet.'

This use has not, however, resulted in a sense on the part of these external users of the computer that they can just come and use it: to the degree that they themselves have built up a personal relationship of ownership with Marjorie's computer, it is a highly attenuated one.

The household may draw on the cultural resources of its social network not just in the processes leading up to a computer purchase, but these networks are also important in supporting the use of the computer once it has been brought home, particularly for solving problems which arise. A friend of Marjorie Brennan's came and helped her to set up the hard disk and organize it when she first bought her second-hand computer. When Claire Matheson has a problem, her son is generally the first person she contacts. If he cannot help, she has a further support network that she has developed through her son. Janet Fuller calls her work colleague Hilary Lacey, but Hilary herself does not know anyone who is more expert with computers than she is, and so relies on manuals and other textual resources such as computer magazines.

Carlos Martinez, like Richard Brown, is part of a peer support network where individuals tend to have well developed areas of expertise: 'I keep in contact with some people that I've worked with, who have gone in different directions, and they've specialized in other areas, so it's worthwhile keeping in contact with them . . . I don't see why I should spend two days finding some information when I can just give someone a ring and get it in five minutes.'

Conversely, there are people who call on Carlos's expertise: 'I had a call from someone last night!'

As we also saw in the discussion of software piracy, the household's domestication of a consumer good like the home computer can only be fully understood in the context of its interactions with the non-commercial social structures within which it is embedded. The household's social networks give it access to cultural resources, but the 'goods' which circulate within these networks operate according to the logic of the gift transaction, rather than that of the commodity. Indeed, these interactions and the mutual obligations which arise because of them provide some of the social 'cement' which binds the contemporary urban community (Gregory 1982; Mauss 1990). Expertise, knowledge and, of course, materials such as copies of software programs, are disseminated within these networks, but not according to the limited principles of 'restricted exchange' which mark economic transactions and which have no necessary ongoing obligations involved. Rather, these interchanges operate according to principles of 'generalized exchange', where the giver gives without expectation of immediate return, and even without an expectation of a return at all from the receiver, because the giver may receive a benefit from someone else within the network (Lévi-Strauss 1969).

Negotiations which take place around the computer, it seems, tend to reflect the broader need for the individuals within a household to manage both their shared access to the household's joint resources, and also the household's embedding within the broader social networks and structures in which it takes part. The processes and strategies which have been described may be seen, then, as reflective of the general household repertoire of techniques of managing their living together. However, the management of the household's pattern of life does not simply emerge from the activities of its members, but must often be actively managed, particularly on the part of the adult household members.

Managing the Computerized Household

Negotiating the Balance of Relationships and Activities

As we have seen, the computer's place in the home is articulated with other structures of domestic activity, and with the relationships between household members. The ownership of the home computer may emerge simply from these patterns of interaction, or may be more complex and contested than this. An individualized relationship of ownership must often be negotiated within a context in which other people are also constructing their own personalized relationships to the computer, and therefore the ability of each individual to do this will relate to broader structures of interaction and hierarchies based on age and gender within the household.

Sometimes the negotiation of solutions to conflicting needs must be explicitly conducted. Before Hilary Lacey switched to a local Internet service provider, both the size of the phone bills and the length of time that Hilary was tying up the phone line had been something of a source of conflict. Her partner Margaret Paine feels that the solution to these problems is a second phone line, but she sees this as something that Hilary should take responsibility for. At the same time, Margaret realizes that since she is the person most inconvenienced by the lack of access to the phone line, she might have to take on the organization of this herself:

> You should see our phone bill: it's just a joke. The last two bills have been $450 and the one before that was $500 and something and none of that's mine ... So we do need two lines now. I'm demanding it. It's her responsibility because she's using it not me. So I want her to take that up and get another phone line put in ... [But] I might make some inquiries because Hilary won't get round to it.

Jim Christou must also negotiate his access to the household phone line with the rest of the family. He has brought up the possibility of putting in a second phone line with his parents, but they were not supportive and so he now tries to avoid tying up the line while other people might be wanting to use it:

> I've brought it up and said 'I want to get another phone line for myself' and they said 'Why do you want to get another phone line?' So I wait until everyone's off the phone and then what I do at the moment is put a notice on the phone saying 'In use, don't touch' so that someone doesn't just pick it up and wreck my whole connection. So I've been doing that and trying to use it at nights when everyone else is asleep so it won't disturb anyone.

Jim's avoidance of using the phone while others might be wanting to use it seems largely to be a method of avoiding a potentially uncomfortable situation, rather than a response to conflicts which have actually happened. These examples illustrate the fragility and subtlety with which the conditions of everyday living are negotiated within the membership of the family, who have lived together over many years and have, generally, a commitment to making the relationship work. The kinds of negotiations which are conducted in less long-term and stable living situations, such as when living space is shared with someone who is almost a stranger, are often more explicit and less likely to be based on implicit negotiations or the adapting of already existing models for behaviour. This is illustrated by the common experience of the single young adult who shares a flat or house with others.

Regine Vassallo has more of a sense of ownership of the flat she shares with another student, since most of the furnishings in the flat are hers, as are the crockery and small appliances in the kitchen, and because she lived in the flat with another person before her current flatmate moved in. Yet when both Regine and her flatmate are at home they tend to spend their time in their rooms, although Regine (and probably the flatmate too) tends to spend more time in the communal areas of the flat when the other is not at home. Living together in relative harmony means that they must delicately negotiate the balance of their use of the household's shared facilities and resources, sometimes non-verbally (such as by not getting in each other's way in the confined space of the flat when they are both there) and sometimes explicitly. For example, they divide up their long-distance telephone charges by going through the telephone bill and working out how much each should pay according to who made each call. On the other hand, they have agreed that Regine's heavier use of local telephone calls is balanced by her flatmate's heavier use of electricity: 'This was her idea – she uses a hell of a lot more electricity than I do because she leaves lights on and she said to me "I'll make you a deal, we'll split the Telstra and the electricity bills in half because you spend more on Telstra and I spend more on electricity" and that's fair enough with me.'

What seems to be important here is not so much whether these charges are actually equally generated, but that the householders agree that this is a fair way to allocate them, as a negotiated position they have both agreed on. The stability of such agreements is, however, dependent on the ongoing goodwill between the people who have agreed to share living space and of course such arrangements are notoriously liable to turn from mutual agreements to sources of conflict should the relationship itself deteriorate.

Tensions within the household sometimes result from someone spending what seems to others to be too long using the computer. As an evaluation, however, how long is 'too long' will depend on the activity. In the Richards household, for example, the only activities which are judged as being 'too long' are game-playing. While Maria Martinez feels that her husband Carlos spends too long using the computer sometimes, this tends to be because she feels that he is working too hard. Carlos protests that he is often unaware of how much time he has spent: 'I get very involved and then you don't notice the time.'

For Hilary Lacey and Margaret Paine, the amount of time Hilary spends on the computer has at times been a source of tension. Hilary has tended to modify her behaviour in order to keep the peace:

> It's very rare that it's not on for a day and if it's not it's only because I've been growled at, you know, 'Get away from that computer' type of thing . . . I get really pissed off . . . but I can hear what's being said though, you know, you can't sit there all the time I suppose, especially if you're in a relationship. (Hilary Lacey)

The tenor of these negotiations is also illustrated from Margaret's point of view. When she feels that Hilary has been spending too much time on the computer: 'I bring it to her attention and she says things like "I'm just going through another phase because I've just learnt how to use 'x' and then it will die down and I won't use it as much." She always has this "bear with me" sort of attitude' (Margaret Paine).

Conversely, however, Margaret suggests that Hilary would never feel that she herself was spending too much time using the computer: 'No. She would like me to use it more so that I wouldn't be complaining about her probably.' Hilary and Margaret each have their own computer, both of which are located together in the dining room (which has been converted for use as an office). They have at times discussed setting up one of the bedrooms as a study. Margaret is quite keen on this idea but Hilary has resisted it, since she feels that she would be able to get away with even less use of the computer if it were moved to a more isolated location: 'I figured that one out early in the piece, definitely,' she said, laughing.

Parental Management of Children's Use

In households with children, the parental role involves the management of children's access to household resources, and often also involves explicitly setting standards and regulations for behaviour. This may be manifested in household 'rules' (Wood and Beck 1994; Hawkins 1998), such as the common 'no food or drink around the computer'. Parents often also serve a gatekeeping function and resolve disputes around the computer, including conflicts over whose turn it is to use it. Domestic regulation of home computer use is often just one aspect of the regulation of media use in general: 'on an everyday level, in individual households, . . . expressed through decisions to include and exclude media content and to regulate within the household who watches what and who listens to and plays with and uses what' (Silverstone, Hirsch and Morley 1992: 20).

In some households, children must ask permission to use the computer. Whether or not they must get permission, or may just turn the computer on and use it if no-one else is using it, is generally related to whether the computer is seen as belonging to a particular household member or members, and whether it is seen as a 'work' or 'leisure' appliance. In the Talbot and Cooper households, for example, where the computer is used by the children for playing games (although the adult household members may use it for more 'serious' purposes), the children will simply turn the computer on and use it, if no-one is using it already. In the Turner household, by contrast, where the computer is strongly identified as a tool that Thomas Turner uses for his work (and which tends to be seen implicitly as more his than anyone else's), the children will tend to ask whether they can use the computer. Elizabeth Martin's granddaughter Sophie must also get permission in order to use the computer: 'Yes, she's got to ask and it depends what mood I'm in whether I let her. If she's done what she has to do. It's not just something I will let her just go use when she feels like it.'

Asking whether or not it is alright to use the computer may simply be a case of wanting to know if someone else is planning to use it, or it may be a matter of requesting permission to use the computer because it is seen as being someone's private property. Or it may be, as in the case of Jessica Lane and her son Michael, a question of whether this is an appropriate activity:

> He might ask if it's okay if he uses the computer but more around is it okay if he spends his time doing that rather than is it okay if I turn this machine on. He might also ask if it's okay if he can watch television or if it's okay if he goes and plays basketball or whatever.

While in most households there is an explicit or implicit rule that there should be no eating or drinking around the computer, the rule may be rather more relaxed for adults than for children. Many adults will say that they sometimes have a cup of coffee when using the computer. Sometimes the injunction about no food or drink around the computer is a specific instance of a general direction that food and drink are limited to particular areas of the house, as in the case of the Manfredotti household. In the Talbot household, too, 'Food doesn't go in the bedrooms anyway, but they used to get an apple and sit at the computer but that's banned now.'

In addition to the common rules about food and drink, in the Cooper household the children are required not to behave boisterously around the computer, since there was an incident in which a CD-ROM slipped down inside the computer. In the Fowler household, too, the general rules parallel those in many of the other households, and again there is a sense that the computer must be protected from children from outside the household who may not have the respect for it that the Fowler children have learned: 'Our next door neighbours don't have a computer and don't go near it. They're not allowed to touch the computer. If other children were to come along and knew how to treat the computer, then they would have access to it' (Doug Fowler).

In this, as in the Richards household, the music from computer games must be turned down, or the person who is playing must use headphones in order to respect the use of the shared space by other household members (Taachi 1998 also illustrates the essentially 'personal' nature of some kinds of sound in the domestic setting, with reference to radio). In households where the children are old enough to be left at home alone, the children are able to enjoy some of the rule-stretching privileges of their parents. As Hawkins has pointed out, such domestic regulations are always contingent and often contain an 'OK when Mum isn't home' clause (1998: 131). Patricia Collins's children arrive home before she does in the afternoons, and she is aware that they may behave differently when she is there than when she is not. Although homework should take higher priority than playing games, she is aware that when she is not there to enforce this priority:

> When I'm not here then much as I would love these nice little children
> to come home and put their school bags in their rooms and then sit down
> and do their homework, I know that doesn't happen. So I feel well let
> them have that relaxing time when I'm not here and then I can gently
> push them or even firmly push them when I get home.

Parents' regulation of their children's computer use tends to be based on and to fit in with their more general attitudes and control of the children's activities. Paul and Maureen Chapman regulate their children's use of such technologies as the television and the computer rather more strictly than the other parents in the study. As Maureen says, 'When they come home from school . . . sometimes they swim, but if they don't go swimming they might sit down and watch television for a while. I see that as part of their unwinding.' But the children are not allowed to watch television once they have had dinner:

> Because the TV's downstairs, which is a totally separate area . . . it's a deliberate act to go and watch TV . . . Our policy is that once the kids have had their dinner there's no television, and that would be the same for the computer too. If you want to entertain yourself you get a book out. And I think at this stage of their development that's the most important thing. (Paul Chapman)

The computer, as an information and communications medium like television, is 'doubly articulated': access must be regulated not just to the object itself, but also to the media to which it gives access (Morley and Silverstone 1990; Silverstone 1989). In general, parents monitor the types of games that their children are allowed to own and play at home in the same way that other media content is regulated. Most are aware of games (generally ones involving violence or adult themes) that are in circulation, and which may be owned by their children's friends, but apply moral or developmental arguments for not allowing their own children to play these games. The Richards would draw the line at games which involve simulated violence against human beings:

> They've borrowed their friends' Street Fighter II and Mortal Kombat . . . they've dabbled in them and been turned off them as well, so I'm glad about that, and if they were interested in buying them I would discourage them. A lot of the video games have shooting in them, or knocking things over . . . I guess where I draw the line is where you have simulated human violence against other humans. (Peter Richards)

Patricia Collins's thirteen-year-old son prefers 'gory' games, she says. Although she would prefer that he did not play these games, she says that they are not a cause for concern for her because they are not realistic. In fact, she is more concerned about violence on television than in computer games:

> It is a bit bloody but I think they've realized it's the pictures that are doing the moving around and not themselves. Apart from the soccer game where because they play soccer I think they see themselves in that a little more . . . Although I really would rather they didn't have some of those games. I think it's worse on television than some of the games on the computer. They're still like cartoons when they're on the computer, they're still not real.

In the Bartlett household the children's ages cover quite a wide range (ten to nineteen). Merilyn has asked the boys to remove games from the computer that she disapproved of, but some of the games she sees as acceptable for a teenager to play, but not for a ten-year-old. One of the older boys has bought a Second World War fighting game for himself, but:

> We sort of restrict that one for the ten-year-old because I wasn't really happy about it. They had 'Doom' on there and they had 'Wolfenstein', now I didn't have a problem with Wolfenstein at all but Doom just bothered me and I asked them to remove it. That was 'bluebeard' [pirated] stuff too. They were quite happy with that, they said, 'Oh yes, it is a bit.' It wasn't from the violence, there were just certain things on it, certain images on it I thought 'No they don't need that one.'

Although Merilyn does not have any problem with her children playing it, Wolfenstein is one game that many parents would not be happy with, judging from the statements of Peter Richards quoted above (and echoed by other parents in the study, such as Carlos Martinez) – it involves Nazi imagery and first person point of view violence against animated human characters.

Children are, however, expected to eventually have internalized these values for themselves, and to become autonomous in applying the correct moral values to their behaviour (Hawkins 1998). Parental regulation of computer game playing (as more generally of computer use) is therefore an integral part of the parental role in managing the children's upbringing. It is part and parcel of the necessity for providing the children with the cultural infrastructure for enabling them to take advantage of life opportunities and to move towards social independence. In the Turner household, as with the Bartletts, the parents' position is not so much one of imposing a regulation on the children, as that the children will themselves come to recognize that such games are 'not good for them'. As Sally Turner puts it: 'With Mortal Kombat, Jonathan knows that he doesn't feel good playing that game even though he might enjoy it very much to start with'.

The children in the Cooper household frequently swap games with their friends, but have developed a knowledge of which are the kinds of games they will be allowed to bring home. Although it seems that Sylvia knows that her children may have access to this material outside the home, she is confident that she has instilled in them the sense that such things are unacceptable materials to bring home: 'I don't encourage those sort of games, they know I don't so they don't bring them home.' The children's sense of which games will be acceptable has been built up partly by having seen the consequences of bringing home games which Sylvia found unacceptable: 'There's one where the man lashed out and chopped off another man's head. It's quite grotesque and we sort of talked about it . . . and they know now that with things like that I will complain about them.'

The Chapmans, whose restrictions on their children's television watching were described above, would apply the same strict standards to computer games: 'It would be not negotiable, they just wouldn't see the point. It's not something that we've ever had to deal with.' In general, then, children often have a clear sense of where the guidelines are within their own particular households, and tend to be aware of the kinds of behaviour their parents will find acceptable.

Conclusion

The household and its pattern of life – as an objectification – forms an enduring structure which is not just a material structure which the individual household members inhabit, but is also incorporated in them. It is also an embodied structure, inscribed on the household members themselves as dispositions (habitus) – routines of behaviour which do not have to be consciously reflected on to be effective. Individuals are supported by the structures of everyday domestic life, in that their needs for everyday living are generally met and they are enabled within it to enact their individual lives and to pursue their goals. But because of their objectivity these structures inevitably act also to constrain the actions of individuals. As forms of objectification, homes are (to recall Lukács' words) 'formations [which] get out of the control of man [sic] and become autonomous powers with an objectivity of their own' (1975: 82).

Domestic roles and patterns of interaction establish resistance to change, and novel activities and objects will tend to follow existing patterns (if a suitable model exists). It is true that, particularly over the long term, there is scope for challenges to existing structures. Some of these structures are so well entrenched that they might even be said to be foundational to the household's very existence. Structures based on age and gender (particularly these roles within traditional family structures, the roles of 'father' and 'mother' particularly) tend to be so pervasive to everyday domestic life that the introduction of a novel technology has little option but to accommodate to these patterns.

Is the Home Computer
Pink or Blue?

As we saw in the last chapter, a home computer is brought into a domestic situation structured through well-established age-based hierarchies, with pre-existing patterns of interaction and activity. Technologies are also involved in the negotiation and renegotiation of gendered relations between individuals within the household. New technologies arrive into an already gendered setting: with a gendered domestic division of labour, gender-specific household technologies, gendered access to the economic resources of the household, and gendered differences in the right to spare time within the routines of the household. New domestic technologies are capable, however, of both perpetuating and challenging existing roles, values and divisions within the household.

There is an extensive academic literature on the relationship between gender and technology, much of it written from a feminist perspective (see Frissen 1992 for a good overview of the issues and a comprehensive review of the literature on gender and new information and communications technologies). Technology has been characterized as a tool of both patriarchy and capitalism, benefiting the interests of men and enterprise by controlling women's work. It is suggested that domestic technology is generally designed by men and imposed on women, who are its main users and that domestic technology has, in general, simply 'reinforced the traditional sexual division of labour between husbands and wives and locked women more firmly into their traditional roles' (Wajcman 1991: 87). There is also considerable evidence to suggest that domestic technologies have been singularly unsuccessful in lightening the burden of women's domestic work, despite these technologies universally being promoted as labour-saving (Cockburn 1992; Cowan 1983).

157

As Kramarae points out, however, 'technological processes developed by men for men are nearly always interpreted by women in ways other than those intended by men' (1988: 2). While valuable in exposing the gendered nature of sociotechnical change, it is important not to portray power relations (as with other social relations) as mediated through technologies in simple, mechanical and deterministic ways.

Technologies may be gendered in their design and marketing and still be capable of being subverted through their creative adoption by women. This is made clear in Rakow's (1988) work on the history of the development of the telephone. The telephone had a paradoxical role in, on the one hand, facilitating the polarization of urban development into suburbs and central business districts, and on the other in helping to alleviate the ensuing isolation for women. The case of the mobile phone also illustrates the complexity with which technological innovations are incorporated into existing roles. While early adopters of the mobile phone tended to use it for business purposes, many women now carry a mobile phone for reasons of personal security and maintenance of contact with the family. This has resulted, according to Rakow and Navarro (1993), in an intrusion of domestic pressure on women into spaces and times where they were previously isolated from it. These authors have identified a trend towards what they call 'remote mothering', in which women exist in domestic and work modes simultaneously. The 'double shift' (in which working women perform a shift at home after their paid work shift) becomes a 'parallel shift'.

There is, then, a rather pessimistic view taken in the literature on gender and domestic technology of the potential of innovations for empowering and liberating women. While it is true that many women live in households with home computers they rarely have time to use, many of the women in this study feel that they have gained self-esteem through the acquisition of technical skills, and assign to the computer a role in maintaining control over their lives. New information technologies are not simply the oppressive tools of patriarchy as feared by some commentators; nor are they utopian instruments of potentiality, as others have uncritically welcomed them.

The Computer and the Role of Mother

It is often suggested that, while the domestic realm is a site of leisure for men, for women it is largely a site of work. As Gray points out in her study of women's use of home VCRs, it is easier for men to be able to 'switch off from the domestic environment and pursue their hobbies and leisure activities' (1992: 243) than it is for women. Women in Gray's study reported 'that they found it difficult, if not impossible, to justify taking time out to do something for themselves', and that if they did (particularly during the day) 'they were constantly haunted by the unfinished tasks with which they were surrounded' (243). This is substantiated by the women in the present study. Mothers, in particular, say that they do not have time to sit down at the computer, particularly when it comes to learning new skills. Women also spend much less time playing computer games than men or children. The women in the present study who do play games are generally the ones without children, although Merilyn Bartlett sometimes uses the computer as an escape from the family, which is assisted by the location of the computer in a family room physically separated from the house.

Gray (1992) investigated the gendering of household technologies by asking her study participants to code areas of the house and the items within it as 'pink' or 'blue'. Kitchens and irons were coded as pink, garages and power tools as blue. On the VCR the controls were generally lilac (play, stop, fast forward, rewind), but the timer switch and the remote control were most definitely blue. It seems clear that the home computer, like the VCR, is neither completely pink nor blue but is lilac in parts, blue or pink in others. It is clear, for example, that computer games are differentially coded. 'Fighting' games, such as Marathon and Doom are highly male-associated, while others, such as Tetris and Solitaire tend to be played by both male and female adults and children. As is frequently noted, however, there are very few computer games oriented towards women and girls (Kinder 1991; Cassell and Jenkins 1998).

Some of the gendered meanings of new technologies are translated from the technology's previously established business and educational settings. Wordprocessing, for example, is often a task delegated to female employees in the workplace. In what seems like a parallel trend, mothers and wives will often take on wordprocessing for other members of the family. As Sarah Richards explains, speaking of her fourteen-year-old son Matthew, 'I can do it much faster than he can. He'll load the dishwasher for me, and I do this for him'. Such processes of negotiation contribute to the construction and maintenance of the gendered social categories of the domestic environment.

New domestic technologies may perpetuate existing roles and values, or may provide a challenge to existing patterns. Particularly in households with children, the mother's role as nurturer, supporter and household manager tends to be perpetuated around the home computer

– as appreciative audience and settler of disputes, for example. Wheelock notes the contradiction that although wives may use the computer less than their husbands and be less interested in it, their traditional role may mean that they 'nevertheless take on a teaching and managing role with the new piece of technology' (1992: 109). Miller and Slater observed amongst Trinidadian couples based in the UK a tendency for the female of the household to act as a kind of social secretary for the family's Internet use. Much of the routine emailing was devolved onto women, even to the extent that they became the mediator for information between their husband and his family. Women were also seen to be assisting their husbands by searching for information. As these authors note, 'women might find the online experience of Internet use liberating, but there were clear constraints on their ability to translate this into offline changes in gender relations' (Miller and Slater 2000: 50).

The pressures to make technologies conform to existing domestic patterns of life, but also their capacity to be used to resist such pressures, are highlighted in Edna Mitchell's study of domestic video game playing. Half the mothers in this study had not attempted to play during the first six months after acquisition, and a further 20 per cent had tried but not continued. One mother who did not play often 'laughed about her own poor performance in comparison with the rest of the family' (1985: 124). She believed that her problem was poor coordination, but that she could become skilful if she played more. This woman's daughter described her as 'cute': 'Well, she's not real good, but she's cute. She's a good sport . . . she tries' (124). The aberrant behaviour of one mother in Mitchell's study, however, raises the possibility that these mothers are simply behaving in accordance with their accepted role within the family, as 'supporters' rather than competitors. This mother 'became an "addict"', monopolizing the video-game set and television bought for her two sons. After achieving the highest scores in the family at Pac-Man, the boys refused to play with her. Their comments reflect their attitude: 'We used to have time to talk and be a family, but now it's always Pac-Man,' suggesting that a mother can only be described as 'cute' while playing a video game as long as she does not become too good at it. This mother, recently divorced, believed that the compulsion 'grew from a desire to show herself and her sons that, as a woman, she too could master the games'. After several weeks of high scores, her interest flagged and life returned to 'normal' (125).

New domestic technologies are capable therefore of both perpetuating and challenging existing roles and values and divisions and hierarchies within the household based on gender and age. Silverstone, Hirsch and

Morley argue that, although the home computer may appear to be a threat to what is taken for granted in the routines of domestic life, 'this challenge is often thoroughly dealt with by the technology's incorporation into the moral economy of the household [and] it is the computer which is, as often as not, transformed by this incorporation, much more than the routines of the household' (1992: 20).

The sedentary nature of computing as an activity, and the need for uninterrupted time to concentrate on some types of computing task, contributes to making computer use difficult to combine with the mother's role where there are small children with frequent demands for attention and assistance. The mother's role as nurturer, supporter and domestic manager tends to be perpetuated around the home computer – as appreciative audience, solver of problems and settler of disputes. Often these mothers are themselves confident and competent computer users, particularly if they work outside the home in occupations which involve the use of information technology. 'I spend all day working on the computer, when I come home I want to do something different', says Sarah Richards, who works three days per week in an office which uses Apple Macintoshes.

Other mothers in my study speak of the difficulty of finding time to sit down at the computer, either to perform tasks they are already familiar with or to develop new skills (cf. Wheelock 1992: 108). Hayley Crowther, for example, refers to the computer as a 'when Jennifer is asleep' activity. The time available to be devoted to such activities is strictly limited, and this mother has higher priorities for these times, such as studying Japanese. Such women often end up feeling left behind by the rapidly developing skills of their husbands and children. The pattern of women's domestic activity – doing many things at the same time, but also 'sitting down' to do something as rare – is, of course, well established in the literature on television audiences (Morley 1995: 174).

For Maria Martinez, there are too many other demands on her time when she is at home (Maria, like Hayley Crowther, has a pre-school child at home), so her main computer use is outside the home, at the college where she is undertaking a course:

I don't find time to really start to discover things here, because there is just so much to do around the place. So I really prefer to go to college, because then you have to go there and sit down and do it. But if you're just at home it's harder, because you always will see something to do around.

Her husband had been telling her that this year should be easier for her, since her second-youngest child had started school: 'But it's not, because he [the youngest] is by himself here and he's after me all the time. So I can't do much, you see.'

Gender may also emerge as a factor in the kind of computer purchased. A computer is often a major expense for the household and must compete with other potential purchases for the allocation of scarce resources. There are often differences between household members in their support of the capital outlay involved in buying the computer. While economic theory tends to treat households as unitary wholes, they have internal gender- and age-based differentials in access to economic resources (Pahl 1990). The internal political dynamics of the household will determine when a computer is actually purchased and what kind is bought. It is often easier to justify the capital outlay when it can be seen as an investment for the future or a necessity, rather than simply as the purchase of a luxury good.

The traditional gender-based role configuration of many households tends to result in these economic considerations serving the interests of male householders and children at the expense of adult female household members. Kirkup (1992: 271) suggests that female hobbies are generally ones which need little capital outlay and have a useful end-product (and may be related to pre-industrial crafts), while male hobbies need a large capital outlay and produce little or no end-product, being done for the pleasure of the activity itself. In the Martinez household, where computing is very much an activity of the father, the computer is an up-to-date model and is an ongoing expense, regularly upgraded or traded up to the latest equipment when new models become available. Carlos's own computer is located in a room set aside as a study (this case is compared in chapter 10 with that of the Fowler household, in terms both of the computer's physical location and the father's role within the household). Chris Talbot, on the other hand, had always wanted a computer, but other priorities always intervened. Her husband, acknowledging her interest, one Christmas bought cheaply a discarded 286 IBM-compatible computer when his employer upgraded office equipment. The computer is located in their three-year-old daughter's bedroom, which means that there is never a convenient time for her to use it: either her children require her to be available in other parts of the house, or her daughter is asleep in the room. This family was planning to move to a bigger house in the near future, and Chris was hoping that she would then have a more convenient spot to locate the computer.

The mother's role within the household is often that of supporter and spectator, rather than participant. Patricia Collins is called on to be a spectator to her children's use of the computer: 'I do watch the children on occasions – they'll yell upstairs "Mum come and see this" and they've just discovered something new and I'll come and look at that.' The maternal role also involves taking on much of the responsibility for managing the domestic space, and for solving day-to-day problems. Sarah Richards often helps the children to find out how to do things on the family's Windows computer, even though she rarely uses it herself. She is able to draw on the general computer literacy and wordprocessing skills she has developed using a Macintosh at work to explore menu options, and is generally able to work out how to do something, even if she has not come across it before. The children are less likely to experiment to try to work something out:

> I just help the kids if they can't do something. Like today, Matthew said 'Can I change one word that I've put right through?' Like he'd put 'Director' and he wanted to put his name, so I showed him how to do that . . . I just go through the menus to see where it is.

Sarah rarely uses the family's home computer herself, however. Sarah's reasons for this are similar to those of Chris Talbot: both women work in offices where they use a computer all day, and say this means that when they get home they are no longer interested in using the computer. When they need to use the computer, to write a private letter for example, it is often easier to do it at work rather than at home:

> This one you have to set it up, get the kids out of the way, turn it on, get in whereas at work it's just all there. Type a letter, print it off and then it's done because you are in that computer mode whereas at home you have to switch over to it. Especially with the kids because they want to sit on you just to see what you're doing, and it's 'I want a go now'. It's actually quite hard for me to do anything like that at home. (Chris Talbot)

Although for many women their use of the home computer is shaped by the constraints of their domestic role, this does not necessarily mean that the computer cannot contribute to their sense of control over their life.

Taking Control of Domestic Technology

While many women find their domestic role limits the benefits they receive from home computer ownership, for many others a significant benefit in self-confidence and self-esteem stems from increasing computing skills. Surveys into gender differences in computer use have identified a 'we can, I can't' paradox – 'a tendency for females to be unsure of their own individual ability to use computers, but to feel that women as a group in general are as able as men in learning about computers' (Makrakis 1993: 191). This phenomenon means that, for many women, there is more at stake than there is for men in developing computer skills. There is uncertainty and lack of confidence to over- come, but there is also a very high potential gain in self-esteem when women successfully acquire mastery in computing, as an outcome of achieving something that one thought perhaps one could not do. Many women express surprise at finding themselves successful.

For Laura Manfredotti, as we saw, the purchase of a computer was instrumental in giving her control over her children's educational development, and she spoke of her sense of control as something she had struggled to achieve. Sarah Richards, who went back to work two years before our interview after sixteen years out of the workforce, found the experience of going back to work difficult, and likened it to stepping back into a previous, less experienced and competent, self:

> Oh, going back to work was just terribly hard. I hadn't worked in an office for sixteen years, and it's really strange. I think you have to go through it to understand it . . . but it's a really strange feeling, because you feel like the junior in the office again, because everything's changed so much . . . Like when you're at home with kids and you're working in school canteens and stuff like that you don't think of technology . . . like 'that's the old me'.

The extended self is constructed through activity and interaction in particular social and cultural contexts. If ontological security is primarily achieved in those particular environments of action with which we are familiar and comfortable, then being thrown back into an unfamiliar workplace environment engenders insecurity and discomfort. In Sarah's case, a familiarity with the technology, gained at home, was instru- mental in providing a handle on the new situation. An important part of Sarah's strategy for re-entering the workforce was the acquisition of computing skills. She says: 'There was nothing like this when I was at work, so I was really nervous about going back to work. I've been really surprised at how easy it's been . . . it's given me a great confidence boost . . . you realize that if you can master that then you can do anything.'

Helen Samuels is in her fifties and bought her own computer when she was made redundant from an educational administration position. She has been using computers since 1985, and in recent years was able to maintain home access to up-to-date computer technology through a series of laptops provided by her employer. She lives alone, and uses email to maintain a network of acquaintances all over the world. The most difficult aspect of being faced with redundancy, she says, was the prospect of losing her computer. Over a two-month period where she thought she was going to lose it, she stopped using the computer completely: 'For that interim period, where I thought I was going to lose my machine, I just gave up on everything . . . because I sort of felt that if you're too dependent on it the loss of it will be too great to bear.'

Helen is one of the many women who belie the generalization sometimes made that women are interested in computers as a means to an end, where it is men who are interested in computers as things in themselves. She, along with Claire Matheson, Hilary Lacey, Sue Kozlowski and other women in my study, would recognize Turkle's description of the attraction of computers to the (male) hobbyist as an aspect of their own interaction with the technology: a 'sense of engagement and energy . . . found primarily in the non-instrumental uses of the technology'. The appeal is 'intellectual, aesthetic, involved with the fun of . . . "cognitive play"' (1985: 184). Women do sometimes buy computers just because they want one to 'play' with, although they might not describe what they are doing by the use of that term.

Technology and Gender Beyond the Home

While home computers are implicated in gender-based roles and relationships within the household, it is also possible that information technology use at home may have effects on gender roles more broadly. Both Jessica Lane and Danielle Singleton felt that their development of computer skills had changed the way they saw themselves, in that this gave them a sense of a professional self:

> I probably see myself as more professional now than I did before . . . I think it is related to the computer because people comment on the professional look of my work and even my son is saying the same thing . . . To a certain extent it probably has changed the way I feel about myself in that way, in that professional sense. In a personal sense it's probably helped me feel more organized which has helped me feel better about myself. (Danielle Singleton)

For Jessica Lane, this has been more of a long-term progression:

> I think, because I've been involved with [computers] for the last twenty years it's more of a progression. It's a progression that I'm very pleased about and there are times that I feel triumphant, I mean like when I had to install a whole lot of lightning strike equipment on my own before Christmas. I actually did it and it all worked. That was a very much a sort of a personal triumph.

This contrasts with the role of information technology in the self-development of someone like Doug Fowler, whose current involvement in computing is a confirmation or reinforcement of how he always saw himself. Knowledge and skills in information technology seem like something he has a natural right to develop, and he has been prevented from developing them only by lack of access to economic resources. Many of the women in the study, on the other hand, were able to reflect on how the broader social structures of discourse and power were implicated in their own pursuit of such skills – both in terms of making these skills desirable and in the kinds of obstacles they might meet.

Some of them, for example, noted the importance of having a command of the 'jargon' in establishing authority in relation to technology, and that this is often something that men and boys have more familiarity with. Developing this command of the language is often therefore an important aspect of an evolving sense of empowerment around this technology. Gail Shaw, whose work involves contact with immigrant women with poor English language skills, feels that the 'digital divide' will continue to be a complex social issue, which improving access to the technology will only go some way towards addressing:

> I feel like, it's sold that there's a whole like subculture of people out there using the 'Net to provide information to people who are disempowered, or where voices aren't heard. But I don't have a sense of computers as being like that, I still have a sense that the people with access to computers are people with money and resources . . . And I don't have the sense of a computer or a new 'zine as being the way that [the women she works with] would actually network with each other or reduce their isolation.

A familiarity with the appropriate forms of discourse and practice in contemporary technological culture – competence in its spaces and times, to recall Glennie and Thrift's (1996) phrase – is most readily accessible to those with the social, economic and cultural resources to engage in them. A sense of alienation – the sense that these spaces and times do not belong to us and that they are not ours to enjoy – acts to discourage us from entering unfamiliar contexts and situations. As Gail says, 'like I'd never gone into a computer café, because I would feel like I didn't know what to do'. Overcoming this unfamiliarity, for Gail as for a number of the other women in the study, is expressly about wanting to understand and be involved in activities they see other people being involved in, particularly men and boys. 'I didn't want to not be able to understand what it is that people are doing. In fact, I think it was a lot to do with wanting to understand what boys were doing, I didn't want to be left behind with all that sort of stuff.'

Computing as social technology is not just about performing certain work or education related functions, but is also a means by which individuals and groups can be enabled to engage in economic, political and cultural life more broadly, as well as a technology for individual self-development and empowerment.

Conclusion

Computers are, in many ways, still designed and manufactured in ways that exclude or discourage women and girls. Parents complain of the difficulty of finding computer games suitable for their daughters, and powerful role models for women are less visible than the stereotyped gendered representations of the computer advertising. The existence of the 'we can, I can't' paradox suggests that the computational reticence described by Turkle (1988) might still be a problem for women: avoiding computers because they symbolize masculine values and ideals. Yet, certainly for some of the women in my study, the existence of these associations seems to be part of the attraction of the computer. By being a symbol of what a woman is not, the computer becomes a (personal at least) symbol of their resistance to cultural ideas of how women are supposed to be, and a source of empowerment, as we saw in the case of the mother in Mitchell's study. Mitchell also observed that although it was uncommon for mothers in her study to play video games, those who did often reported 'a sense of growing competence and pride in achievement' (1985: 132).

Both Helen Samuels and Sue Kozlowski report that their computer skills have had a profound empowering effect on their lives:

It has become a really powerful and yet almost invisible part of my life, in the sense that I do feel empowered by it, in that it helps me do what I do, but it also is empowering in that it ratifies my problem-solving skills always. That mastery, that 'Yes!' [Helen Samuels]

Coming from an electronic music background, I feel I've lived and breathed technology, and that I'm a product of it. It is empowering. Once it was mysterious, now there is no mystery, but the awe is still there. [Sue Kozlowski]

Van Zoonen proposes that gender should 'be conceived, not as a fixed property of individuals, but as part of the ongoing disciplinary process by which subjects are constituted, often in paradoxical ways' (1992: 20). Similarly, Cockburn stresses the relationality of gender: 'gender identity is what people do, think and say about material and immaterial things *in relation to* other people conceived of as sexed' (1992: 40). I am also arguing in this book that the interactions between people and technological and other objects should be viewed relationally, and it is clear that the gendered associations of objects are an intrinsic aspect of this relationality. The flexibility of computer technology, then, via its incorporation into the domestic sphere, may facilitate a reshaping of the cultural associations of gender and information technology (Berg 1994). Claire Matheson expresses satisfaction in a tone of wry amusement at 'not being a typical grandma'. Helen Samuels explicitly allies her computing activities with her ability to assert that she 'doesn't fit any of the stereotypes'. Yet it is the lack of clear public visibility of women such as these – their lack of representation in widely available forms of objectification – that allows the stereotypes to be perpetuated, and allows other women to be unsure of their technological ability and surprised at their eventual success.

The Domestic Ecology
of Objects

It was suggested in chapter 2 that the physical presence of material objects may allow them to act as a kind of personal psychic scaffolding. Home, in particular, is a place in which the familiarity and continuity of the material environment of objects provides us with a space of 'maximal practical know-how: knowing what everything is for and when it ought to be used' (Hage 1997: 102). It is a place of embodied familiarity, where we hardly need to wake up in the middle of the night to be able to make our way to the bathroom or the fridge. For the extended self, as a self-in-relation to the objects by which it is constituted, the objects of home clearly form a privileged domain. As we have seen, however, the extended self does not simply map onto such assemblages of objects, but is constructed dynamically in interaction with them. Neither are the objects themselves disposed in static arrangements, but in their meanings and uses they are constituted by their incorporation into everyday praxis.

The artist and designer Douglas Fitch (1995) describes how contemplating Pompeii led him to think of furniture as the space solidified around human activities:

> Once, a long time ago, a mountain exploded near Pompeii and in a single moment, everything that had been *between* suddenly *became*. All that space between people, the room in their rooms – even the space inside their mouths – was filled up with lava, and what had been merely invisible space became object . . . There are lessons from Pompeii about taking space for granted. After seeing it, I started to think about furniture as being the space solidified around human activities. The chair, for example, I suddenly saw as the result of making the space around a sitter solid. (50)

Human activity, however, is just that – it is *activity*. Even when seated we frequently change position in order to remain comfortable: the most comfortable chairs and sofas often seem to be the ones which will support a range of different positions. When Mount Vesuvius erupted and Pompeii's space solidified, all activity immediately ceased.

Furniture is therefore not simply the space solidified around human activities, but bears a more complex relation to those activities, in which the space is not a passive stage, but itself preserves the potential for interaction and particularly for flexibility in interaction. When the space between subject and object itself is filled, there can be no activity, no interaction: the existence of the space between objects (and humans and objects) establishes a productive relation between them and allows them to interact. Spatial organization is itself a modality of objectification:

> Culturally and socially, space is never simply the inert background of our material existence. It is a key aspect of how societies and cultures are constituted in the real world, and, through this constitution, structured for us as 'objective' realities. (Hillier 1996: 29)

Furniture as Solidified Space

Fitch also describes the task of assembling the home by bringing together objects – the bricolage of home-building – when moving into a new apartment:

> When I relocated to a two-bedroom apartment in New York City, it took me an entire year to completely move in, for various reasons. But that extended time afforded me the opportunity to explore my relationship to the space I was moving into and to study, over time, the elements I was adding. Its existing contents – appliances, cabinets, walls, doors, room dividers, cable TV hookups – seemed like a bunch of large found objects with which I would assemble a new way of life. The challenge was in combining the existing components – detritus of previous human/object interrelationships – with new ones, including myself and a roommate. (50)

A single object, such as a home computer, needs such complex collaborations of other objects within the domestic space in order to function properly within the domestic pattern of life.

In constructing a personal 'living appliance', the components we use, as we saw above, may be more or less materially (and symbolically) resistant to adaptation. The fabric of the building itself provides little scope (in the short-term) for change, although there will be the choice of allocation of rooms to functions. New houses, for example, are frequently now built with a room designated as a 'study' or home office, while older housing does not have such spaces as formally designated, but may have other spaces (such as bedrooms) which can be allocated to this purpose. Much of the adaptation of these spaces is performed through locating furniture within them, as a means of further defining the proper use of the space and supporting those functions within the space. Indeed, in the French language the terms *mobilier* (furniture) and *immobilier* (real estate) give this sense of the home as constructed from both movable and immovable elements.

If we may think of the home computer as a kind of domestic appliance, then might we not also think of such organizations of domestic objects as having an appliance-like character? Having assembled a personal domestic environment for ourselves, it must function effectively as the locus of the practices of our everyday living, as a 'machine for living' in Le Corbusier's famous phrase. For Le Corbusier, the home as a machine for living would be an engineered, hygienic and mechanically efficient space for living, in which every element has its correct place, in tune with the advances in technology and manufacturing processes (such as the theories of F.W. Taylor) of the twentieth century. In this way it would resemble other products of industry such as ocean liners, motor cars and aeroplanes (Curtis 1986). Most importantly, such housing could be mass-produced, and indeed would provide mass-housing, in planned urban communities.

However, the image of the domestic environment as a DIY bricolage of objects found at hand in the cultural environment is rather different from the one that the father of Modernist architecture envisaged in using this phrase. The term bricolage (Lévi-Strauss 1966: 16–33) has gained broad currency to refer to cultural processes which involve creative symbolic combination and recombination. This is also the sense in which the term is used within this book, but here the usage is particularly apt, since in common French usage bricolage is used to refer to do-it-yourself construction, as opposed to more professional or engineered forms of construction. This is precisely the distinction made here between the home as a 'machine for living' which is a bricolage construction of its inhabitants, and not as an engineered product of large-scale manufacturing processes.

The home-building practices of contemporary western householders involve the translation of symbolic and material goods originating in large-scale social processes, particularly those of mass consumption, into the concrete and particular contexts of everyday domestic life. Home-building is not just, however, about the management of the affective and social relationships of home, but is also a material practice by which the physical environment of home is assembled. The process of home-building is not one in which the home is manufactured and then lived in, but its construction is more like that of the bird's nest described by Michelet in chapter 1: although the materials from which it is built are brought into it from outside, the home is 'modeled by fine touches', and is, in the final analysis, 'a house built by and for the body . . . in an intimacy that works physically'.

Figure 9 shows the 'computer room' in Sue Kozlowski and Phillip Healey's two-bedroom apartment, which contains their four networked computers (three PCs and one Sun Sparcstation). The objects in this room – furniture, the computers themselves, and ancillary objects such as the rubbish bin, the empty coffee cup, and the large quantities of books, papers and disks – seem to form the space into a 'machine for living'. While many home offices might be thought of more function-ally as 'machines for working', this one is a space for performing a range

Figure 9 Sue Kozlowski and Phillip Healey's 'technological cocoon': four computers set up in one of the bedrooms of their two-bedroom unit.

of kinds of activities, and not just for working. The couple can 'sit down together here, chat to each other, be doing different things at the same time': the chair on the right of the image is Sue's, while the workstation on the left is Phillip's.

Sue and Phillip spend a lot of their time at home in this room, much more, they say, than they spend in the living area of their apartment. Indeed, the living area looks as if they have never really finished moving in. A number of framed art-works lean against the walls, because they have never 'got around to putting them up'. The living area is likely to stay this way, since Sue and Phillip are planning to move again, partly because they would like a bigger space for the computers, and so that they can also set up Sue's electronic music equipment in the same space. The computers are used extensively for communication (email, news-group reading and posting, browsing the Internet and publishing web pages), for experimentation and learning about the technology.

Indeed, this room seems to operate for this couple as a kind of technological cocoon. Within it, although their embodied selves are physically located there, the technologies within the room give them a two-way window to the external world, particularly when their local computer network is connected to the Internet (at the time of the study they were thinking of putting in a second phone line so that they could stay connected continuously). The poster on the door says 'A World of Information': it is on the outside of the door, so that when the door is closed it seems to indicate both the room's contents and its purpose. The material objects in this room, then, structure a space for the bodies of the home's inhabitants within which the patterns of their everyday living can be enacted.

Constructing the home as inhabited space requires more than the provision of the material infrastructure as an engineered, designed space for living. As we saw in the discussion of objectification in chapter 2, it is the case with all mass-manufactured objects that they are taken up by individuals who reshape and adapt them to their own purposes. In doing so, each individual attempts to build for themselves a personal-ized place in the world, through adapting (or adapting to) those materials which are found at hand in the cultural environment.

Patterns of computer use, as we have seen in previous chapters, are constructed in complex ways. They do not emerge straightforwardly as a natural consequence of how its designers anticipate it will be used. Fundamentally, technologies are embedded within and in an essential way constituted by particular sets of human praxis. Any technology takes on its meanings and uses from its cultural context and environment of use, and does not necessarily take on the same roles when relocated to another cultural context (Ihde 1993).

Indeed, Ihde insists that technologies are fundamentally relational. Human–technology pairings must be considered as the units of analysis: one must speak therefore of 'a human-technology relation, rather than abstractly conceiving of them as mere objects' (1993: 34). Technologies in use are always contextual and relational, 'they "withdraw" in use and become partially transparent means by which humans relate to an environment' (1993: 108). Ihde uses the term 'technical' to refer to the physical characteristics of a technological artefact, essentially the material condition for its functional effectiveness. Functionality is not fixed once and for all by these characteristics – which 'may be designed or they may be discovered' (73) – there is the intrinsic possibility of flexibility in use. A technology is therefore, perhaps, not so much a particular kind or class of artefact, to be contrasted with objects which are not technologies. On the contrary, any artefact in use – that is, involved in human–artefact interaction – has a technological aspect.

This tool-like functionality – how the object performs the physical/material effects that it does in our interaction with it – is an aspect of many everyday objects, including such things as tables, chairs, cups, blankets and so on. The physical/material characteristics of an object do, however, predispose it to perform certain kinds of function (that is, to be involved in certain kinds of praxis): any large flat-topped surface within a range of suitable heights is potentially a table, for example. To suggest a more sophisticated example, the magnetic metal door of the contemporary fridge predisposes its use as a notice board and display area. This use, although peripheral to the fridge's main purpose of food storage, is enhanced by its role as a centre which is visited frequently by household members. As this example demonstrates, an object's physical characteristics may result in its being used in ways unforeseen by its designers, (although the proliferation of fridge magnets indicates that such successes tend not to go unnoticed for long). This example also clearly shows, however, that domestic objects are not used in isolation but exist as elements in the household's total assemblage of artefacts and technologies, and are built into its patterns of activity and interaction – its 'pattern of life', as has been stressed throughout this book. As Ihde suggests, 'technologies in ensemble are probably more like cultures than like tools' (1993: 42), and therefore how each element is used must be seen in the context of how this totality operates.

Sue Kozlowski and Phillip Healey's computer room is therefore a 'machine for living' in this profound sense. The material ensemble of the room – both the mundane elements like the desks and chairs and the technological ones like the computers and the room's reticulation into utility networks (telephone, electricity) – structures a space for the body of its inhabitants, which supports the praxis of their living in the room. Such technological ensembles are surely the contemporary equivalents of the earliest of human inventions, shelter and storage technologies (Sofia 1995).

As we have seen, the home computer adds certain types of functionality to the domestic ensemble. In examining the functionality of the home computer, then, and in investigating which alternative household arrangements it may be introducing or displacing, it is necessary to think outside the narrow confines of the obvious communication and information technologies which are generally indicated in discussions of technological convergence (television, telephone and VCR). The ways in which the physical space and objects of the household functions as a 'machine for living' adapts to the changing functionality of the collection of objects within it (the setting aside of rooms as home offices, for example, and the appropriation by home computers of other pieces of furniture such as desks and chairs). The functionality of any one object is thus dependent on the supporting functionality of a large range of other objects, and other uses of a room will shape how the object is used.

Computers in Relation to Other Household Objects

Computers tend to be large, fairly immobile objects, and generally have a defined physical place within the household. The allocation of household space, and its segregation into rooms with different purposes is considered in the next chapter. In general, however, the disposition of the computer within the home also involves the use of furniture such as desks and chairs at least, and often also such objects as filing cabinets, bookcases, books and large numbers of small objects such as papers and disks. The computer cannot therefore be seen simply as an independent object within the home, but is one which forms one node in a network of objects which are disposed within the household in relation to each other. It is just one element in the total ensemble of domestic objects.

Further, it is important to emphasize that the ensemble of domestic objects is not a static disposition of objects, but is one which is dynamic and active. Small portable objects, in particular, can be highly mobile, such as computer disks which travel between the home and work. The movement of small objects traces the locus of activity within the space of the household. Children's toys, for example, at times appear to adults to move around the home without human intervention. Household 'mess', which must be actively managed as a distinct domestic activity, is a reflection of and necessary concomitant to this mobility.

In relation to the home computer, for example, pieces of paper are often mediators of an activity which is partly computer-based: John Powell keeps bank statements in two sheaves held together with bulldog-clips which hang on hooks on either side of the window frame. On one side are the ones which are still to be input into his financial accounting program and on the other are the ones which have already been entered. The movement of pieces of paper between one sheaf and the other traces the progress of the activity of maintaining his financial records on the computer (Pellegram 1998 analyses paper as material culture in an office environment). Many of the images of home computers which have been reproduced in this book clearly show that the computer, rather than being an object disposed statically within the home, is the centre of many intersecting domains of activity which involve the movement of people as well as other objects.

Computers 'Collaborating' with Other Objects

Jim Christou is a 25-year-old computer programmer who has two self-contained rooms (a sitting room/study and a bedroom) within his parents' house. He spends most of his time at home here, where he has had cable television installed for his own use (his parents and sister were not interested in it). Jim tends to have the television on most of the time, and has his sitting room set up in such a way that he can see the television easily when he is using the computer:

> Like at the moment, when the cricket's on and I'm watching that, you don't really want to watch it for seven hours straight, so I'd have it on and every now and then you'd hear something and turn away from the computer. If I'm watching like a series or a show or something then I'll leave the computer, go and watch, then come back to it.

In households with both a computer and a dedicated games machine, game-playing activity can be distributed between the two. The games machine may be used when someone is already using the computer (as we saw in the case of the Collins household, shown in figure 8), or the reverse may take place. In some households the computer becomes redefined as for 'serious' use, rather than for playing games. In the

Figure 10 Charlotte Thompson's computer. Computers are often surrounded by other 'collaborating' objects such as furniture and small moveable objects like books, disks and pieces of paper.

Manfredotti household, for example, the children have become bored with the games on the computer, and tend to use the Nintendo for playing games instead. While there is often, then, a complementarity between the role of the home computer and dedicated electronic games machines, there is also complementarity of the computer's relationship with other kinds of objects.

Some of the householders in the study are very aware of the ergonomics of computer workstation set up, both through employment experience, but also through the marketing of specialized computer furniture such as adjustable desks and chairs and accessories such as wrist pads and anti-glare screens. Although Hilary Lacey, for example, is generally concerned to minimize the cost of her computer, she has invested money in a good keyboard and is aware of the ergonomics of her computer set up, such as having the monitor at the right height. Jim

Christou is a member of his workplace occupational health and safety committee, and has brought some of the work-based principles of ergonomics to his home set up:

> I've got pretty much an ergonomic chair, but the computer desk is sorely needed, I've just got a flat desk at the moment for the Macintosh. . . I'm considering getting some other ergonomic furniture. I slouch a lot. I do stretch and stuff, and I've got computer glasses that I don't always use, but I do try to use them. And I try to look away a lot and blink and that.

Charlotte Thompson also makes an effort to apply ergonomic principles to her workstation, although she does this by bringing together items she finds around the house, rather than by acquiring specialized furniture: 'Even if I haven't got a typist chair – like that I have at work – then I am quite conscious at least of getting it at the right height for my eye level. . . I do find the right chair in the house and usually set things up on telephone books to get the right height.'

Many of the study participants had adapted existing furniture within their homes to accommodate their computer. Laurence Harrison, however, had constructed specialized built-in furniture for the computers, modifying a built-in wardrobe by taking off the doors and building in a desktop and wall shelving (figure 11).

Danielle Singleton had bought specialized computer covers to protect her computer, but at the time I interviewed her had fallen out of the habit of putting them on the computer when it was not in use, although at one stage she says that she had been quite fastidious about this. The interplay of convenience and comfort in the emergence of habits and routines is clear here, as it was in the case of Hayley Crowther's routine of studying when her daughter was sleeping, rather than using the computer.

Other participants use a variety of methods to either protect the computer or appropriate it visually and make it comply more closely with the aesthetic style of their household. Regine Vassallo drapes a crochet shawl over her computer, because 'it gets really dusty', she says. Both Ann Harrison and Gail Shaw have themselves made covers for the computer in their household, which in both cases was a kind of gift or domestic craft offering for their partner. Laurence had asked Ann to make the cover for the Commodore (shown on the left in figure 11), when it was still a 'new toy', although this request was also justified by the original location of the computer in their previous house, in a garage which could be dirty. Gail Shaw made curtains for her partner

Figure 11 The Harrisons' computers. Ann Harrison made covers for the Commodore when it was still a 'new toy'. Laurence Harrison has converted a built-in wardrobe into a computer workstation.

Felicity's room, and made a computer cover to match from the left-over fabric:

> A small home-maker gesture. I made her curtains for that room. Partly because I was exasperated with what she was using, and partly because I thought she'd really like some nice curtains. And I'd never tell her how much the fabric cost . . . And I thought out of the leftover bits, a cover for the computer would be really good.

Although such collaborations between domestic objects as have been described tend to have a utilitarian justification, it is not uncommon for people to decorate their computers with objects in a manner which seems more aesthetic or ironic than functional. Both the Chapman household and Margaret Paine have teddy bears on their computers as decoration:

I've got a little teddy bear on the top . . . A friend gave it to me as a gift and I sat it on top of my computer and then after a while I thought 'I like that there.' It's like a little friend sitting there looking at me and I've kept it there and I know it annoys the shit out of Hilary. She always says 'What's that teddy bear doing there?' It's really tiny and I just say 'Tess gave me that.' She says 'Yes?' I think it's fallen off once and she kind of put it on the table and I put it back on the computer. That's where I want it to be. (Margaret Paine)

The Chapman's computer is shown in Figure 12. This computer is located in the bedroom of the Chapman's eldest son, who is a university student. This computer is rarely used, however: as is clear from the photograph, the computer was unplugged at the time of the interview.

Marjorie Brennan keeps a clear white crystal on the top of her computer. This item was also given to her by a friend as a gift, and is said to bring 'clarity of thought'. Marjorie does not subscribe to a belief in the potency of such crystals herself, but thought that the top of the computer would be a suitable spot to place the crystal. (Although she was not sure whether by being there it symbolized her own clarity of thought or that of the computer.)

Figure 12 The Chapmans' computer had a teddy bear resting on the keyboard on the day of the interview (note also that this computer is unplugged).

For Ruth Bourke aesthetics were an important element in the kind of computer she bought. She likes the compact 'look' of the portable Macintosh Classic, and also the fact that the computer is small enough that the desk can also be used to do other work: 'I just like the idea that it is small and it is compact and it doesn't dominate a room. You can shove it to the back of the desk and you can do something in front of it.'

For Margaret Paine, the look of the area the computer is in is also important: 'I just hate to think what it would look like without the proper computer tower that I've got . . . We've got a black filing cabinet which is between the two computers and we've got a black dining room table, so all charcoal and black matches.'

For Jessica Lane, whose computer is located in her main living space, the computer's styling offends her general sense of how things should look:

> I don't find it aesthetically pleasing in the lounge room but that's where it is. And I've no longer got it on the workstation so it's not ergonomically set up because I do have a fairly strong sense of aesthetics so I've got it on the nice old wooden table in the lounge room and the chair that I sit on is a nice old wooden swivel chair. I have difficulty in my house – I find it easier to make things look nice than to actually make things comfortable. I can't make things comfortable but I can make them look right. So that's the way the computer's set up.

On the other hand, when Jessica's computer was in the study, it did not matter as much what it looked like: 'whereas when it was in the study it was fine, and totally ergonomic, and I wasn't looking at it all the time, purely functional'. Jessica would ideally like to be able to hide her computer away inside a piece of furniture which corresponds to a different aesthetic to the contemporary functionality of the computer's design:

> I would prefer it to be something that I could put in a beautiful antique wooden cupboard that would open up into an ergonomic work station when I wanted to use it, and then it could be closed away when I wasn't using it . . . If one had the money you could have it made up but I'm limited by finances. If I had the money I could probably find a nice wooden cabinet and have it adapted or whatever, or specially made so that I could have that but I can't even afford to have the actual telephone point moved.

Incorporating the computer visually into the home environment is thus an important aspect of the domestication of the technology for many householders, and the aesthetic is a further dimension of the household's appropriation of the object. The appropriation of the object is not, however, only attributable to the human householders: as these examples make clear, the computer is also capable of appropriating other household objects to itself.

Indeed, to some extent, household objects are also able to appropriate their owners. Claire Matheson, for example, has five pairs of glasses, which are disposed around the house and used for different purposes:

> One very rarely gets used, which is that pair over there, which are just for looking at that screen [the 386] and they don't do anything else. If I'm typing in the database thing then I use these [bifocals which are around her neck, on a glasses 'chain'] so that I can see the screen through the top, and I can read my information here. Where that one there [the 486] is at a different distance, and I use my music glasses for that one. And I have one pair of music glasses for the computer, and one pair of music glasses out near the piano, so that I'm not racing from one end of the house to the other, which is a nuisance, and to me it was worth having an extra pair of glasses.

Claire's fifth pair of glasses are her reading glasses. This particular ensemble of objects and their owner is an example of the technological phenomenon of 'prescription': the need for us as human beings to behave in certain ways, because of the functions that have been built into the objects we use. In the strand of the literature on the sociology of technology which is known as actor network theory, the notion of 'actor network' is adopted as a heuristic, and the functionality of non-human artefacts is based on the delegation of human capacity for action (Akrich and Latour 1992). Having delegated potential human action to a non-human actor, however, there is often a trade-off in that the lack of flexibility in the behaviour of non-human as compared to human actors is that these artefacts often impose behaviour back onto humans (referred to as prescription). These prescriptions incorporate assumptions about the characteristics and behaviour of the human user, which complement those of the technological artefact. Users who do not display these characteristics may effectively be discriminated against by the technology (as is the case for automatic doors, which will often not open for children or for people who approach them too quickly).

Claire's need to have the right glasses available at the right time means that, although she herself has organized her domestic space in this way, her everyday praxis must now fit in with the structure she has created:

> If one is missing, I miss it dreadfully. I couldn't find these [the ones she is wearing around her neck] the other day, and half of me was thinking at that stage 'I don't think I'll get these again'. But when I couldn't find them I missed them, because I couldn't do what I wanted to do, which was putting the database in. And I had to put one of my reading glasses up to read the stuff, and then put those ones on [the computer/music glasses] so that I could see what was happening on the screen. It was a real nuisance.

The relationship between the computer and other household objects is also illustrated by competition, rather than collaboration, between the computer and other objects for their use in activities.

Computers 'Competing' with Other Objects

A number of authors have reported that heavy computer use tends to result in less watching of television (Wheelock 1992). Among the participants in the current study, television was one activity which was said to have been displaced by computer use (although, as we saw above, some people are able to use the computer and watch or listen to television at the same time). However, a number of other kinds of activity were also mentioned.

Margaret Paine, for example, has noticed that since she bought the computer her habit of writing a daily diary has fallen off:

> I've always been fanatical about writing a daily diary. And, like, I've got diaries from the last seven or eight years that I've lived in Australia and I've got each year's diary. Since I've bought the computer I'm not writing in my diaries and I feel really heartbroken about that because it's been really important for me to keep that daily diary and I can time it as to when I got the computer to when there's slowing down in my writing habits . . . I do it much less frequently.

Friends have suggested to her that she should write the diary on the computer instead, but Margaret feels that this is not personal enough: 'My handwriting in my special diary with my special leather cover is much more personal.' The transition from handwriting to computer writing involves much more, then, than simply switching from one medium to the other. The physical praxis of handwriting engages with objects which have particular tactile qualities – the look, feel and smell of a leather cover, with their associations of luxury and history – which contrast markedly with those of the computer and its connotations of contemporary professional life.

If, as was suggested in chapter 2, the presence of material objects in our environment acts at a level below that of consciousness to provide us with a kind of psychic scaffolding, and within which what I have referred to as a kind of cultural proprioception is enabled, then such changes in technology may have profound effects on the self in relation to writing. Other forms of activity with a practical outcome are also clearly affected: a number of study participants also commented on how the computer seemed to displace craft activities, such as knitting, needlework and sewing, or the playing of musical instruments. It might be suggested, therefore, that in our 'living with things' (Dant 1999) in the contemporary world, our interactions with the materials and objects we are surrounded by is increasingly becoming technologically mediated, even within the intimate locale of the domestic sphere.

Some formerly quite common domestic objects have been supplanted by the arrival of the computer. Many of the study participants had typewriters before they had computers, and Jim Christou's sister does not have a computer but does have a typewriter. As Janet Fuller puts it, there's no need for a typewriter when one has a computer: 'I have an old typewriter and it's always kind of handy to have a typewriter or now it's like a computer because it's better than a typewriter.' Ruth Bourke gave her typewriter away once she got her computer. She feels that the computer has not, however, simply taken the typewriter's place, but has given her additional possibilities and made it possible for her to start a university course, which she does not feel she would have been able to do with just the typewriter.

John Powell, in talking about whether or not to use the computer for some kinds of tasks or to do them the 'manual' way, compares the issue to that of whether or not to grate cheese in the food processor:

> I sort of think of the computer a bit like I think of this thing [the food processor]. You know it can do all these sort of things, you know . . . you can grate cheese with it, but is it actually easier to sort of take this out, put in the cheese grating appliance, plug it in, grate the cheese then take this off and wash it, or would it be easier to get the grater out and just grate the cheese?

In a similar vein, Elizabeth Martin speculates on whether it is worth starting the computer up to look something up on the CD-ROM encyclopaedia:

We actually do use it on occasion for her homework. It's like 'we'll just get the encyclopaedia and look it up'. But it takes such a long time to do that sometimes, I've got to turn it on and wait until it comes up, put the CD in just to get this one bit of information and then turn it off and I'm just wondering whether it's really worth the effort.

In many households there is a sense that both the computer and dedicated electronic games machines (such as Nintendo and Sega equipment) have displaced more traditional gaming methods, such as card and board games. The Cooper household has always had a 'culture' of playing games, but is finding that the computer has displaced some of this activity:

We have always had that culture of playing games, cards or whatever. That's how I grew up. Say, like every Sunday we do a quiz that's in the paper. That's like a little thing that I did with my family and we do it now. Someone comes and they'll say 'Have you done the quiz yet?' and so I think that when we come together often it's expected that some sort of game follows. (Sylvia Cooper)

Although they do still play card and board games, particularly when the family gets together, Sylvia feels that their use of their Sega game system is an extension of this culture of communal game-playing within the family. Indeed, it has to some extent taken the place of the non-electronic types of game. In this as in many of the study households, computer or electronic game-playing is a common joint activity, either for children playing together, children playing with an adult, or adults playing together. In the Cooper household, while the children tend to prefer to play on the computer, their parents will frequently play together on the Sega:

We play Columns on the Sega and the kids play on the computer usually. We have competitions. To see who's going to make the cup of tea and things like that . . . We probably would do it at least a couple of times a week. Of a night, usually when the kids have gone to bed. (Sylvia Cooper)

This behaviour appears not to be unusual. Peter and Sarah Richards report that when they first bought an Atari games machine for their children, they themselves 'used to sit up until midnight playing it'. Perhaps the willingness to be engaged in such 'playful' pursuits is part of the constitution of the relationship of these couples.

In the Collins household, although both a computer and a games machine are owned, the computer is preferred by the children, so it tends to be a case of whoever gets to the computer first plays on that, while the other takes a turn on the Nintendo. Both the computer and the Nintendo are located downstairs from the main part of the house, in a family room which was built onto the house a couple of years before. Patricia Collins feels that the Nintendo does not get as much use as it did before the computer came into the household. Patricia feels that her son's level of use of the computer or the video games machine, particularly as a joint activity with his friends, is also related to the age group he is moving into:

> It's got a bit to do with him getting older as well. Once upon a time they would play cricket up on the road perhaps even go out and throw balls to each other. There's not much of that happening now. I don't think that he would do that now anyway, even if the computer wasn't there. I think the Nintendo would get more use if the computer wasn't there.

In the Bartlett household, where there are four sons aged between ten and nineteen, games machines also take up some of the overflow of game-playing from the computer:

> We do have the old Atari system, with joystick thing plugged into the television and they've got Gameboys and things like that. If it's school holidays they'll alternate [between games machines and the computer] and if I drag the Atari stuff out and say here it is stick it on, they'll play that. The Gameboy is used constantly or not at all – if it happens to be in the line of fire they'll grab it to play. (Merilyn Bartlett)

If the computer may be seen to be both collaborating and competing with other household objects, we must also consider the extent to which the computer may be viewed as a space containing other 'objects' such as software and electronic documents, rather than a simple object. As a domestic space, the computer itself must be actively managed and kept organized.

Computer 'Housekeeping'

In most households, computer 'housekeeping' tasks, such as backing up important files or keeping the hard drive organized and tidy, are taken on by one person in particular. In the households where there is one person who has a clear proprietorship over the computer it tends to be this person who undertakes housekeeping tasks associated with the computer. In the Turner household, for example, although the computer 'technically' belongs to the family as a whole, in practice Thomas Turner uses it most and has exerted proprietoriality over the computer. Thomas is also the one who keeps the hard drive organized. Each member of the family has their own folder:

> If you open the computer it's got the hard disk. You open the hard disk it's got 'Applications' for the software, then it's got 'Users' and then you click on 'Users' and it's got 'Jonathan', 'Michael', 'Thomas', 'Sally', and then within mine it's got other folders, 'Tax', and 'Current Jobs' and all this sort of stuff and then 'Masters'. So yes, so things are organized. (Thomas Turner)

In the Martinez household, Carlos and his eldest son do the computer housekeeping together:

> Now and then I check that everything seems to be OK and sometimes we'll get together [with Jonathan], and that is one thing that we do together is clean up the drive together. And before we do the defragmentation we'll say 'Get rid of this, this. I like it but I'm not using it' and so on. (Carlos Martinez)

Defragmenting the hard drive is a procedure that most householders would not undertake as part of their routine maintenance of the computer. Over a period of time, through successive deleting and overwriting of files on the hard drive, the information can become inefficiently stored and defragmenting the disk rearranges the information so that it can be read efficiently by the computer, resulting in some performance improvement. Making backups of the information on the computer is another kind of 'housekeeping' task, and households vary in the degree to which they do this. In the Cooper household, there is no internal organization to the computer, all the files are in together, and individuals are expected to take care of backing up their own files if they want to make sure they are kept.

While for many computer users their housekeeping of the computer's internal space reflects more general domestic patterns, Thomas Turner feels that it's possible to be more organized within the virtual space of the computer than it is in 'real' life, because the computer forces a choice about where a file will be located:

> I'm very lazy when it comes to organizing things but I find I'm really organized on a computer. And the thing I like about the computer is that you can open all these things out and then you just click on them and they all close and then you switch the computer off and when you come back to it you know it's all there. Whereas with papers, it's all over the place and I hate it.

In the Richards household, it is Peter who has oversight of the information on the hard disk. Each of the children has their own floppy disk on which they store their own data, and for which they are responsible themselves: 'I make sure that things go into folders on the hard disk. The children do all their own work on floppy disks.' If one of the children leaves something on the hard disk, Peter puts it onto their disk for them. The activity of keeping the computer organized is thus similar to that of other household space, where some members of the household may leave objects 'lying about' for other people to 'tidy up'. Indeed, Peter actively tidies the hard disk: 'I'll often tidy it up. I can't keep my office one as tidy, but I can keep this one tidy. It has to be fairly tidy because it's got various users and they have to have space to put their stuff when they come to use it.'

Peter's habit of neatness is reflected also in his general behaviour around the house. Sarah says that she can 'handle more mess' than Peter: he is often the one to tidy up and is responsible for all of the household vacuum cleaning. Peter also feels that it is easier to stay on top of things at home, since work is too busy to be able to spend time there keeping things tidy. 'It's probably also that I can't keep my office under control at work, so I think I want home to be more of a haven.' In this household, then, although there is a gendered division of household labour (Sarah does all the cooking, for example), it tends not to be the 'traditional' one in which the woman is responsible for the inside housekeeping tasks such as vacuuming while the man is responsible for 'outside' tasks such as taking out the garbage and mowing the lawn (Goodnow and Bowes 1994).

In many of the images of home computers included in this book, the computer is surrounded by the by-products of everyday domestic activity – by 'mess'. Indeed, household mess can be seen as the normal state of entropy of the household's objects, which is routinely overcome by the reverse entropic activity of 'tidying up'. People vary in the degree to which they experience stress as a result of living amongst their own or other people's 'mess', and in their responses to living with mess, and these variations are probably to some extent determined by upbringing, and by their formation within the environments of childhood. In some households, one or more people have such a low tolerance for mess that tidying is a high priority activity and the house is kept extremely tidy. In other households it seems that the disorder produced by the ongoing activities of the household's occupants is a perfectly acceptable environment. 'Tidying' is therefore one of those activities of home-building by which we make household space habitable, whatever that means to us.

What to one person will appear to be a hopelessly messy desk, for example, to its owner may be a highly efficient work space. Each item having been placed in its location as a result of its owner's ongoing activities, the desk's state at any given time is essentially an externalization (objectification, even) of ongoing processes which are also partially internal to the owner. The relationship between the owner and the desk is therefore one in which there is synchrony between the state of the desk and the owner him or herself, the objects on the desk interfacing with the owner's expectation of where to find each item. This is indeed a critical point: the owner needs to be able to find each item as and when it is needed, without having to think about it too much, or having to search for it. The purpose of tidying up, then, can be seen to also fulfil a similar purpose, and hence the adage 'a place for everything and everything in its place'.

The processes of home-building require such housekeeping activities. It is only when objects can be relied upon to stay in their places that the home's ability to provide a maximally familiar environment is fulfilled. Further, to refuse to reimpose such order may be a strategy for asserting ownership over such spaces. It is difficult to imagine that a messy desk could have more than one owner: when work space is shared (in shared offices, for example), the shared space is generally left orderly when each user leaves it available for others. To leave a desk messy is to assert one's proprietoriality over it, as if to say to passers-by, 'I haven't finished here, please leave this as it is'.

Conclusion

Home is an objectification of its members in the sense developed in chapter 2, and is thus a structure in space and time made up of material objects and established patterns of activity, as well as ideas, meanings and values. Although it is created by its members, it exists outside of them but not independently of them. Nor do they live independently of it: although home is generally a structure which supports and enables the everyday life of its inhabitants, their actions and activities are also constrained by it. The computer's relationship to the other 'movable' objects of the home is, as we have seen, the result of complex dynamic processes of negotiation, involving not just its human 'owners', but also the objects themselves and their existing interactions and relationships. It is also necessary to consider how all these relationships are given structure by the physical dwelling itself.

t e n

Machines for Living

The relative inflexibility of the material construction of the home contrasts with the flexibility which we saw in the last chapter can be achieved with the use of furniture to create a material structure which supports the ongoing patterns of activity of the household. In the case of housing stock, flexibility may be gained by adapting rooms to different uses, or by renovating or extending the fabric of the home. The bulk of Australian housing stock incorporates a set of standard assumptions about how these buildings will be inhabited as homes, including areas for everyday living (lounge, family, dining rooms), for food preparation and laundry, for sleeping, and for outdoor leisure. These functions may not map easily onto the inhabiting customs of people who arrive in Australia from other cultures.

Vietnamese migrants in Australia, for example, must select from available houses the ones which most closely conform to geomantic prescriptions and which can most easily be adapted to their accustomed pattern of life (Thomas 1999, chapter 3). While in Vietnam the extended family often lives under one roof, Australian houses are generally not big enough to accommodate such large numbers of people. Further, the configuration of spaces within the home, and the articulation of internal and external spaces are also quite different from those of houses in Vietnam. As Thomas describes, 'Vietnamese people often find it hard to accustom themselves to the difference between the size, shape, layout and use of rooms in Australian houses and those in Vietnamese houses' (55). In Vietnam, for example, kitchens are often much larger than they are in Australian houses, as several people are often involved in food preparation at the same time. More particularly, 'the relatively fixed definitions of living, dining, sleeping and cooking spaces of the typical Australian house appear to be inappropriate to communal living styles' (59). Thomas describes a number of strategies used by Vietnamese people to adapt this housing to their accustomed style of living. But it is clear that the materiality and physical inflexibility of housing construction necessitates that this adaptation is mutual, and that the Vietnamese people must also adapt their pattern of life because of constraints and prescriptions imposed on them by Australian housing forms. Those of us who have been brought up with such housing have conformed in developing a culturally customary pattern of life largely without being aware of it.

Computers are generally large appliances (although they vary in their portability). They therefore tend to be set up in a particular location and used there (in the present study, the only laptops in use within the study households were either second computers or ones which had been brought home from work). Since the pattern of life of the household's inhabitants involves the material spatial structure of the home just as it is involved in temporal structures, the location of the computer in the home will affect how and by whom it is used. The exception to the observation that computers tend to be relatively static objects within the household is an instructive case, that of the computer in the Fowler household.

Case Study: A Computer Without a Location

Households are often not secure and happy places for their members. The kinds of strategies of mutual accommodation which were described in earlier chapters do not always allow individual household members to maintain ontological security. For people in difficult life situations this may be true most or all of the time, while for others – probably, in fact, for all of us – there are times within an otherwise secure existence that our ontological security is undermined. It would be easy, within a study based on a relatively brief contact with each household, to give the impression that everyday domestic life for the people involved, and in particular the role of the computer within the home, is on the whole smooth and successfully managed. Although instances of 'conflict' and 'tension' around the home computer have been described, such conflicts all seem superficial and easily resolved within the normal domestic mechanisms for resolving such disputes – and certainly they do not fundamentally threaten the integrity of the household or any of its members.

In the Fowler household, as we saw in chapter 7, there is some tension around the computer. It may be seen as Doug Fowler's personal link to a fantasy world of science fiction and technological mastery, a kind of escape mechanism from a real life domestic situation of very limited material resources and therefore little other freedom of self-expression. The ambiguities around the place of the computer in the Fowler household are illustrated by the computer's lack of an established location within the household space. Most of the time it is located on a small table at the foot of a staircase, which is a kind of 'dead' space at the end of the corridor just outside the lounge room. If the computer is not on it, Bev uses the table to put the basket of clean washing on to keep it out of the way, since the back door of the house is at the other end of the corridor. This is not a good location for sitting to use the computer, since it is clearly more of a place where the computer can be out of the way, without taking up any more 'useful' space within the house. The issue of the computer's spatial location within the household seems to provide a symbolic indicator of the computer's place within the household – or rather the denial of a place to it. Essentially it is an item which is accorded no space of its own, and its changing temporary locations reflect its transient claims to different kinds of legitimacy within the household.

When Bev uses the computer, she moves it onto a coffee table in the lounge room, which legitimizes her use as a 'family' use. During one school holiday, the computer was moved into the couple's seven-year-old son's room for several days 'as a reward'. Sometimes the computer is set up on the dining room table, particularly on Friday nights when Doug has a regular get-together with his friends. While this is quite a good location from the point of view of having space to use the computer, it can only ever be a highly temporary arrangement, since the dining room table is needed for other activities: 'It really only ever comes to the dining table if it either needs to be worked on or friends of mine bring their computers'.

It might be argued that the layout of the Fowlers' house should be examined as a possible source of the spatial limitations placed on the computer. However this would be to deny the part that intra-familial negotiations (explicit or implicit) around the use of household space play in such allocations. The Martinez family, for example, lives in similar public housing not far from the Fowlers, and indeed has four children compared with the Fowlers' two. Yet within the Martinez household, Carlos has a dedicated study which contains his computer, a room with a lockable door so that the children can be excluded both materially and symbolically. The family's second computer, which is the one the children are supposed to use (although they also have limited access to Carlos's machine) is located within the bedroom of the eldest son. The Martinez family has more bedrooms available than the Fowlers, but some of their children must share a bedroom in order for there to be space for Carlos to have his study. Within the space of this household, then, the father is accorded a clearly marked space for his own personal use. It is tempting, rather than reading the allocation of space within these two households in terms of limited availability of spatial resources, to instead view the position of the computer as an index of the role of the father within the two households. While both households would be classified as low income and both live in rented public housing, Carlos Martinez has professional expertise and qualifications and works part-time as a college lecturer as the household's sole income-earner. On the other hand, Doug Fowler has been unemployed long-term and appears to have no prospects of employment within the foreseeable future. In terms of the normative gendered role models for domestic life, then, Doug is someone who could be seen as clearly not having 'earned' the traditional male position of 'head of household', and is therefore denied the traditional domestic rewards of the position, such as the kind of privileged access to the household's financial and spatial resources that Carlos Martinez enjoys. This denial is, however, tacit and conducted through techniques of passive resistance, rather than because it is explicitly articulated or overtly negotiated.

The computer, for Doug Fowler, then, is perhaps able to provide him with an escape into a domain within which he is able to achieve some imagined status through the development of technological problem-solving skills. That Doug certainly uses the time spent on the computer to escape from the mundane demands of everyday domestic life (which, because he is unemployed, is primarily spent at home) is illustrated by the following exchange:

> *Bev Fowler*:   I could go out and say 'can you wash up while I'm out?' and he was on the computer when I left and he still is when I come back and he says 'Guess what nothing's done'.
>
> *Doug Fowler*:   And I've been doing nothing on the computer but fiddle. Check files out, deleted files, maybe run a couple of programs, played a game or two, and done nothing and I could do it for three, four, five hours.

The potential for such a structure of domestic activities to result in tension and conflict within the family is clear, although this could not be fully explored within the interview situation of the present study.

The Spatial Organization of the Home

Some households have more space as a resource at their disposal than others. A single person living in a two- or three-bedroom unit or house will clearly have much more disposable space than six people living in a three-bedroom house. Households containing more members may therefore have less choice about dedicating space to the computer. However, as the Fowler and Martinez households illustrate, the allocation of space in the household depends on the negotiation of access to the space of the home as a material resource, and on the meanings and values attached to the activities involved with the computer.

The computer's location within the space of the household can be illuminated by examining a number of different dimensions of the spatial organization of the household: that of spatial isolation (a bedroom at the end of a long corridor, for example) versus accessibility (a location at the centre of household activity); that of the personal space of one individual versus a location in communal space; and that of space coded for work versus that associated with leisure.

The computer's place within the household is affected by the relative isolation or accessibility of the space that it is in, compared with other spaces within the household (Hillier 1986). In the Bartlett household (which, apart from the parents, includes four boys aged between ten and nineteen), the computer is located in an external family room which is physically separated from the rest of the house by a small courtyard. The isolation of this location means that it can be used as a peaceful haven from the stresses of living in such a busy household: 'Sometimes the reason why they are out there is because they want a bit of time out or a bit of peace and quiet or something' (Merilyn Bartlett).

Merilyn feels that this is an ideal location for the computer, since in the rest of the house its use would clash with other activities, such as sleeping if it were in a bedroom, or with television watching if it were in the combined lounge/dining area. Merilyn herself is able to use this space and this activity to get away from the demands of motherhood:

> Somebody invariably wants me for something and . . . I very rarely actually get to sit down and just have switch off veg time. I don't watch television for that reason . . . but if I can quietly disappear out into the computer room, do a bit of work, or play on the computer or whatever, or just sit and read the Encarta, and have three quarters of an hour peace and quiet to myself.

Paradoxically, the computer is part of the structure of the home but is able to provide an escape from it. As Douglas argues, the household exerts a powerfully tyrannous hold over the minds and bodies of those who inhabit it (Douglas 1991: 303), and it is therefore perhaps necessary for it to contain such (illusory) escape mechanisms.

In other households, the computer is located in the mainstream of the household's activity. In the Richards household, for example, the layout of the house is organized around a large L-shaped area with the dining room on the one side, a family room on the other, and the kitchen in the middle. Bedrooms and the more formal lounge area are located off this main space. The computer is situated in the family room area, a location which is central to the activity of the household.

In the Cooper household, the computer is now located on a desk in one corner of the lounge room. Several other locations within the house have been tried, however:

> It did actually go upstairs for a while. It was in the corner [the current location] and that was OK because I would do a lot of work when the kids had gone to bed, like at night and that was quite a good time to sit there and do some. That way it wasn't disturbing everyone as it would if it was upstairs like other people in bed. So that was quite good. It went upstairs for a while, we rearranged a few things but now it's gone back in the corner. (Sylvia Cooper)

Sylvia feels that when the computer is downstairs there tends to be more joint use. Having the computer in the midst of household activity means that sometimes people will be lining up to use it, 'whereas if it's upstairs it's sort of like out of sight out of mind'.

As we have seen, the home computer may act as one of the domestic 'escape' mechanisms by which the members of the household are enabled to cope with the inherent paradoxes and constraints of living together. These mechanisms also generally include an allowance for individuals to have some level of personal privacy. Even when people do not isolate themselves spatially, they may be able to achieve a sense of isolation simply by engaging in an activity which takes the user 'elsewhere' mentally. The level of concentration and engagement in playing an immersive computer game, for example, is often comparable to that achieved when reading a novel.

A second dimension of household spatial organization within which the computer's location is implicated is that of private (individual) space, versus public (communal) space. Where a computer quite definitively belongs to one individual within the household and is only used by that person, then the computer is generally located within the private household space of that person. This is the case, for example, with Regine Vassallo's computer.

In Felicity Attard and Gail Shaw's home, the computer is located in the small spare room, which is also where their medium-term house guests, Joe and Barbara are staying.

> It's always been the spare room, and also the computer room. It has a bed in it for when people come to stay. But then we've always had people staying: Felicity's brother stayed for quite a long time when he moved from Adelaide. We used to share with another friend when we first bought the house, that seemed like an easy way to get over the first hurdle of moving in together. And at that stage Felicity didn't have the big room, she had this room and Felicity owns the computer, so it was in there with her. (Gail Shaw)

At that time, another woman was sharing the house with them, and had her own computer in her room, and therefore at that stage each computer was in the bedroom of the person who owned it. When this woman moved out and Felicity moved into her room, the computer stayed in the third, smallest, bedroom. This room is now dual-purpose: it is the spare room if someone comes to stay, but also the computer room. The computer is a portable Macintosh Classic II and is sometimes moved out of the room to be used on the dining room table or in the desk in either Gail's or Felicity's rooms:

> When Joe and Barbara first came, we both felt sensitive about them having that small [single] bed, so we offered them one of our rooms, or alternatively that we could move the computer out. But they said they were fine in there, and in lots of ways it's a more private space down here, because we were up there [at the other end of the house]. So I feel now, like it is their space, and the last thing I want to be doing is being in their space doing computer stuff, because that would mean that it's not their space. But I don't say all of that, I say 'Do you mind if I take the computer now?' [laughing]. Like 'do you mind if I get this out of your way?', but then it goes back again, because for some reason I want clear desk space in my room, or it feels like we're not going to be using it for a while, or once we got onto the Net, the phone plug is out here, so it has to be hooked up from in there. (Gail Shaw)

If Barbara and Joe are not home, however, the computer tends to be used in place, rather than moved.

At one point the Turner household had located the computer in the parents' bedroom:

> When we first had it I was doing a lot of private work. There was a lot of pressure to get reports done and because it was in the house in the bedroom Sally would be wanting to go to sleep and I would be working away there and printing, 'bzzzz' . . . Yeah, Sally got the shits. (Thomas Turner)

As these two examples show, where a space has multiple uses it is possible for them to be incompatible, but workable in the short term (as a temporary arrangement which is not terribly convenient).

The computer's place in the home is therefore influenced not just by the relative isolation or accessibility of its space, or whether that space is someone's private space or is communally used. The ambiguity of the computer's status, as both a work tool and something associated with leisure activities, particularly when it comes to game-playing, is also articulated with the other uses of the space it is located in. The Turners' computer is now located in a study which has been built into the back of the garage, underneath the main level of the house. In order to reach this room, which is generally kept locked, it is necessary to go out of the house, down a flight of steps, and through the garage to the study. The room was built as a work area for Thomas Turner, and is very much set up as a work space for architectural drafting, with a drawing board, filing cabinets and so on. Before the garage was converted to create the study, the computer was located in the main communal living area of the house:

> There was a time when I had my drawing board in the corner over there by the bookshelves and I had the computer on the drawing board, or before that it was sitting on the desk in the bedroom. We also put the two boys together in a room at one point and I had the study up here at the back and I had it in a similar set up to downstairs but it was up here. It's generally not been like the TV, it's certainly not been part of the furniture. It's moved around. (Thomas Turner)

The Turner children used the computer more when it was more available, but this has also been affected by the arrival of a Nintendo games machine in the house.

Fred and Irene Farrell also found, through comparing different computer locations, that the issue of the isolation or accessibility of the computer affects its broader 'place' within the household. They had their previous computer in a small study which was relatively isolated from the flow of household life. When they got the new computer, they moved the dining room table slightly to accommodate the computer in a space at the junction of the dining and lounge areas of their open living space:

> Our son said that it has to be in the living space. Well, you see, we had the other one in the spare room. It's no good if someone's going to use it if they have to remove themselves from the family flow, and they're isolated … My son said that it has to be in with the family … That's what he's come to see, through experience. And we could see it that first Christmas that it was here, that people just flowed towards it. You could imagine how difficult it would be if it was somewhere else. There'd have to be a special trip, you know. Here, if Irene's working on it or something you can just look over their shoulder. (Fred Farrell)

Figure 13 The Farrells' computer is located in a spot carved out between the lounge and dining areas of their open plan living area.

As we have seen, domestic space is structured around a number of dimensions which segregate and segment its space. The use of different spaces within the home, and therefore of the objects which are located within those spaces, is profoundly influenced by these processes of spatial differentiation. Having divided up the domestic space in this way, rooms are allocated to specific purposes, and named accordingly, as kitchens, dining rooms, family rooms, living rooms, bedrooms, studies and so on. Each kind of space is associated with certain kinds of domestic activity, which may be transferred to a home computer once it is located within such a space. Conversely, however, it is possible for the associations of the computer to symbolically 'stretch' the meanings and uses attached to the space, and transform it in turn. The surprisingly common choice of the dining room as a location for the home computer illustrates this trend.

Computers in Particular Locations

The provision of a separate 'dining room' is extremely common in Australian housing stock. Generally located next to the kitchen, when it is not a separate enclosed room the dining room often also acts as a transitional space between the kitchen and the lounge area, with its comfortable seating (and usually a television). Even quite small flats, such as the two-bedroom flat occupied by Regine Vassallo and her flatmate, will have an area designated as 'dining' space, even if this is simply one end of a single lounge/dining room. It is also common for Australian houses which have been built within the last twenty years or so (or those which have been extended during this time), to include a room designated as a 'family room'. The family room often also is furnished with comfortable seating and a television, but is usually for more informal use (including often informal dining), particularly in households with small children (in which the family room often contains many of the children's toys). The lounge room is often left as a more formal, adult-oriented space, and may be kept free from toys and general household mess (in a manner rather like that of the formal parlour or sitting room of earlier times).

The dining room is an interesting room within contemporary Australian homes, in that, if it were only used for dining, it would be an extremely under-utilized space. In practice, dining rooms or areas are frequently used in a much broader way. If the comfortable seating of lounge rooms means that they are generally seen as spaces suitable for relaxing, the table and seating of the dining room is such that the space lends itself to more 'work-like' uses. Children often do their homework at the dining room table. One of the study participants, Katherine Scarborough, on the basis of her experience of providing freelance accounting consultancy services to small business owners, observed that such people would frequently work on their accounts using a laptop computer at their dining room tables. Similarly, when Gail Shaw brings home a laptop from work to complete some task, she generally uses it on the dining room table. The dining room table may lend itself to providing a venue for discussions with a visitor whose purpose is relatively formal: the interviews which form the basis of the empirical part of this research were conducted around a dining room table more than in any other location within the house.

While in some cases the computer is set up in a corner of the dining room (such as in the Farrell household), in others the dining room may be completely converted to be used as a study/computer room (in Hilary Lacey and Margaret Paine's house, for example).

It seems that dining rooms may be available for such reconfiguration because of their under-utilization, but also because of the ambiguity of their status with respect to the work/leisure axis. They are therefore often suitable for locating a home computer in houses where there is no space available to be designated as a 'study' or 'family room'. The fact that many home computers are located in rooms designated as dining rooms is particularly interesting considering the seemingly universal injunction that there should be no food or drink around them, and suggests that such spaces are clearly seen in terms symbolically much more broad than their name would imply.

As we saw in chapter 3, images which juxtapose food and computers seem to be a common strategy for the domestication of these technologies on the part of computer marketers – showing consumers that these are appliances just like other domestic technologies and can be used throughout the home. However, for home computer users themselves this understanding of the computer's potential place within the home does not need to be literally taken up. There is a refusal to see computers and food and drink as objects which can be juxtaposed within the domestic space, and an insistence that they need to be kept physically separate, even though it may be possible under controlled circumstances for them to share the same space. The exception, in which adults will have a cup of tea or coffee with them when using the computer, resonates with the acceptability of this as workplace behaviour, and suggests that what is going on here is an insistence on the part of householders that computer use is seen as 'serious', work-like behaviour.

As we have seen in this chapter, households have a range of strategies for organizing and structuring domestic space so that such differentiation of activity can be made and maintained. A computer may be located in a space coded for serious work-like use, if this is what its owners want to do with it, or a space may be reconfigured to include these uses. In Katherine Scarborough's house there would be plenty of space to allocate a room to use as a study, but Katherine chooses to locate the computer in the main open area of the house:

> I've got a three-bedroom house so I could easily have one room set up as an office but I feel cut off if I do that so I'm the kind of person that really likes to live in one room . . . I spend most of my time in this family room. I've got one section set up like an office, I've got lights and everything there and an office desk and a typist's chair . . . and I've got a phone on an extension cord there and my answering machine and all that.

Before she moved into the house she is currently in, she lived in a place where she had a room set up as an office, but 'hated going in there'. She has always had a dedicated space for the computer, but finds that if it is in a separate room this discourages her from using it. The sense of being 'at home' in our everyday living space is therefore homogeneous throughout the space. Partly this is because of comfort (bedroom offices may be cold in winter), or may also be because the space is differentiated for different purposes.

For people such as Jane Middleton and Charlotte Thompson, who do a significant amount of their employment-related work at home, their differentiation of space within the household is an important way of creating boundaries between their home and work lives (Nippert-Eng 1995). For Marjorie Brennan, too, it is important to set boundaries between work at home and the rest of her home life. Marjorie's computer is in a room set up as a study at the front of her house. This room is often cold, however, especially in winter, so she will also often work in her living room:

> I do work out here and then I will do work in the office on the computer. I was considering, just because it is winter, bringing the computer in here. Just to be warmer . . . but I'm just weighing that up because I need to separate work and private space . . . I was just thinking about that because it is a nice outlook here and work and whether that would be more productive, I don't know.

Figure 14 Marjorie Brennan's home office is often cold in winter, but she prefers to keep work and private living space separate. (The small clear crystal on top of the computer is just visible in this image.)

Hilary Lacey and Margaret Paine considered setting aside a spare bedroom as an office, but chose to transform their dining area instead, choosing deliberately to blur the boundaries between work and home:

> We've got a lounge room which turns into a dining room and then the kitchen, it's like a 'L' shape. Where one part of our living space is lounge and TV, where the dining is supposed to be is now where the computers are set up which is in between, I guess, the kitchen and the lounge room. Mine's right next to the glass sliding doors that look out onto the back bush [so] you've got that on one hand and high technology on the other. But it's nice, it's a nice spot to be. The dining room table is there but it's sort of tucked away. We have plants and stuff around it. Now it's definitely an office look ... What we've done is made it look like we've actually blurred those boundaries. (Hilary Lacey)

In addition to the dining room as a common computer location which is in a communal living area, computers are frequently located within the main 'lounge' area of the house itself. Claire Matheson's main living area is L-shaped, with the lounge area in one arm (containing the lounge suite and television), and the 386 computer is located in the other, which is more an informal sitting room. Her new 486 machine, which she was having some difficulties with when I met her (although it will eventually replace the 386), had been set up with the Commodore in the lounge room area. She is still undecided about where the 486 will eventually be located, since she can see advantages in both locations: 'Well, this one kinda landed here, when it arrived, and I found I liked it here, because I can do the computing and watch the telly at the same time.' Although being able to watch television at the same time as using the computer is something of an advantage, Claire does not feel that she misses being able to see it if she is around the corner where the 386 is located. She can still put the television on and be able to hear it, or alternatively not put it on at all:

> A lot of the television stuff you don't need to watch, you can just listen to it. And if there's something that I really want to see, I'll get up and come and have a look at it. But most of it's just listening . . . Until this [the 486] came here I didn't really watch much television . . . Until this was here, I hardly ever watched television – I could go for days and not turn it on.

In fact, since the computer has been located in the lounge room, Claire has been watching more television than would be usual: 'Yes! My priority would be computer over television, but here I can combine the two.'
Jessica Lane's computer is now located in the lounge room:

> When I first bought it, it was in my study and I would sort of have a workstation and stuff and I worked in there and that was great, that was when I was actually focusing on a project. Then when I stopped doing that and I came to work here it was sitting in the study not being used very much at that time . . . Then I moved it into Michael's room and he decided he didn't want it in his room. Then when I bought the modem, and the telephone connection is in the lounge room. Also I thought that I might use it more if it was in the lounge room because the fire's also in the lounge room and the television's in the lounge room, and I often play around on [a bulletin board] or whatever whilst I'm watching television you know. So I thought that it would get more use in the lounge room.

In Patricia Collins's house, as in many others (the Bartlett family's house is another example), the family room is an alternative living space where adults and children can choose their own activities, without getting in each other's way:

> We built the extension, and when we got a computer it was going to go down there. It was originally sort of like a family room so that anybody could go down there. Before the computer they used to go down and play the Nintendo. It was up here to start with until the extension was built, then the Nintendo went down. We put their study desks down there and Caroline has had very good use out of that room. They can go down there and get out of our way so that's good. Also if they're up here already involved in a program we can go down there and get out of their way too.

Where a computer is located in a room that is also someone's bedroom, in general this is because the computer is primarily for the personal use of the room's occupant and may be seen as their exclusive personal possession. Regine Vassallo's or Jim Christou's computers would be examples here. Jim, for example, has two rooms within his parents' house, where he has all his entertainment and study needs met (although he is still able to depend on his parents for more bodily needs such as food and laundry).

In two of the study households (that of Peter and Sarah Richards, and Sally and Thomas Turner), the computer was at one point located in the parents' bedroom, although this arrangement proved only temporary. Both the Richards and the Turners had had their computers in the bedroom but found it an unsatisfactory arrangement, since one partner would be working on the computer while the other was trying to sleep. It seems not uncommon for such an arrangement to be tried, although I have not come across (or heard anecdotally about) any cases in which this has proved to be anything other than a temporary arrangement. This is not to say that such an arrangement cannot work. But in order for it to be a stable arrangement, the two uses of the room – sleeping for the couple, and using the computer for one or both of the partners – must be organized in such a way that they are not brought into conflict. As a private and isolated space (in the terms of the dimensions discussed above), the bedroom is a space that is conducive to work, but this would only be the case when it is not being used for its main use (sleeping).

It is also possible for the computer to be located in a bedroom, but to also be available for public use. In the Martinez household, the family's second computer (the 386 which was their main computer before their 486 was acquired) is now located in the eldest son's room, and is in principle available for the use of all the children. In practice, however, there are more up-to-date games on the other computer and so the younger children tend not to be interested in using the 386: 'No, they don't want it any more. There's better games on the other computer. They don't want to play those other games any more.'

In Chris Talbot's home, the computer's location in her three-year-old daughter's bedroom is one that is problematic, and as this example shows, computing is not the only kind of activity that is limited for mothers by the demands of their children and the configuration of household space and objects. Chris's sewing machine is also in her daughter's bedroom, and so her use of the sewing machine is restricted in similar ways to her use of the computer, since the space that she would normally use for sewing is the desk in her daughter's room that the computer sits on.

Figure 15 Virginia Parsons's computer, located in a spare bedroom which is also used as a dressing room.

In households where there is adequate space, a room is often set aside as a 'study'. These rooms often also contain a bed, and double as a spare bedroom for when people come to stay. Such rooms may, however, be out of the normal flow of household activities, unless the room is regularly used for work or educational purposes. The isolation of such rooms can otherwise result in the computer being 'out of sight, out of mind' and therefore getting little use. Janet Fuller, for example, now has the old 286 computer she bought from Hilary Lacey permanently set up in the spare room but she currently does not use it much. When she first had it she would move it out into the lounge room to use it.

This brief survey of computer locations within the study households is not, however, exhaustive of the possibilities for locating a computer, or for overlapping uses of household space in ways that are productive for a household's members. One of the more unusual uses might be that of Virginia Parsons's household, in which the computer is located in a spare bedroom which, in addition to the computer, is also used as a dressing room (figure 15). The objects with which this computer is surrounded – a medicine bottle beside the computer, toiletries on the dressing table, a spare shoe lying on the floor – demonstrate the flexibility of the home computer as a component in the domestic ensemble of objects as a 'machine for living'.

Conclusion

Technological objects – and here it must be recognized that most (perhaps all) objects have some technological role – are embedded within and in an essential way constituted by the particular sets of human praxis they are engaged in. The function of an object is an aspect of the human–artefact relationship, but is also constituted through the relationship between the artefact and other objects. Single objects, even such highly technological objects as the home computer, do not function independently but need the collaboration of the other objects of the home in order to perform their functions properly within the domestic pattern of life.

Home computers, as household objects, collaborate with a broad variety of other objects: furniture, other technological objects such as televisions, telecommunications devices and games machines, and small objects such as books, papers, disks, coffee cups, waste paper bins and pairs of glasses. With other objects their relationship is more competitive and over time some of these objects may be entirely displaced within the home (typewriters are a clear example of this process). If, as Fitch suggests, these objects can be thought of as the space solidified around human activities, then they form the home into a machine for living not by staying in their places, but in our interactions with them, and in their configuration. And, as Hillier insists, space itself is not a passive stage, but perhaps, indeed, 'space is the machine' (1996).

The dynamic nature of the material home is also indicated by the need for active management of its arrangements of objects: home-building practices necessarily include 'housekeeping' tasks, which are generally undertaken by particular household members as part of the domestic division of labour. 'Tidying up' – the reimposition of order within the spaces of the home (including the internal space of the computer) – is a strategy for maintaining control over the domestic ensemble and may also constitute a form of proprietoriality. Both tidying up and, paradoxically, leaving mess too, appropriate the space of the home by asserting or changing the arrangement of objects within it. These are therefore both practices by which relationships of ownership of domestic space may be constructed and maintained.

Domestic objects, then, do not exist in isolation from each other, but are elements in the household's total assemblage of artefacts and technologies, forming a 'machine for living' which is the material and technological underpinning of the household's unique pattern of life. According to the perspective developed in this book, the extended self, as a subject-in-relation to its objects, is constructed dynamically and dialectically in particular, local and concrete contexts of interaction with the material and immaterial objects of its social and cultural environment. This definition encompasses the relationship between the home and its inhabitants, and the 'home' is therefore clearly recognizable as a form of objectification. It is principally an outcome of the activities of its members, but is not their creation alone. Indeed, it is a necessary condition of the existence of contemporary homes that they are embedded in both global-scale structures of commodity production and more local social structures (such as work and school environments). Further, the home as objectification is more than simply the collection of objects it contains. It is, indeed, the household's 'pattern of life' in its broadest sense: complex and amorphous, simultaneously both abstract and concrete, and constituted in praxis. It is a structure composed of material objects, patterns of activity and temporal rhythms, hierarchies of power and routines of interpersonal interaction, is manifested in domestic systems of value, and is embedded within a broader social and cultural context which sustains it.

Constructing the Self through Objectification

For some people, information technology is so much a part of their everyday lives that it is no longer in question as part of who they are. They have achieved a sense of being 'at home' with the technology. It has been so thoroughly incorporated into their subjectivity that the process by which it became that way is no longer readily accessible to the observer. This is true, particularly, for people who have used and owned computers since the mid-1980s. For others, the incompleteness or newness of this process affords the opportunity for closer observation. Uncertainty about the outcome of this process is illustrated through the affective dimensions of the incorporation of the home computer into individual lives, in both positive and negative senses, including anxieties and fears and inevitable frustrations, including at times a fear of losing control verging on a sense of loss of ontological security. Laura Manfredotti's feeling of being 'nervous and feeling like an idiot because I didn't know anything', and Sarah Richards's 'I was petrified. I thought "I'll never be able to do this!"', contrast with the excitement of a new computer keeping people up late into the night, and the strong sense of empowerment expressed by women like Helen Samuels ('That mastery, that "Yes!"') and Sue Kozlowski ('the awe is still there').

The lack of familiarity and fear is particularly intense when a piece of complex technology is new and doesn't behave as expected:

> You tend to panic. You think it's broken and you think that will incur expense, that's one of the problems, I think. It's total unfamiliarity with it, and it's also that you've laid out quite an amount of money on it, and there might be some really expensive harm done to it. And you get frustrated, you don't think properly . . . When you look back . . . you just

laugh at the trouble you had, and the worry that it caused you, and that sort of thing. (Fred Farrell)

Both Jessica Lane and Claire Matheson had installed new hardware accessories which involved opening the computer up: 'There are quite a few things I do with my heart in my mouth. Install a modem: "whoah". Like I don't have that technical background so, you forge on, but you forge on with lack of confidence.' (Jessica Lane)

Claire Matheson installed her own CD-ROM, after suggesting to her son that he should come and do it for her:

> I said to [her son], you'll have to come home now and put this in for me, and he said, 'No, no, you can do that'. So I did. It was very scary. Very scary. But I did it . . . you plug it in, and then you have to connect the little cables and it's very tight in there, but it works . . . This is just so highly technical. I just thought it was out of my league.

Ontological security is tied, in the contemporary world, to our reliance on technologies to function as expected. When things go wrong, such as a car breaking down when we are far from habitation, or a computer breaks down and we lose valuable files, the sensation can be more than frustration and anger, but can be experiences as an assault on our ontological security itself. Charlotte Thompson had a problem to do with the battery running flat on her computer:

> I assumed that it would never let me down and like I got a real shock when that happened. I was quite afraid of them when I started but then I got to trust it that it wouldn't do anything awful to me. Then the battery went, it just started to wear out and it didn't warn you and it didn't say that the battery's going. So that gave me a bit of a shock and then I didn't want to use it for quite a few months. I was quite injured (laugh).

We can see here that a sense of discomfort – of not being at home – arising from lack of trust in the computer can lead to someone being discouraged from using it. As we have seen, the activities which are likely to build themselves most successfully into our lives over the long term are those with which we are familiar and comfortable. There is often a heightened sense that things might go wrong with any piece of complex technology, but this fades as things do not actually go wrong, and confidence is developed: 'You think you could do something potentially disastrous but once you've allowed yourself to do those things, whatever they are nothing really happens and you develop that confidence that you can.'

During my discussion with Jane Middleton and Charlotte Thompson, the topic shifted from that of the computer breaking down to that of a car breakdown. As Charlotte put it, 'you take things for granted and then all of a sudden [something happens] and then you go into some odd place that reminds you of somewhere else, some place where you don't have any control but it's attaching to something primeval'. Charlotte described it as a moment of finding yourself 'out on the bleak precipice':

> The world does change, in those dramatic shifts when all the things you've taken for granted and then there's a big something and it's all up for grabs, just briefly. Like if your car goes or your computer they're a little bit similar . . . The world does sort of change colour a little . . . With the battery thing, it was more the feeling like the car. The first time it happened, because I had started to trust it. You develop a lot of confidence, as you get to be an adult, as well I can find out why and I or someone else can fix it. You develop that strategy against that being out on the bleak precipice . . . All those mechanisms when they fail, even just a computer, it just reminds you of that moment, of feeling powerless and not knowing. (Charlotte Thompson)

While the emphasis in this book has been on the potential for objects to become incorporated into the extended self, as these examples show objects also resist our appropriation of them and that incorporation into the self. Some kinds of objects remain intrinsically alienated or are able to become suddenly alien and perhaps even dangerous. Many of the objects in our homes remain to some degree alienated in this way. This might be because of the kind of technological capacity for failure which Charlotte spoke about, or because they are the personal possessions of someone else in the house, or because they are located in a domain which 'belongs' to someone else – a child's bedroom, the power tools in the garage, and so on.

To return to Winnicott's account of the individual's psychogenesis in the parent's gradual disillusionment of the infant: the environment is not under our magical control. The extent to which it remains under control depends on the activities of other people, and on the reliability of the material objects and technologies we are surrounded by, those 'faithful witnesses' who stay in their place to give us our place (to return also to Romanyshyn's description of possessions). The process which has been described in this book, it must be emphasized, is one of personal investment of the self in objects:

> I feel overall that the technology is empowering, if it does what it's meant to do and I understand it. But there's a process involved in which I need to engage with it in order to understand it, and that's what's hard. It isn't a function of itself, it still needs me to engage with it, and that's a problem. It's like being confronted with a whole new body of knowledge that you need ... I feel like I just have a surface relationship with both of them [the car as well as the computer], like there's only so far I can go. It's almost like there's some utopia out there, like some promised land, and I'm never ever going to reach it. It's always evading me, and even if I was going to really get my running shoes on I would never get there. [And in that utopia] you've got control, over what's happening. Like the fact that I'm constantly lurching for someone else to help me find things out, even though I can learn the steps, I feel not very in control about that. But I feel much more in control this week than I did a month ago. (Gail Shaw)

The objects with which we interact within the contemporary western world are increasingly socially and culturally complex objects like the personal computer, which have profound symbolic and functional depth, but which are also, as we have seen, implicated in mediating a complex and rapidly changing cultural world. Information and communications technologies do not just mediate communication in a narrow sense, but also mediate our relationship to cultural form more generally. This book has also, then, attempted to give an insight into the changing nature of our relationship to a broad range of cultural forms, and how we access, acquire and consume them, including both physical and 'virtual' or digital goods.

There is an investment of the self in personal possessions, through which both self and objects become deeply implicated in each other. In the case of our personal possessions, this investment is both an affective emotional attachment, and an investment in the construction of our personal machines for living, since we assemble these objects collectively as a technology to support everyday life. The self-in-relation to its belongings is not so much a bounded entity in interaction with its environment, but is an extended self, an interface with complex topology which, in its most intimate moments, completely blurs the boundary between self and object. If the object itself is lost, then it can feel like part of the self has gone too.

Katherine Scarborough's Story

It has been suggested that some objects may act in an 'anchoring' mode, preserving and maintaining a sense of the self as it has been achieved, while others may be more like 'handles' or 'bridges', giving access to a developmental potential for the self. As has been stressed throughout this book, material objects do not fulfil this anchoring function by remaining literally static, but by appearing in their expected places and behaving as we expect them to in everyday interaction, providing us with a kind of psychic/material scaffolding within which we maintain a proprioceptive sense. Further, as components of the extended self, they do not act in isolation, but as elements in the overall material, social and cultural environment of the self. Everyday life is able to remain so largely habitual, and does not need to be available for conscious reflection at all times, because of the continuity of this familiar environment and the embodied cultural and practical competences which allow us to inhabit it as consumers, parents, workers and so on. Indeed this continuity, it has been proposed, amounts to a kind of cultural proprioception. A sense of belonging and competence in the spaces and times of everyday life is generated by the material continuity of the social world and its perceptible cultural forms, because these support and structure the sense that we have of our place in the cultural world and mediate the way that we act in it.

Central to this view of the self, then, is the potential for self-transformation through the cultural processes of objectification. However I have not, up to this point, offered a clear example of self-transformation through home computer ownership. Although the 'cyberspace' literature is filled with such stories (see Turkle 1995, for example), it has been argued here that the processes of objectification are manifested in the flow of many objects and discourses. It therefore makes little sense – and indeed goes against the grain of the overall thrust of the argument – to attribute such a potential to a single object (albeit a complex technological one). Taken as a whole, the empirical material presented here is evidence of a collective shift in the subjective relationships of the study participants to the cultural environment in which they have lived over a period of time stretching between the mid-1980s and the present. This shift has affected individuals differentially, and in all cases the home computer is but one element within an effectively boundless array of mutually interacting cultural objects.

I am, however, making a strong claim within this book about the potential (even necessity) for transformation in subjectivity through these processes of interaction with the objective cultural environment. One example is therefore offered of how home computers, through being a material projection of an imagined possible self, have been instrumental for one of the study participants, Katherine Scarborough, in the personal changes she experienced over a five year period. I will allow Katherine to tell this story largely in her own words.

The first home computer Katherine used was a Macintosh Classic which she would bring home from work:

> I would have had the feeling [the novelty of having a new computer] when I borrowed the Classic in '91. I lived in a little flat in Wollongong and I only worked one day a week . . . and I was going through a really – well I had just left my marriage of 30 years and so on. And that computer was – it was just a little old grey, black and white – I used it, it was my friend. And I was so excited that I had it. I played music but I didn't even buy a television. What was it's name? – Emily . . . and Emily and I were buddies. Emily and I spent, non stop, sometimes she was on twenty-four hours at a time. I would have gone crazy I think without Emily and so I was so excited to have it and you could put your hand in the top of her and pick her up and just go where ever you wanted to go. I used to borrow my mother's car and I would take Emily home [from work]. She definitely saved me, it was wonderful.

Eventually, Katherine bought her own computer, a Macintosh which a work colleague had bought only a couple of months before but was selling because of moving interstate: 'So when I got the LC . . . maybe because it had belonged to someone else, even if it was for three months or two months, I don't know but it was great to have it but it didn't . . . it wasn't the same . . . No, it was something to work with but it wasn't like Emily.'

Katherine named the hard disk on this computer 'Fire Woman':

> I called that one 'Fire Woman' because I'm a fire sign. I'm an Aries and I was going through my, sort of I was asserting my authority and my place as a woman in the world. And I just felt, I don't know, I mean I've never regarded myself as a fire woman at all . . . because I'm introverted, but I don't know I think maybe I needed it. I needed to arouse some fire within me because I had been battered around emotionally. So, yes, it was a question of a part of myself I wanted to awaken. [EL: It's like an affirmation?] Yes, yes that was exactly why I did it.

This computer was stolen in a burglary, and after a difficult two-month period without a computer, Katherine bought another one with the insurance money:

> Now this one, 'Spirit of Life' is, I guess is where I am now. Because I feel I'm coming out of the other side of this horrible five year cycle that I've just been through, and so I'm becoming much more my own person and I guess the person I was always meant to be but it was stifled because of the relationship I was in.

I asked Katherine whether she felt that she had incorporated the 'Fire Woman' assertiveness and no longer needed to affirm it in the same sort of way: 'Yes. That's right, yes. It's interesting that you should bring that up because I did that but I never really investigated why I did it. And, why I no longer felt the need to call the next one "Fire Woman".'

The depth of Katherine's response to the loss of the computer named 'Fire Woman' is an indication of the extent to which the personal relationship of ownership with such objects may be profoundly affective. This computer carried an enormous emotional investment for Katherine:

> I was devastated when it was stolen, I was devastated. I felt violated anyway, because people do when their homes are broken into and you know your knickers are lying all over the floor and all the drawers are all emptied out, it's awful. But I kept looking at that space on the desk and crying. It was terrible . . . I had to reorganize the desk because every time I saw the empty space it made me depressed.

If such objects are able to give us our place in the world by staying in their place, then their loss may literally be experienced, temporarily at least, as a loss of self. The self is, however, constituted not simply through its relationships with individual objects, but through its belongings in the broadest possible sense, including to abstract objects such as knowledges and objects which are not physically present. It is clear from Katherine's experience that the relationship is not simply disconnected when the object is physically lost. Paradoxically, while the self-in-relation may be constituted through the totality of such relationships, individual objects may be effectively interchangeable (a paradox which is also noted by Csikszentmihayli and Rochberg-Halton 1981: 164)

Katherine's new computer is different in the way the hard drive is organized, and the operating system is a later version and is thus more complex. This is one of the reasons for her relative lack of comfort with it, compared with the computer called 'Fire Woman'. Our level of comfort with our familiar habitual environment arises because we 'know' it at a level which is below conscious reflection. It is precisely this embodied knowledge which has been referred to as a proprioceptive sense in relation to our familiar environment. It should by now be clear that this sense is not just our relationship to the local physical objects we are surrounded by, but also to geographically distant, or intangible and abstract entities (such as the Internet, or absent family members). In the case of the home computer, our sense of comfort in using it is related to such a sense of knowing how it is organized, how to perform everyday tasks, and where in its internal spaces our electronic objects (documents, programs, games) can be found. Changing to a new and more complex computer is often disorienting and discomforting at first: Katherine Scarborough therefore now has a sense that she only 'knows' parts of the new computer, compared with the computer named 'Fire Woman', which she felt an intimate sense of familiarity and comfort with.

Katherine's story, however, clearly demonstrates the potential for such objects to act as 'handles' to a potential self which may be only dimly imagined. It is also clear that this is a process taking place through long-term interaction – in Katherine's case the transformation in her confidence in herself took place over a period of five years – and is essentially a process by which the ontological security of parts of the self which might previously have been in question stabilize and we come to feel at home through the accumulation of experience and knowledge in inhabiting them.

Conclusion

The relational notion of ownership which has been developed in this book extends the conception of ownership as rights and the notion of ownership as appropriation by seeing ownership as a social process and as a cultural activity. An important component of projects of home-building in contemporary society, our possessions are in general initially encountered as mass-produced commodities. Our association with them is directed towards the production of a place to be 'at home' in the world. In its most abstract formulation, the relationship of ownership is a mutually constitutive subject–object relationship in the full sense of objectification: we are constructed as subjects through these processes of interaction with the object world, just as our objects (such as the home) are constructed through them. The relationship of ownership is one of mutual belonging: we do not simply appropriate objects to the self, but they also 'appropriate' each other, and (individually and collectively) they 'appropriate' us in turn.

It may be contended that 'ownership' does not exhaust the range of subject–object relations which are constitutive of the self through processes of objectification. If, however, the extended self is seen as a self-in-relation to its belongings in the broadest sense, then narrow legalistic definitions of possession encompass only the very tip of the iceberg of those objects and relationships by which the subject is constructed. I have, indeed, used the term 'ownership' within this book in a broader sense than many of the householders would recognize or acknowledge. John Powell, for example, has emerged over time as the major user of the computer in the household he shares with Hayley Crowther and their two-year-old daughter Jennifer. As we saw, Hayley finds that the demands of looking after their daughter tend to be incompatible with a sedentary activity like computing, and she would rather spend the limited time she has available for such activities doing other things. I asked Hayley if she felt that the computer was more John's than hers: 'Ermm . . . I think I possibly do in a way, I hadn't really thought about it in terms of ownership. I mean I don't feel that I have to ask him permission for it . . . I feel that I've got as much right to use it as he has.'

This is not to suggest that everything which a person encounters, has knowledge of or interacts with in its everyday environment is a 'possession' in a uniform sense. What I hope to have opened up for investigation and debate within this book, however, is a conceptual space in which many different kinds of ownership might be recognized and examined, not all of which will convey legal or economic rights and responsibilities. We do often feel that certain tangible and intangible entities are 'ours': the local park, the street, the suburb, the nation, our workplace, and so on. If a sense of ownership is constructed through engagement in interaction and activity, then what does this mean for the development of a sense of ownership to such abstract entities as academic disciplines and other 'imagined communities', or for the development of an institutional structure like a university? Perhaps, as I have suggested here, a useful way forward may be in defining ownership relationally and as constituted through everyday interaction and practice.

In Miller's formulation of objectification, goods which are acquired in commodity-form transactions (as alienated goods) can be recontextualized and appropriated to 'inalienable cultural material' (1987: 17). For Miller, inalienability is not an intrinsic link between people and objects, but 'the inalienable is deemed to exist only in as much as a given cultural tradition constructs its relationships of material culture that way' (Miller 1998b: 131). This view parallels the concept of inalienability found within the anthropological literature, where gift transactions are defined as the exchange of 'inalienable' things between people who are in a state of reciprocal social dependence, while commodity exchange is characterized by reciprocal independence and 'alienability' (Gregory 1982). The association between inalienable objects and a person or group is so strong that even when given to someone else they retain some of their association with the giver. Inalienability is explored further by Weiner, in developing the category of 'inalienable wealth':

> Whatever happens to these objects, they are perceived to belong in an inherent way to their original owners. Inalienable possessions are imbued with affective qualities that are expressions of the value an object has when it is kept by its owners and inherited within the same family or descent group ... The primary value of inalienability, however, is expressed through the power these objects have to define who one is in a historical sense. The object acts as a vehicle for bringing past time into the present, so that the histories of ancestors, titles or mythological events become an intimate part of a person's present identity. (1992: 210)

Thomas has pointed out some of the difficulties with this definition: 'Is it really the case ... that a thing can never be definitively transmitted, such that it belongs in an unqualified sense to someone else?' (1991: 24). He proposes instead that 'both inalienability and alienability must be imprecise terms which may refer to various bonds between persons and objects, or the erasure of such bonds' (39). Taken together, then, the notions of alienability and inalienability may be seen to express the degree of association between a person and an object. Both Weiner's inalienable wealth and the fully alienated commodity form represent the extremes of association possible, or are perhaps 'ideal-type' forms which exist only approximately in real life.

The problem then is perhaps the seeming binarism of the terms alienable and inalienable, and a failure to recognize that these are relational terms. An object is not alienable or inalienable in and of itself, but is only so in relation to a particular individual or corporate group of individuals. The notions of alienability and inalienability therefore express something about the relationship between particular people and the object, and in particular, whether or not there is an imminent likelihood of the transfer to someone else and how such a transfer would affect the current relationships to the object. The strict binarism alienability/inalienability therefore obscures one of the important aspects of the relationship of ownership as it has been elaborated throughout this book. That is, the need for such relationships to be negotiated at the level of everyday activity and interaction, and the possibility for ownership claims to be conflictory and contested.

Ownership, to be sure, is a phenomenon which is framed by social and cultural conventions, and is often constituted through socially sanctioned actions and practices. These will regulate how goods may be transferred between individuals and groups in such a way that both the new associations of ownership and the transformation of the old one are socially recognized. The question of how such associations are operationalized in everyday practice is, I would argue, an empirical one, and it has been one of the central aims of this book to explore in detail this empirical issue for the specific case of contemporary home computer ownership.

Is it possible, then, to argue that the processes of objectification result in the production of 'inalienable' culture? I believe that it is. Lukács (1975: 532) elaborates the origin of alienation for Hegel: social institutions and forms appear to individuals as existing outside of them and constraining their actions. But this seemingly autonomous and objective social reality in fact arises from collective human activity. The actions of human individuals are therefore capable of generating objective social form which is perceived as existing outside of and independently of the individual, and it is this separation that is the essence of alienation. Alienation may thus be seen simply as a recognition of the objective nature, when seen from the point of view of the individual, of social and cultural form. Both technological determinism as a way of thinking about sociotechnical systems and the home as objectification as it has been characterized in this book are alienated forms in this sense. Both alienation and, conversely, inalienability may therefore be taken to be aspects of the complex and dynamic topology of 'potential space' (in Winnicott's terms), the relational interface between the self in interaction with its environment. The dialectical and processual relationship between alienability and inalienability is thus an expression of the inseparable interrelationship between the 'me' and the 'not-me'.

Alienation and inalienability are clearly not fixed states, but end-points on a continuum of incorporation of the world into the extended self, a continuum which is indexed through familiarity and comfort and the sense of ontological security. Objects and activities are able to move both inwards, towards greater attachment to the self and inalien-ability, and outwards, towards detachment and alienation. This book has tended to concentrate its attention on those processes through which commodities and technological objects are de-alienated as they are brought into everyday domestic life, rather than on those equally important and still poorly understood processes through which cultural form is able to become increasingly alienated, particularly from the people responsible for its production. Everyday domestic life, however, clearly involves both processes of appropriation (reducing alienation) and divestment (increasing alienation), both of which have been illustrated here.

If possessions, as it has been argued, can provide a personalized scaffolding for the self, at several points throughout the book this has been described in terms of the self *creating* this personalized environ-ment. The processes through which the computer *finds* a place within the pattern of life of the household have also been described. It must however be conceded that such constructions tend to ascribe agency to the human actor at the expense of the object. I am not, however, proposing that agency should simply be recognized as having been delegated in some way to objects by human actors (as actor network theory suggests). On the contrary, there is a fundamental misrecogni-tion of the nature of structure and agency within both of these constructions – 'creating' on the part of the subject and 'finding its place' on the part of the object – which is caught up in the dialectical interdependence of subject and object as they mutually construct each other through the processes of objectification. Social reality is at the same time both created and found (Winnicott 1971; Silverstone 1994).

Where, then, is the inalienable? Through everyday interaction, the human subject establishes/finds its own subjective relationship between the 'me' and the 'not-me'. Alienation is therefore perhaps a quality of the relationship to the world which may be overcome through coming into the kind of relationship which has been described in this book as one of 'ownership'. Processes of appropriation work to bring objects and knowledges closer and into a more intimate and enduring relationship with the self. Individual objects are not inalienable in and of themselves, as Katherine Scarborough's loss of the computer she named 'Fire Woman' indicates. It is indeed the totality of a subject's objects – in the form of the extended self – which constitutes the inalienable self, and which makes that subject at the same time both a unique individual and a product of its social and cultural environment.

This book has attempted to show the detailed dynamics of everyday objectification, as complex processes which are grounded in the concrete specificity of particular people, times, places and practices of daily life. In this context, highly technological commodities such as the home computer are of particular interest because of their close association with and integration into sweeping contemporary social and cultural changes. For, as Miller suggests, 'consumption is concerned with the internalization of culture in everyday life' (1987: 212).

Building this technology into the domestic context – through practices of home-building – transforms the symbolic qualities of the technology, but it also transforms to some degree the domestic context itself. The home into which the information appliance has been incorporated becomes more workplace-like, as some of the dominant cultural meanings and associations of the computer are imported into the domestic setting. Home 'offices' are set up, teleworking becomes possible, and domestic activities and community work take on some of the character of office administration. It remains to be seen over the coming decades how the new information and communications technologies – particularly the Internet – will transform homes, and whether these changes will be as profound those which have accompanied the incorporation of television into the home over the last fifty years.

As more and more people come to own computers, and as more and more children grow up in homes where there has always been a computer – just as many of us now have had no experience of domestic life without television – the technology will become no longer handle-like, but will form part of the established cultural milieu. These technologies will perhaps not for much longer, then, have the same cultural potency as they have for those adults who were brought up without them (such as those who were interviewed for this study), and who therefore feel them particularly as a lack in their lives and for whom they are able to provide a 'handle', both to the future and to the self.

Appendix: The Study Participants

A total of 95 individuals, living in 31 households across a diverse range of household types participated in the study. The literature on the use of information and communications technologies in homes has tended to concentrate on a narrow range of household types, typically two-parent households with school-aged children. Hence the study aimed to investigate the experiences of home computer users living in a range of different kinds of household, for example households of older people or single-parent households. The inclusion of a range of different household typeps allowed the study to provide a more complex and nuanced analysis of the range of experiences and processes of home computer ownership than would have been possible had a narrower range of household types been included.

The households participating in the study were recruited using a number of methods: through computer training classes conducted by the author (continuing education courses offered to the public, and to university administrative staff), via the local Macintosh computer reseller, through a notice put up in the local library, through informal contacts at the author's daughter's school and through 'snow-ball' contacts (study participants putting the researcher in touch with other potential participants). All but one of the participant households (the exception is Gail Shaw and Felicity Attard's household) resided in the western Sydney area, within a region bounded by Katoomba in the west, Richmond in the north, Penrith in the south and Parramatta in the east. Most of the interviews took place in the home of the participants, while a small number took place in other locations (such as the participant's workplace).

The majority of the initial formal interviews were conducted in 1996, with subsequent informal follow up with many of the participants.

223

The Study Households and their Computers

Bartlett: Merilyn (30–40, part-time casual clerical work), Stephen (40–50, engineer), Paul (19, stockbrocker trainee), Edward (17, apprentice fitter/machinist), Joel (15, at school), Allan (10, at school).

> *Computer*: 486 IBM compatible, bought in 1994. Stephen has a friend who is a computer dealer, and they bought from him. They had been talking about getting a computer for about 5 years before actually purchasing one.
>
> *How the computer is used*: Merilyn uses the computer for wordprocessing (swimming club secretary and household management). Stephen uses it for wordprocessing (genealogy research). The children use it for games, school and higher education assignments. Merilyn and the children play games.

Bourke: Ruth (60+, retired high school principal)

> *Computer*: Macintosh Classic II, bought in 1994 when Ruth retired.
>
> *How the computer is used*: Used for study (master's degree in local history), for letter writing and administration (secretary of the local University of the Third Age and church secretary). She has also done resumés for friends and family members.

Brennan: Marjorie (30–40, part-time community nurse and part-time research assistant)

> *Computer*: Mac SE, bought second-hand in 1994, to write MA research thesis.
>
> *How the computer is used*: Uses the computer mainly for thesis writing, also sometimes for bringing work home.

Brown: Richard (70+, retired fitter and turner. Now teaches computing for University of the Third Age), Sally (60+, retired)

> *Computer*: 486 DX IBM compatible with CD-ROM (upgraded from 286). Bought in 1992. (Former computer: Commodore 64, bought in the late 80s when someone asked him if he was interested in a computer which was an unwanted gift.)
>
> *How the computer is used*: Richard does tutorials, lesson preparation for U3A teaching, plays games, wordprocessing, consulting CD-ROMs (e.g. Encarta). Sally uses the computer occasionally for wordprocessing, consulting CD-ROMs (e.g. Family Doctor).

Chapman: Maureen: (40–50, teacher); Paul: (40–50, teacher and careers adviser); Martin (20, university nursing degree student); Gordon (17, apprentice electrical engineer); Lisa (9, at school), Dale (8, at school), Benjamin (6, at school)

> *Computer*: Apple IIE, given to them in 1996 by the Farrells in exchange for a bottle of red wine.

How the computer is used: Children use educational software and games (brought home from school by Paul Chapman), eldest son uses as a wordprocessor for university assignments. Paul also brings a work computer home which is used by the family. At the time of the study this was a Macintosh 475.

Christou: Jim (20–30, analyst programmer, also part-time undergraduate commerce student. Lives at home with parents and sister)

Computers: Apple Power Macintosh 6200/75, TV tuner card, modem. Bought 1996. Commodore Amiga 500, bought in 1988. Commodore 64.

How the computers are used: Jim dials in to work to work from home, check email and surf the Internet. Develops web pages and publishes online Sci-Fi media guide. Some wordprocessing. Hasn't yet started programming on the Macintosh. The Amiga is still plugged in but hasn't been turned on for a while. The Commodore 64 is packed away in a box somewhere.

Collins: Patricia (widowed, 40–50, university admin. worker, also doing a college certificate in urban horticulture); Caroline (15); Sean (13)

Computer: Apple Power Macintosh (DOS-compatible option), bought in 1996.

How the computer is used: The computer is mostly used for games. Sean also uses the computer for wordprocessing homework assignments. Caroline is working on developing typing skills using a typing tutor program and is wading through a games sampler CD. Patricia uses the computer for TAFE assignments and playing games. Her partner hasn't used the computer at all.

Cooper: Sylvia (40–50, community nurse); John (40–50, tradesman); Tom (Sylvia's brother); Colin (13); Vicki (11); Russell (9)

Computer: IBM 486, bought in 1994. Ostensible justification for the purchase was as a Christmas gift for the whole family, although it was precipitated at the time by Sylvia going on to university study. (Former computer: the family had a Commodore, but did not think of it as a computer, rather as a games machine. It 'died', then there was a gap before they bought the computer.)

How the computer is used: Sylvia uses the computer for bringing work home and household administration, and previously also for university assignments but this is now completed. Children play games.

Farrell: Irene (60+, retired teacher/librarian, still does casual work at local library); Fred (60+, retired high school principal)

Computer: Macintosh LC 630, bought in 1995. (Former computer: Apple IIE, bought in 1986. Given away in 1996 to Chapmans in exchange for a bottle of red wine.)

How the computer is used: Irene uses the computer for family history (research and writing up) and other wordprocessing. Fred doesn't use the computer (although he has done a small amount of wordprocessing).

Fowler: Doug (30–40, long-term unemployed); Bev (40–50, not employed but does volunteer work and is treasurer for school canteen); Neil (8); Vivienne (6)

Computer: IBM-compatible 486, built up from spare parts given by a friend. Has spent about $100 on parts: floppy drive, keyboard, I/O board, sound blaster card. (1996)

How the computer is used: Doug tinkers, plays games. Bev uses it for accounts work (treasurer of school canteen). Sometimes plays games. Children: playing games, wordprocessing (e.g. letters).

Fuller/Smith: Janet (30–40, community nurse); Graham (30–40, clerk)

Computer: 286 IBM-compatible, bought in late 1995, second-hand from Hilary Lacey. Janet intended originally to give the computer to her godson, but then decided to keep it for herself.

How the computer is used: Not used much. Janet plays games, and if friends come with their children she will put it on for them. Graham also plays games.

Harrison: Ann (40–50, clerical/administrative work for local government); Laurence (40–50, clerical/administrative work for local government)

Computer: 'Revved up' 286 IBM-compatible, bought in 1995. Commodore 128, bought around 1989. Not worth selling it, kept out of interest. (Former computer: Commodore 64, bought in mid-80s. Sold to a friend when Commodore 128 bought.)

How the computer is used: The 286 allows Laurence to run similar software to that at work, and gives him a chance to experiment, keep up and improve DOS skills. Ann uses the 286 for wordprocessing and occasional spreadsheet use. The Commodore is still used occasionally, to do things that cannot be done on the DOS machine.

Kozlowski/Healey: Sue (20–30, contract IT support work); Phillip H. (40–50, contract systems analysis and HTML programming)

Computers: Sun Sparcstation (jointly owned), bought in late 1995, second-hand. Professional Unix computer. Named Juno. 486 IBM-compatible, belonging to Phillip. Named Betty. This is Phillip's '2nd or 3rd' computer since he had his first computer, a 286, which was stolen several years before. Bought in mid-1995. 486 IBM-compatible, belonging to Sue. Named Janus. This computer acts as the network server for their home ethernet network. This computer was bought in 1994 because Rosie, the 386, was too slow and limited. 386 IBM-compatible, belonging to Sue. Named Rosie. Bought in 1993 to replace an Atari (which formed part of Sue's music studio) which was stolen.

How the computer is used: Computer systems as a whole are used for developing professional-level information technology skills (both are hoping to move from contract IT work into permanent employment). The local network can be connected to the Internet via modem and the couple is also thinking about setting up as a web server.

Lacey/Paine: Hilary (30–40, youth health counsellor, currently undertaking BA Women's Studies); Margaret (40–50, youth health counsellor, currently undertaking a postgraduate degree in adult education)

Computers: IBM-compatible 486, belongs to Hilary. Bought in late 1995, built up cheaply by a small local dealer. Hilary upgraded because of the frustration of struggling with an old computer when Margaret had a much more up-to-date one. Macintosh 475, which belongs to Margaret. Hilary also has dedicated use of a work laptop, a 486 with external modem. (Hilary's former computers: first computer was a 286 Toshiba laptop bought in January 1995 just before she started her university course. This computer died just as a university assignment was due so she bought another 286 machine second-hand. This computer was sold to work-colleague Janet Fuller when the new computer was bought. She still has the dead laptop in a cupboard somewhere.)

How the computer is used: Hilary uses her computer for university assignments, bringing work home and Internet communication. Uses the Internet to research assignments, uses email extensively including participating in discussion lists (particularly ones related to queer sexuality and theory). Margaret uses her computer for personal correspondence (family and friends in New Zealand), bringing work home, personal financial records management and university work. Sometimes plays games but during semester tends to be focused on university work.

Lane: Jessica (40–50, electronic bulletin board manager, community organization); Michael (11)

Computer: Apple Macintosh Classic II, bought for Jessica in 1993 by her father

How the computer is used: Jessica uses the computer for bringing work home, dials in to the bulletin board system she administers. Also personal correspondence. Michael uses the computer to play games.

Lester: Joy (50–60, college business communication teacher, published writer, currently deferring her PhD studies); Larry (60+, retired)

Computers: Apple Macintosh Quadra 660AV, bought two years before when Larry retired. Apple Macintosh Powerbook laptop, bought at the end of 1991 or early in 1992. (Former computers: Joy's first computer was an Apple IIE bought in 1984 or 1985. This was upgraded to a Macintosh Plus around 1987. This computer is currently with one of the couple's adult children.)

How the computers are used: Both play games. Joy uses the computers for writing and multimedia projects, for bringing work home, and for email and bulletin board communication. Larry uses it for transcribing material for a joint project. They also use it together for monitoring the performance of a share portfolio (a Saturday morning regular activity).

Manfredotti: Laura (30–40, home duties and voluntary work); Max (30–40, truck driver); Angelica (15); Paul (14); Steven (11); Josh (6).

Computer: Apple Macintosh LCIII, bought in 1994, exclusively to contribute to the children's education.

How the computer is used: Children, particularly the eldest, use the computer for school work. Laura uses the computer for wordprocessing and financial records (related to community work). Children tend to play games on the Nintendo rather than the computer, although at the weekend there will be some on the console and some on the computer.

Martin: Elizabeth (50–60, secretary/receptionist, widowed); Sophie (Elizabeth's grand-daughter, 9)

Computer: Macintosh Performa, bought at Grace Bros (six months interest free deal), in 1996.

How the computer is used: Elizabeth uses the computer for managing personal financial records, playing games, typing up recipes for a friend. Sophie plays games, writes stories and does drawings. They look things up together in the encyclopaedia for Sophie's homework.

Martinez: Carlos (40–50, works part-time as college electronics teacher); Maria (30–40, home duties); Jonathan (15); Roger (7); Allan (5); Paul (3)

Computers: 486 IBM-compatible, bought in 1994; 386 IBM-compatible, bought in 1991. (Former computers: Carlos built his first computer from parts (including the boxes) in 1984. It had 94K memory and ran Wordstar wordprocessing program. Second computer was a Commodore Amiga.)

How the computer is used: Carlos uses the 486 for compiling lesson plans and course materials for work, studying computer-based training development. Maria does a small amount of wordprocessing. Jonathan: uses 386 to teach himself about computers, school work and games. Smaller children: school work, games, drawing.

Matheson: Claire (50–60, semi-retired music teacher)

Computers: IBM-compatible 486, bought in 1995, because her son left home and took his machine with CD-ROM with him. IBM-compatible 386, bought in 1994, second-hand. Commodore 64 (uses television as monitor), bought in 1988 as her son's computer when he was at school.

How the computer is used: Claire plays games, explores shareware CD-ROMs, wordprocessing. The 386 is only being kept because there are teething problems with the 486. The Commodore is still used to manage eisteddfod databases. Claire has also built a database on the 486 to store the data from and analyse a survey on tinnitus.

Middleton: Jane (30–40, education resource centre director, also MA student); **Thompson**: Charlotte (40–50, cultural development manager for local government)

Computer: Apple Macintosh LCII, belonging to Charlotte. Bought in 1993 to bring work home.

How the computer is used: Charlotte uses the computer for bringing work home. Jane primarily uses Charlotte's computer for university assignments, but is also able to bring home a work computer and tends to do this to avoid the need to negotiate with Charlotte over competing deadlines.

Parsons: Virginia (50–60, continuing education manager); Harry (60+, retired)

Computer: IBM 386 bought second-hand in 1994. A friend's daughter's boyfriend who worked for a computer company got it for her, and installed a new hard drive.

How the computer is used: Mainly used at the time of the study for playing games. Was previously used more for bringing work home.

Powell/Crowther: John (30–40, general medical practitioner); Hayley (30–40, speech pathologist by training, currently mainly home duties but works one day per week); Jennifer (2)

Computer: Macintosh LCII, bought in 1993.

How the computer is used: John uses the computer for work (spreadsheet for medical centre expenses) and for managing the household finances (using an accounting package). Hayley uses the computer only rarely to do personal and work-related correspondence (such as annual Christmas circular). Jennifer plays on the computer (preschool software).

Richards: Sarah (40–50, administrative work at local university); Peter (40–50, middle manager (administrative) at local university, currently undertaking MA (Communication and Cultural Studies); Jessica (17); Matthew (14); Sam (12); James (6).

Computer: 486 DOS/Windows, bought in late 1995 on a 9 per cent reducible interest deal (less than mortgage interest rate at that time). (Former computer: Amstrad from a large retailer who later stopped selling computers, no hard drive. Given away when new one bought.)

How the computer is used: Children use the computer for school work, especially the eldest who is doing the HSC in the year of the study. Adults use it for wordprocessing. Children and Peter play games. Peter also uses a spreadsheet to manage the household finances. Sarah doesn't use the computer much, although she occasionally does wordprocessing for the son who is in high school.

Samuels: Helen (50–60, educational administrator, Regine Vassallo's mother)

Computer: Pentium 100 Windows computer, bought in 1996. Helen was made redundant and organized to be paid money instead of leave owing, so that she could buy a top of the range computer. (Until this time she hasn't had to buy one for her own use because she has had dedicated use of a work laptop for several years.) (Former computers: Helen's first computer was an Apple IIE, bought in 1985. She upgraded in 1989 to a Macintosh Plus, bought in 1989. This computer is now at her adult son's place. Helen also bought a 486 MS-DOS machine in 1994 for her daughter (Regine Vassallo) who was starting a university computing degree and living at home at that time. Regine moved out and took the computer with her.)

How the computer is used: Helen uses her computer for university assignments (wordprocessing and Internet research, desktop publishing). Likes to tinker: e.g. transferring Mac graphics to IBM-compatible format. Participates in email discussion lists and corresponds with acquaintances she has met online. Keeps tax records and other household management tasks on spreadsheet or database. Her son and his family come to use the computer, sometimes when she is not there.

Scarborough: Katherine (50–60, finance officer, education resource centre)

Computer: Apple Power Macintosh (DOS-compatible option), bought in late 1995 with the insurance payout from the household burglary in which her first computer was stolen. (Former computers: Apple Macintosh LC520, bought in 1994. It was just over a year old when stolen in a burglary. Katherine divorced from her husband around 1990. There was an IBM-compatible computer in the household during the marriage.)

How the computer is used: Bringing work home, playing games (sometimes also when she has insomnia), personal correspondence. Supports Katherine's freelance consultancy sideline in providing financial software support and training to small businesses. Katherine's daughter and granddaughter also use the computer when they visit.

Shaw: Gail S (30–40, trainer, health industry); Attard: Felicity (30–40, community housing worker); Franklin: Joe (20–30, unemployed); Langley: Barbara (20–30, unemployed)

Computer: Apple Macintosh Classic II, bought by Felicity in 1994

How the computer is used: Gail and Felicity live together and own their house. Joe and Barbara are long-term guests. Gail uses the computer for assignments, personal correspondence, other 'life administration' tasks. Felicity uses the computer for maintaining financial records for a community organization and other personal administration. No-one plays games on the computer (none installed). Joe and Barbara have not used the computer.

Singleton: Danielle (30–40, college teacher, also consultancies); Ian (12)

Computer: Apple Macintosh Classic II, bought in 1993.

How the computer is used: Danielle uses it for work and household management (wordprocessing, information organization). Ian uses it for school work, writing stories. Both play games.

Talbot: Chris (20–30, administrative work at local university); Geoffrey (30–40, science museum technician); Matt (7), Rebecca (3).

Computer: 286 IBM-compatible given to Chris by Geoff as a Christmas present in 1996. Geoff's employer called for tenders for old computer equipment. (Former computer: Had another old 286 given to them in 1995 that 'died'.)

How the computer is used: Gets very little use. Really only used for playing games (by all household members), although it has been used once or twice for wordprocessing.

Turner: Sally (30–40, administrative work at local university, also doing an undergraduate degree by distance education); Thomas (30–40, architect, also doing a master's degree); Jonathan (11); Michael (6)

> *Computer*: Apple Macintosh SE, bought in 1990 when Thomas was working freelance from home. (This household bought a Power Macintosh between the first and second visits to interview them.)
> *How the computer is used*: Most use of the computer is for the adults' study. The children mainly use it for playing games, drawing, some school work and creative things like birthday cards.

Vassallo: Regine (Helen Samuels's daughter, about 20, university computing undergraduate student, also works part-time as a computer support officer). Shares rented accommodation with another student.

> *Computer*: 486 SX 33 IBM-compatible, bought in 1994 by her mother when Regine was living at home. Having a computer at home meant that she didn't have to spend evenings and weekends on campus using laboratory equipment
> *How the computer is used*: University work, Internet (particularly IRC), plays games. Uses computer's CD-ROM as music system, often on in background when computer is not being used itself. Flatmate doesn't have access to Regine's computer.

Bibliography

Adrian, R. (1995), 'Infobahn blues', [Online], available from http://www.ctheory.com/article/a021.html [accessed 24 October 2001].

Akrich, M., and Latour, B. (1992), 'A summary of a convenient vocabulary for the semiotics of human and nonhuman assemblies', in W.E. Bijker and J. Law (eds) *Shaping Technology, Building Society: Studies in Sociotechnical Change*, Cambridge, Mass: MIT Press.

Allon, F. (1998), 'Geographic promiscuity, mobility and the "problem of home"', in C. Houston, F. Kurosawa and A. Watson (eds) *Imagined Places: The Politics of Making Space*, Bundoora, Vic.: School of Sociology, Politics and Anthropology, La Trobe University.

Apple Computer Australia (1996), *The Impact of Computers on Australian Home Life*, Sydney: Apple Australia.

Australian Bureau of Statistics (2001a), *Household Use of Information Technology, 2000*, Catalogue number 8146.0, Canberra: Australian Bureau of Statistics.

—— (2001b), *Use of the Internet by Householders, November 2000*, Catalogue number 8147.0, Australian Bureau of Statistics.

Bachelard, G. (1994), *The Poetics of Space*, Boston: Beacon Press.

Baudrillard, J. (1996), *The System of Objects*, London: Verso.

Belk, R.W. (1988), 'Possessions and the extended self', *Journal of Consumer Research*, 15:139–68.

Berg, A.-J. (1994), 'Technological flexibility: bringing gender into technology (or was it the other way round?)', in C. Cockburn and R. Furst-Dilic (eds) *Bringing Technology Home: Gender and Technology in a Changing Europe*, Buckingham: Open University Press.

Bourdieu, P. (1977), *Outline of a Theory of Practice*, translated by Richard Nice, Cambridge: Cambridge University Press.

Branzi, A. (1988), *Learning from Milan: Design and the Second Modernity*, Cambridge, Mass.: The MIT Press.

Bryant, A. (1988), 'The information society: computopia, dystopia, myopia', *Prometheus*, 6 (2, December 1988):61–77.

233

Campbell, C. (1992), 'The desire for the new: its nature and social location as presented in theories of fashion and modern consumerism', in R. Silverstone and E. Hirsch (eds) *Consuming Technologies*, London: Routledge.

Caron, A.H., Giroux, L., and Douzou, S. (1989), 'Uses and impacts of home computers in Canada: a process of reappropriation', in J.L. Salvaggio and J. Bryant (eds) *Media Use in the Information Age*, Hillsdale, N.J.: Lawrence Erlbaum and Associates.

Carrier, J. (1990), 'The symbolism of possession in commodity advertising', *Man*, 25 (4):693–706.

Cassell, J., and Jenkins, H. (1998), *From Barbie to Mortal Kombat: Gender and Computer Games*, Cambridge, Mass.: MIT Press.

Centre for International Economics (2001), *Save–Home: Valuing the Benefits of Home Internet Access*, Canberra: National Office for the Information Economy.

Clarke, A. (1998), 'Window shopping at home: classifieds, catalogues and new consumer skills', in D. Miller (ed.) *Material Cultures: Why Some Things Matter*, Chicago: University of Chicago Press.

Cockburn, C. (1992), 'The circuit of technology: gender, identity and power', in R. Silverstone and E. Hirsch (eds) *Consuming Technologies*, London: Routledge.

Cowan, R.S. (1983), *More Work for Mother: The Ironies of Household Technology from the Open Hearth to the Microwave*, London: Free Association Press.

Csikszentmihayli, M., and Rochberg-Halton, E. (1981), *The Meaning of Things: Domestic Symbols and the Self*, Cambridge: Cambridge University Press.

Curry, A. (2000), 'What are public library customers viewing on the Internet? An analysis of Burnaby transaction logs', [Online], available from http://www.bpl.burnaby.bc.ca/weblog.htm [accessed 24 October 2001].

Curtis, W.J.R. (1986), *Le Corbusier: Ideas and Forms*, New York: Rizzoli.

Dant, T. (1999), *Material Culture in the Social World*, Buckingham: Open University Press.

Dittmar, H. (1992), *The Social Psychology of Material Possessions: To Have is to Be*, Hemel Hempstead: Wheatsheaf.

Douglas, M. (1991), 'The idea of home: a kind of space', *Social Research*, 58 (1):287–307.

Douglas, M., and Isherwood, B. (1996), *The World of Goods: Towards an Anthropology of Consumption*, London and New York: Routledge.

du Gay, P., Hall, S., Janes, L., Mackay, H., and Negus, K. (1997), *Doing Cultural Studies: The Story of the Sony Walkman*, London: Sage Publications.

Fitch, D. (1995), 'Looking at what's not there – yet', *Metropolis* (November):50–1.

Frissen, V. (1992), 'Trapped in electronic cages? Gender and new information technologies in the public and private domain: an overview of research', *Media, Culture and Society*, 14:31–49.

Gates, B., with N. Myhrvold and P. Rinearson (1995), *The Road Ahead*, New York: Viking Penguin.

Giddens, A. (1990), *The Consequences of Modernity*, Cambridge: Polity Press.

Glennie, P.D., and Thrift, N.J. (1992), 'Modernity, urbanism, and modern consumption', *Environment and Planning D: Society and Space*, 10 (4 (Aug)):423–43.

—— (1996), 'Consumers, identities, and consumption spaces in early-modern England', *Environment and Planning A*, 28:25–45.

Goodnow, J.J., and Bowes, J.M. (1994), *Men, Women and Household Work*, Melbourne: Oxford University Press.

Gottdiener, M. (1995), *Material Culture and Postmodern Semiotics: Material Culture and the Forms of Postmodern Life*, Oxford: Blackwell.

Gray, A. (1992), *Video Playtime*, London: Comedia Routledge.

Gregory, C. (1982), *Goods and Commodities*, London: Academic Press.

Haddon, L. (1988), 'The home computer: the making of a consumer electronic', *Science as Culture*, 2:7-51.

Haddon, L. (1992), 'Explaining ICT consumption: the case of the home computer', in R. Silverstone and E. Hirsch (eds) *Consuming Technologies*, London: Routledge.

Haddon, L., and Silverstone, R. (1993), *Teleworking in the 1990s: A View from the Home*, Brighton: Science Policy Research Unit, University of Sussex.

—— (1996), *Information and Communication Technologies and the Young Elderly*, Brighton: Science Policy Research Unit, University of Sussex.

Hage, G. (1997), 'At home in the entrails of the west: multiculturalism, 'ethnic food' and migrant home-building', in H. Grace, G. Hage, L. Johnson, J. Langsworth and M. Symonds (eds) *Home/World: Space, Community and Marginality in Sydney's West*, Sydney: Pluto Press.

Hawkins, G. (1998), 'TV rules', *UTS Review*, 4 (1):123–39.

Hegel, G. (1977), *Phenomenology of Spirit*, Oxford: Oxford University Press.

Hillier, B. (1996), *Space is the Machine*, Cambridge: Cambridge University Press.

Hirsch, E. (1992), 'The long term and the short term of domestic consumption: An ethnographic case study', in R. Silverstone and E. Hirsch (eds) *Consuming Technologies*, London: Routledge.

Ihde, D. (1993), *Post-phenomenology*, Evanston, Ill: Northwestern University Press.

James, W. (1981), *Principles of Psychology, Vol. 1*, Cambridge, Mass.: Harvard University Press.

Kinder, M. (1991), *Playing with Power in Movies, Television, and Video Games: From Muppet Babies to Teenage Mutant Ninja Turtles*, Berkeley: University of California Press.

Kirkup, G. (1992), 'The social construction of computers: hammers or harpsichords?', in E. Kirkup and Keller (eds) *Inventing Women: Science, Technology, and Gender*, Cambridge: Polity Press.

Kramarae, C. (1988), 'Gotta go Myrtle, technology's at the door', in C. Kramarae (ed.) *Technology and Women's Voices: Keeping in Touch*, New York: Routledge and Kegan Paul.

Lally, E. (1999), 'On (not) being there when Deep Blue beat Kasparov', in A. Greenhill, G. Fletcher and E. de la Fuente (eds) *Rethinking the Social (Proceedings of a conference held July 1998)*, Brisbane: Griffith University.

Latour, B. (1988), 'Mixing humans and non-humans together: the sociology of a door closer', *Social Problems*, 35:298–310.

Lévi-Strauss, C. (1966), *The Savage Mind*, London: Weidenfeld and Nicolson.

—— (1969), *The Elementary Structures of Kinship*, Boston: Beacon Press.

Levy, S. (1984), *Hackers: Heroes of the Computer Revolution*, Harmondsworth: Penguin.

Lukács, G. (1975), *The Young Hegel: Studies in the Relations between Dialectics and Economics*, Translated by R. Livingstone, London: Merlin Press.

Lunt, P.K., and Livingstone, S.M. (1992), *Mass Consumption and Personal Identity*, Milton Keynes: Open University Press.

Lupton, D., and Noble, G. (1997), 'Just a machine? Dehumanizing strategies in personal computer use', *Body & Society*, 3 (2):83–101.

Macpherson, C.B. (1978), *Property, Mainstream and Critical Position*, Toronto: University of Toronto Press.

Makrakis, V. (1993), 'Gender and computing in schools in Japan: the 'we can, I can't' paradox', *Computers and Education*, 20:191–8.

Matthews, M.H. (1992), *Making Sense of Place*, Hemel Hempstead: Harvester Wheatsheaf.

Mauss, M. (1990), *The Gift*, New York and London: W.W. Norton.

McCracken, G. (1988), *Culture and Consumption: New Approaches to the Symbolic Character of Consumer Goods*, Bloomington & Indianapolis: Indiana University Press.

Michelet, J. (1858), *L'Oiseau*, 4th edition, Paris: La Hachette.

Miller, D. (1987), *Material Culture and Mass Consumption*, Oxford: Blackwell.

—— (1990), 'Appropriating the State on the Council Estate', *Man*, 23:353–72.

—— (1998a), *A Theory of Shopping*, Ithaca, New York: Cornell University Press.

—— (1998b), *Material Cultures: Why Some Things Matter*, Chicago: University of Chicago Press.

Miller, D., and Slater, D. (2000), *The Internet: An Ethnographic Approach*, Oxford: Berg.

Mitchell, E. (1985), 'The dynamics of family interaction around home video games', in M.B. Sussman (ed.) *Personal Computers and the Family*, New York: Haworth Press.

Morley, D. (1995), 'Television: not so much a visual medium, more a visible object', in C. Jenks (ed.) *Visual culture*, London: Routledge.

Morley, D., and Silverstone, R. (1990), 'Domestic communication – technologies and meanings', *Media, Culture and Society*, 12 (1):31–55.

Murdock, G., Hartmann, P., and Gray, P. (1992), 'Contextualizing home computing: Resources and practices', in R. Silverstone and E. Hirsch (ed.) *Consuming Technologies*, London: Routledge.

Nielsen//Netratings (2001a), 'Popstars – the biggest online buzz since Big Brother', [Online, press release dated 15/3/01], available from http://nielsen-netratings.com/pr/pr_010315_uk.pdf [accessed 24 October 2001].

—— (2001b), 'Sports tipping the latest online kick for Australians', [Online, press release dated 11/4/01], available from http://nielsen-netratings.com/pr/pr_0104112_au.pdf [accessed 24 October 2001].

Nippert-Eng, C.E. (1995), *Home and Work: Negotiating Boundaries through Everyday Life*, Chicago & London: University of Chicago Press.

Noble, D.F. (1984), *Forces of Production: A Social History of Industrial Automation*, New York: Alfred A. Knopf.

Noble, D. (1986), 'Computer literacy and ideology', in P. Watkins (ed.) *High Tech, Low Tech and Education*, Melbourne: Deakin University.

Noble, G., and Lupton, D. (1998), 'Consuming work: computers, subjectivity and appropriation in the university workplace', *The Sociological Review*, 46 (4):803–27.

Norman, D. (1998), *The Invisible Computer: Why Good Products Can Fail, the Personal Computer is so Complex and Information Appliances are the Solution*, Cambridge, Mass.: MIT Press.

Pahl, J. (1990), 'Household spending: personal spending and the control of money in marriage', *Sociology*, 24 (1):119–38.

Pellegram, A. (1998), 'The message in paper', in D. Miller (ed.) *Material Cultures: Why Some Things Matter*, Chicago: Chicago University Press.

Postman, N. (1993), *Technopoly: The Surrender of Culture to Technology*, New York: Vintage Books.

Press, L. (1993), 'Before the Altair: The history of personal computing', *Communications of the ACM*, 36 (9):27–33.

Rakow, L.F. (1988), 'Women and the telephone: the gendering of a communications technology', in C. Kramarae (ed.) *Technology and Women's Voices: Keeping in Touch*, New York: Routledge and Kegan Paul.

Rakow, L.F., and Navarro, V. (1993), 'Remote mothering and the parallel shift: women meet the cellular telephone', *Critical Studies in Mass Communication*, 10:144–57.

Rheingold, H. (1994), *The Virtual Community: Finding Connection in a Computerized World*, London: Secker & Warburg.

Robins, K. (1994), 'Forces of consumption: from the symbolic to the psychotic', *Media, Culture and Society*, 16:449–68.

Romanyshyn, R.D. (1989), *Technology as Symptom and Dream*, London: Routledge.

Ryan, A. (1984), *Property and Political Theory*, Oxford: Blackwell.

Silverstone, R. (1989), 'Let us then return to the murmuring of everyday practices: a note on Michel de Certeau, television and everyday life', *Theory, Culture and Society*, 6 (1):77–94.

—— (1993), 'Time, information and communication technologies and the household', *Time and Society*, 2 (3 (Sept)):283-311.

—— (1994), *Television, Technology and Everyday Life: An Essay in the Sociology of Culture*, London: Routledge.

Silverstone, R., and Haddon, L. (1993), *Future Compatible? Information and Communication Technologies in the Home: A Methodology and a Case Study*, Brighton: Science Policy Research Unit, University of Sussex.

—— (1996), 'Design and the domestication of information and communications technologies: technical change and everyday life', in R. Mansell and R. Silverstone (eds) *Communication by Design : The Politics of Communication Technologies*, Oxford: Oxford University Press.

Silverstone, R., and Hirsch, E. (eds) (1992), *Consuming Technologies*. London: Routledge.

Silverstone, R., Hirsch, E., and Morley, D. (1991), 'Listening to a long conversation: an ethnographic approach to the study of information and communication technologies in the home', *Cultural Studies*, 5 (2):204-27.

—— (1992), 'Information and communication technologies and the moral economy of the household', in R. Silverstone and E. Hirsch (eds) *Consuming Technologies*, London: Routledge.

Simmel, G. (1990), *The Philosophy of Money*, translated by T. Bottomore and D. Frisby, London and New York: Routledge.

Skinner, D. (1992), Technology, Consumption and the Future: The Experience of Home Computing, PhD, Brunel University, Uxbridge.

Slack, J.D. (1984), 'The information revolution as ideology', *Media, Culture and Society*, 6:247–56.

Sofia, Z. (1995), 'Of spanners and cyborgs: "de-homogenising" feminist thinking on technology', in B. Caine and R. Pringle (eds) *Transitions: New Australian Feminisms*, St Leonards: Allen & Unwin.

Spigel, L. (1992), *Make Room for TV: TV and the Family Ideal*, Chicago: University of Chicago Press.

Staudenmaier, J. (1995), 'Henry Ford's relationship to "Fordism": ambiguity as a modality of technological resistance', in M. Bauer (ed.) *Resistance to New Technology: Nuclear Power, Information Technology and Biotechnology*, Cambridge: Cambridge University Press.

Taachi, J. (1998), 'Radio texture: between self and others', in D. Miller (ed.) *Material Cultures: Why Some Things Matter*, Chicago: University of Chicago Press.

Taussig, M. (1993), *Mimesis and Alterity*, New York & London: Routledge.

Thomas, M. (1999), *Dreams in the Shadows: Vietnamese-Australian Lives in Transition*, Sydney: Allen & Unwin.

Thomas, N. (1991), *Entangled Objects: Exchange, Material Culture and Colonialism*, Cambridge, Mass.: Harvard University Press.

Turkle, S. (1985), 'The psychology of personal computers', in T. Forester (ed.) *The Information Technology Revolution*, Oxford: Blackwell.

—— (1988), 'Computational reticence: why women fear the intimate machine', in C. Kramarae (ed.) *Technology and Women's Voices: Keeping in Touch*, London: Routledge & Kegan Paul.

—— (1995), *Life on the Screen: Identity in the Age of the Internet*, New York: Simon & Schuster.

Turkle, S., and Papert, S. (1990), 'Epistemological pluralism: styles and voices within the computer culture', *Signs: Journal of Women in Culture and Society*, 16 (1):128–57.

van Zoonen, L. (1992), 'Feminist theory and information technology', *Media, Culture and Society*, 14:9–29.

Vogler, C., and Pahl, J. (1994), 'Money, power and inequality within marriage', *The Sociological Review*, 1994:263–88.

Wajcman, J. (1991), *Feminism Confronts Technology*, Sydney: Allen and Unwin.

Warde, A. (1994), 'Consumption, identity-formation and uncertainty', *Sociology*, 28 (4):877–98.

Webster, F., and Robins, K. (1986), *Information Technology: A Luddite Analysis*, Norwood NJ: Ablex Publishing Corporation.

Weiner, A.B. (1992), *Inalienable Possessions: The Paradox of Keeping-While-Giving*, Berkeley: University of California Press.

Wheelock, J. (1992), 'Personal computers, gender and an institutional model of the household', in R. Silverstone and E. Hirsch (eds) *Consuming Technologies*, London: Routledge.

Winnicott, D.W. (1945), 'Primitive emotional development', in *Collected Papers: Through Paediatrics to Psychoanalysis*, London: Hogarth.

—— (1963), *The Maturational Processes and the Facilitating Environment*, New York: International Universities Press.

—— (1971), *Playing and Reality*, London: Tavistock Press.

Wood, D., and Beck, R.J. (1994), *Home Rules*, Baltimore: The Johns Hopkins University Press.

Young, J.A. (1992), 'Business 2001', *Financial Executive*, 8 (6):56–7.

Index